ALBA ROSA

ALEXANDER WOLFHEZE

Alba Rosa

❧

TEN **TRADITIONALIST** ESSAYS

ABOUT THE **CRISIS** IN THE

MODERN WEST

ARKTOS
LONDON 2019

Printed in the United Kingdom.

ISBN   978-1-912975-09-9 (Softcover)
                  978-1-912975-10-5 (Ebook)

EDITING, COVER
AND LAYOUT   John Bruce Leonard

 Arktos.com   fb.com/Arktos   @arktosmedia   arktosmedia

Take my shoes off
And throw them in the lake
And I'll be
Two steps on the water

—KATE BUSH
'HOUNDS OF LOVE'

Dedicated to our people:

ceci tuera cela

CONTENTS

ALBA ROSA

LIST OF ILLUSTRATIONS

Before the High Altar of History

'Rose du Midi', South Rose Window, Notre Dame de Paris (ca. 1250–
60 — an offering by King Saint Louis). The central *médaillon* shows
Christ Triumphant, i.e. Christ as depicted in the Book of Revelation,
with the Sword of Truth coming from His mouth; He is surrounded by
the saints and martyrs that bore witness to Him on Earth. The vision
of the Rose du Midi will have been one of the last earthly sights of
Dominique Venner as he was standing before the High Altar.

Preface

L'heure viendra cependant où, dans un monde organisé pour le désespoir,
prêcher l'espérance équivaudra tout juste
à jeter un charbon enflammé au milieu d'un baril de poudre.

[Yet the hour will come when, in a world organized for despair, preaching hope will
be the same as throwing a glowing coal in a keg of gunpowder.]

—GEORGES BERNANOS, *MONSIEUR OUINE*

THE HIGH ALTAR OF HISTORY

MANY YEARS HAVE PASSED SINCE THE AUTHOR, in his second high school term of German language instruction, first saw the writings of *Die Weisse Rose* — a long time ago, in the long-drowned world of pre-digital learning and unpractical bookish wisdom. Facing the sweetly romantic theme of the 'rose of purity', the boys in class resigned themselves to a long and boring session — the girls eagerly grabbed their poetry albums. At that time, forty years after the Second World War, German language education was still somewhat 'tainted' in the Netherlands — a fact hardly counterbalanced by the latent but pervasive anti-Semitism still experienced by those pupils suspected to be of Jewish stock. On this occasion, however, the teacher managed to gain the full attention and appreciation of his reluctant class. It appeared that the 'rosy theme' concerned a small group of German students — not much older than the pupils who were reading their typed essays four decades later — who had actually paid with their lives for a few sheets of brave, but unwelcome prose and verse. If it was the guillotine that put a full stop behind their words, perhaps their words actually deserved some attention. Of course, after the end-of-term exam, not much would be remembered of what was learnt that day, except the naked name — *nomina nuda tenemus* — and the vague impression of a wrongly scripted David-and-Goliath tale. The theme of the history of *Die Weisse Rose* — the almighty giant of the totalitarian dictatorship that crops a few loud boys and girls at the neck for the sake of the politically correct remainder of a sleeping nation — was simply too far remote from the actual realities of the free and democratic Netherlands of the mid-'80s. At that time, totalitarian repression and brutal dictatorship were only found in remote, primitive regions of the world — and behind the Iron Curtain. There, the Bolshevik world still brought forth brave warriors of the pen, worthy successors to *Die Weisse Rose*: *samizdat* heroes such as Aleksandr Solzhenitsyn with his *Odin den Ivana Denisowitsa* and Vaclav Havel with his *Moc bezmocnych.*

Who could have guessed, at that time, that the theme of *Die Weisse Rose* would one day gain concrete relevance, a relevance extending beyond mere historical curiosity, for the proudly free and exemplary democratic Dutch nation — or for any progressive Western nation? Who could have guessed that one day, totalitarian ideology and dictatorial politics would not be brought *into* the Netherlands by foreign occupiers — as the Germans did during the Second World War — but be brought *forth* by the Dutch soil itself? What about the assumption that German National Socialism had been a unique aberration in Western history — an unfortunate, but entirely plausible *Sonderfall* from the point of view of historical-materialist theory? What about the assumption that Russian Bolshevism and its imperialist metastases in Eastern Europe and overseas were equally unfortunate, but essentially temporary phenomena, owed to 'underdevelopment' — and destined to disappear with material 'progress' and advancing 'enlightenment'? And were these historical-materialist assumptions not soon proven true by subsequent history: by the fall of the

Berlin Wall, the Soviet Union and Apartheid — and by the rise of the EU, the euro and the World Wide Web? The events and rhetoric of the early nineties seemed to be the ultimate confirmation of historical-materialist teleology: with George Bush launching the 'New World Order' and Francis Fukuyama announcing the 'End of History', the post-historical, Postmodern Era had begun.

How could the sporadic incidents of 'Black Hawk Down', '9/11' and 'Abu Ghraib' be anything more than easily removable dust specks on the stainless record of the New World Order — insignificant bumps on the highway to a utopian 'Brave New World' of global peace, freedom and democracy? How could any critic of this glorious vision be more than an 'angry white man' and a pitifully 'unstable person', fully deserving his sad fate? From this perspective, it is entirely plausible that only twelve years after the murder of patriotic Dutch prime ministerial candidate Pim Fortuyn (6 May 2002), his assassin was again a free man. The court decided that the murderer, obligingly characterized as a 'lone wolf', was simply an 'overly conscientious' Social Justice Warrior. The victim, despite his posthumous election as 'second greatest Dutchman in history', had been widely portrayed in the media as a 'danger to society'. From this perspective, it becomes also entirely plausible that the dramatic suicide of cultural critic Dominique Venner, in front of the High Altar of the Notre Dame de Paris (21 May 2013), should have been followed within twenty-four hours by a half-nude act of mockery by a Social Justice Warrior member of the militant feminist action group 'Femen'.

But what if there actually existed entirely different perspectives on such events? Was it not actually true that this 'sextremist' Femen activist, this blasphemous empress of dystopian anti-Tradition, stood without clothes? Was it not actually true that she was shamelessly profaning hallowed ground — and that the word 'hell' was written on her naked belly? And what about the ancient words of the Bible: *Babylon the Great, Mother of Harlots and Abominations of the Earth, ...drunken with the blood of the saints, and with the blood of the martyrs...*? Is it possible that these words were somehow applicable not only to that one *Anti-Notre Dame* of Femen, but also to the whole New World Order that she represented? And, if so, then how had it been possible for such a horrible new regime to rise up in the heart of Western civilization, without being properly noticed, without being bravely denounced and without being seriously resisted? Had similar questions not plagued the students of *Die Weisse Rose*, and had they not reached terrible conclusions? They had been born too late and their questions had been asked too late as well — ten years after the National Socialist *Machtergreifung*. But the brave sacrifice of *Die Weisse Rose* will not have been in vain if later-born youngsters can understand it correctly — if they learn to act punctually whenever they learn about a new totalitarian *Machtergreifung*.

THE CULTURAL NIHILIST MACHTERGREIFUNG

If there is one political fact that is daily evidenced by the Western media, it is this: that the elites of the Postmodern West are immune to societal realities and societal discontent. The more strongly the Western baby boomer elite is disturbed by intrusions of reality and choirs of criticism, the faster its 'enlightened' philosophy and 'progressive' ideology transform themselves into absurdist dogmas, and the tighter it wraps itself in sub-rational reflex responses: it systematically grinds down all forms of 'inconvenient truth' and unwelcome critique, transmuting them into 'narcissist supply' for its own instinctive defence mechanisms. It is only by means of a radical tunnel vision and an activist *Flucht nach vorne* that the baby boomer elite can still maintain the comfort zone of its own existential bubble world. Thus, simple libertarianism is transformed into militant secularism, simple materialism is transformed into status consumerism, simple social Darwinism is transformed into sadistic hyper-capitalism and simple individualism is transformed into malignant narcissism: *Cultural Nihilism* is born.

The first incarnation of Cultural Nihilism is found in the well-fed baby boomer in his role as the permanently adolescent *Rebel without a Cause* (the '60s and '70s). Quickly enough, his politically correct anti-authoritarian personality dissipates into a vague 'lifestyle' fashion statement (the '80s and '90s). Next, this archetype is stabilized in a next generation of opportunistic party-line yes-men, resentful feminists and ambitious diversity creatures (the '2000s and the '2010s). The *Social Justice Warrior* is born.

Faced with the real world of adult responsibilities, the Social Justice Warrior soon takes refuge in a collective existential bubble, constructed around the pseudo-occult utopia of *liberté, égalité, fraternité*, a utopia that quickly shifts from ideal to doctrine. Power and privilege gravitate into the 'black hole' of this bubble, attracted by the titanic force of totalitarian anti-morality. First, the growing power monopoly and the all-levelling *Prinzipienreiterei* of the baby boomers absorb the media and the political sector; next, they absorb the justice system and the educational institutions. The *hostile elite* is born.

Once defined, this autonomous power sphere quickly detaches itself from democratic controls and legitimate national authority by transnational alliances with international 'high finance', multinational corporations and cosmopolitan interest groups: it disappears across the political event horizon of the Western peoples. *Globalism* is born.

Unease and criticism of the real-world implementation of globalism are easily deflected by standard references to intangible processes such as 'market competition', 'European law' and 'international treaties'. These seemingly unassailable forces provide the hostile elite with a convenient lightning rod to deflect patriotic and identitarian criticism: such criticism is easily dismissed as irrational and futile. Even the most articulate counterarguments are narcissistically 'mirrored', misrepresented as 'populist sentiments' and 'social pathologies'. This mechanism explains the patronizing and stigmatizing elite vocabulary, which consistently misrepresents non-Cultural Nihilist ideas and attitudes as 'bellyfeel' and 'racism'. Thus, undisguised demophobia and hysterical witch hunts — 'pre-modern' phenomena that were supposed to have been the exclusive preserve of decadent aristocrats and narrow-minded clerics — suddenly re-conquer the public arena. Now, the self-reinforcing psychodynamics dominating the mental bubble of the hostile elite reach *the point of no return*. *Oikophobia* is born.[1]

At this point, the globalist hostile elite becomes clinically psychotic: solid arguments, irrefutable proof and obvious injustice are purposefully ignored. Throughout the entire Western world, the situation is the same: symbolic gestures and cosmetic measures aside, climate catastrophe, neo-liberal 'shock therapy', mass-immigration, indigenous impoverishment and social implosion are simply avoided. Even the most obscene results of globalist 'policy' — South African 'farm killings', British 'grooming gangs', Dutch 'lover boys' — are simply 'killed by silence' in the mainstream media. Even the most spectacular popular uprisings against the hostile elite — 'Brexit', 'Trump', 'M5S' — are simply laughed away. The *Cultural Nihilist totalitarian dictatorship* is born.

Meanwhile, the hostile elite has already found an easy solution to the excess of indigenous discontent ('angry white men'): *ethnic replacement*. The baby boomer hostile elite simply re-directs its Cultural Marxist dialectics, shifting it from 'class struggle' to 'anti-identity politics'. The unspoken motto of the elite is clear: if the people do not wish to play along, we will simply create another people. Its informal 'Kalergi Plan' aims at the formation of an identity-less *méti-métèque* population to replace the indigenous European peoples. To this end, the rapidly reproducing peoples of Africa and Asia provide an inexhaustible supply of aspiring colonists. Following the historical trajectory of colonial repatriation and guest labour of the '50s and '60s, the hostile elite effortlessly shifts to 'family reunification' and 'refugee resettlement'. But this is a process requiring historical stamina: thus, in the short run, the hostile elite is forced to simultaneously continue work on the socio-cultural deconstruction of the native European peoples. This means the systematic application of institutional power and a ceaseless indoctrination of the indigenous populace with the aim of causing social implosion. The combination of socio-economic pressure ('privatisation', 'market reforms') and subtly manipulative 'psyops' (intellectual 'dumbing down' in education, anti-identitarian 'role

---

1 'Oikophobia' as defined in Wolfheze, *Sunset*, 194.

models' in the media) results in the required cocktail of existential insecurity and cognitive dissonance. Thus, sui-genocide and mass-immigration are complementary strategies: ethnic replacement has started.

Hence, the circle closes: the Cultural Nihilist *Machtergreifung* is a fact.

'In the First Circle'

Some years ago the author returned to his own country after a long stay abroad, and he soon discovered how much — and how quickly — it had changed. Most of the old churches of his city had been handed over to new sects, shut down or turned into commercial real estate. The parks of his city had been mostly relinquished to impudent drug dealers, drunken seasonal workers and anti-social lowlifes. The streets of his city are no longer fit for innocent bikers, unaccompanied girls or strolling families: excessive car ownership, violent youth gangs, disgraceful unseemliness and endemic street crime dominate the public space. That space is shifting towards Third World conditions, reflecting the population make-up. Downtown working-class neighbourhoods are followed by suburban commuter neighbourhoods. The largest cities are followed by the smaller cities. The first signs of this creeping process are the closure of up-market shops and the faltering of postal services. Next to disappear are the pillaged ATMs and over-burdened public transport services. By that time, nearly all decent people who are able to move will have fled — including most wage-earners and entrepreneurs. Remaining behind are the poor, the sick and the elderly, abandoned to hopeless lawlessness, criminality and filth. The homeless sleep in cellars and halls of decaying buildings, vagabonds relieve themselves in the parks, uncollected garbage piles up in the streets and rats make their way back into the city for the first time in over one and half centuries. Public safety and the rule of law are mere memories: failing law enforcement and judicial impunity have created ethnic no-go areas, non-stop crime waves, open drugs trade and structural social malaise. Social and cultural facilities are rapidly being liquidated: retirement homes, psychiatric wards and public libraries are shut down — nursing care, homeless shelters and debt relief programmes have been pared down to the point of obscenity. The first failures in electricity and water delivery indicate the fact that *le voyage au bout de la nuit* is well under way.

The catastrophic transformation at the micro-level is mirrored in social implosion at the macro-level. Unprecedented levels of youth unemployment are hidden — and 'paid forward' at the expense of future generations — under the cover of study debts for useless education, endlessly repeated 'work internships' and bureaucratic 'occupational therapy'. Unprecedented social polarization is hidden under the cover of institutionalized welfare fraud, deliberately tolerated criminality and self-perpetuating consumer credit, destroying societal cohesion and civic virtue. Administrative chaos is concealed under the layers of a monstrous bureaucracy, improvised legislation and ad hoc 'semi-private' institutions, destroying the rule of law. Commercialization, internationalization and feminization have reduced most forms of education to contentless pastimes that shroud a reality of 'low threshold' incompetence, anti-intellectual levelling and cynical 'monetary efficiency'. In this way, the centuries-old academic tradition of the author's *alma mater* has been pulverized between the millstones of *business model, affirmative action* and *diversity*, reducing it to a hallucinatory 'Harvard on the Rhine', a 'gender neutral' theme park for a gilded youth of 'snowflake' millennials, Asian 'internationals' on safari and 'refugee' students in permanent remedial training. In high schools and vocational training institutes, national education has decayed to a point of 'low literacy' that precludes a functional society in the long term: society is approaching the terminal stage of genuine 'idiocracy'.

These symptoms, however, only represent the visible signs of a profound societal metamorphosis: the invisible transformations are much more worrisome. The rhetorical facade of 'environmental awareness' and 'greening' hides the abhorrent realities of an accelerating climate catastrophe and an intensifying 'bio-industry'. Nobody dares to mention it, but even the natural seasons that the author still remembers from his childhood have been abolished: Dutch winter landscapes are now only found in museums and Dutch ice skates are now only useful in indoor facilities. Nobody dares to mention it, because the newest automobile fashion and the next flying holiday take a higher priority. Similarly, nobody wants to know the real price that must be paid for the prosperity cult of meat consumption: the indescribable horror of industrialized animal torture and, increasingly, of 'ritual slaughter'. The hidden desecration of nature is mirrored in the simultaneous desecration of culture. The serene façade of social liberty covers the brutal reality of totalitarian matriarchy with its myriad 'alternative family groups' and 'lifestyle options' ('Living Apart Together', 'Living Together Apart', 'single-parent families', 'same-sex marriages' etc.). This is the real ground zero of social implosion. The physically and psychologically damaged youngsters that finally climb out of the multi-layered hell of this 'new freedom' cannot be anything else but the *schrecklichen Kinder der Neuzeit*, the 'terrible children of the New Age', providing the negative energy that propels the downward spiral of social implosion.

And what is happening in the Netherlands, seen and unseen, is happening on a large scale in the entire West. And there is something even more sinister underway: over, under and beside the converging emergencies of Cultural Nihilism there is a deadly and hushed-up emergency more urgent than all others: ethnic replacement. Masses of immigrants, the 'adopted children' of the baby boomer hostile elite are preparing to take over the inheritance of the self-annihilating West. The young people of the West, after having been disfigured, abused and rejected, are now supposed to silently suffer exclusion in their own countries, from their own cultures and their own identities. Every attempt at redressing this unjust verdict is met with outright repression in politics, in the law courts and in the media arena. Thus, most of the young Westerners, fearing to lose their quiet little corner in the first circle of the hell of Cultural Nihilism, bear this undeserved fate in silence. Most of all, the author is writing for them — to let them know that what has been their indigestible past and their unacceptable present does not have to be their future. To let them know that an unexpected harvest of a profoundly different future can still arise from what was sown, long ago, deep in the ancient soil of the Lands of the West. That this harvest of courage, loyalty and honour can be found within them — as it was in *Die Weisse Rose.*

Verily, verily, I say unto you, Except a corn of wheat fall into the ground and die, it abideth alone: but if it die, it bringeth forth much fruit.

—JOHN 12:24

Acknowledgements

The author wishes to express his gratitude to *Studiegenootschap Erkenbrand*: to his colleagues and comrades he extends a warm welcome to the first printed reflection of the long-lost words that they first found the courage to speak again — *pedo mellon a minno*. He also wishes to thank Arktos' Editor-in-Chief John Bruce Leonard for his patient support — and for reviving the long-lost art of conversation: *rara temporum felicitas, ubi sentire quae velis et quae sentias dicere licet.*

Alba Rosa

Preliminaries

Background

Ｔｈｅ ᴇɴɢʟɪꜱʜ-ʟᴀɴɢᴜᴀɢᴇ, ɪɴᴛᴇʀɴᴀᴛɪᴏɴᴀʟ ᴇᴅɪ- tion of *Alba Rosa* provides a Traditionalist perspective on the Cultural Nihilist Crisis of the Modern West, illustrating its symptoms by an investigation of the 'test case' of the author's own nation, the Netherlands. It should be emphasized that *Alba Rosa* does *not* provide a treatise on Traditionalism itself. Although the essays collected in *Alba Rosa* do contain some remarks about Traditionalism in general (cf. Chapter 6, 'The Regression of the Castes') and some elaborations on specific Traditionalist themes, the author does not intend to analyse Traditionalism as a philosophical and historical phenomenon — let alone 'prove' it. If 'proof' for Traditionalism is possible at all, it is sufficiently provided in the classic literature of the Traditionalist School; the Bibliography provides an elementary reading list for interested readers. The specific position that the author takes regarding Traditionalist thought and Traditionalist methodology is sufficiently explained in his recent book *The Sunset of Tradition and the Origin of the Great War*. In this regard it is important to state that if *Alba Rosa* occasionally refers to *Sunset*, the reader is in no way assumed to be familiar with the content of *Sunset*; *Alba Rosa* is an entirely self-sufficient 'stand-alone' publication. The functionality of *Sunset* was primarily *historiographical*, whereas the functionality of *Alba Rosa* is primarily *metapolitical*. The common element of *Sunset* and *Alba Rosa* is their shared basis in Traditionalist thought. Thus, both works offer a similar and new — because non-historical-materialist — perspective, but on two entirely different subjects. On several occasions following the publication of *Sunset*, the author was asked to project the cultural-historical analyses of *Sunset* forward to the present day — a truly formidable undertaking. But the lamentable paucity of contemporary Traditionalist resources to deal with contemporary realities — particularly acute in Dutch-language countries — convinced the author to make an attempt: *Alba Rosa* is the result.

The readers of the international edition of *Alba Rosa* are asked to bear with the author as he illustrates the predicament of the Western peoples with various examples from the contemporary Dutch situation: they will find that there are many useful lessons to be learnt from the 'test case' of Dutch Postmodernity. In many ways, the Dutch nation constitutes one of the early pioneers — one of the 'guide nations' — of Western Modernity, alongside Great Britain and America: the course it navigates through Postmodernity may well indicate the future course of the more 'conservative' nations of the West. In this sense, other nations may profit from paying attention to the fate of the small Dutch nation; they may profit by the (largely negative) example of the Dutch people's present plight. At various points, *Alba Rosa* touches upon the role of other Western nations at the present stage of the Crisis of the Modern West — Germany in Chapter 1, Britain in Chapter 7, America in Chapter 8 — but the author does not presume to prescribe remedies for their specific national problems. Rather, he wishes to point out the heritage that they hold in common, the plight that they share and the possibility of finding common remedies. Cultural Nihilism poses a mortal danger to all Western nations — a danger well illustrated by monstrous 'super-state' projects such as the 'United Nations' and the 'European Union'. The survival of the Western peoples depends on a double exit strategy from Cultural Nihilism: a fundamental reassertion of national identity and a pragmatic alliance against globalist subversion. Such an alliance requires a fundamental shift in the metapolitical and geopolitical discourse of the West; *Alba Rosa* aims at contributing to this shift. From a Traditionalist perspective, Neo-Eurasianism currently provides the best chance of achieving this shift; the first chapter of *Alba Rosa* is therefore dedicated to a Traditionalist assessment of Neo-Eurasianism.

The background to *Alba Rosa* requires yet another remark, namely with regard to what may be termed its 'religious perspective'. Traditionalist thought is organically — one might even say symbiotically — related to religion, not only in general terms but also in specific terms. Every authentic Traditionalist thinker and scholar is associated with a specific 'religious' Tradition, without considering that specific Tradition to be *universally superior*. To the extent that it is authentically followed and experienced, each specific religious Tradition is intrinsically and undeniably superior to all others for individuals and groups *within that Tradition itself*. The Traditional School recognizes a universal *Sophia Perennis*, a shared Eternal Truth, in all authentic Traditions, but it simultaneously recognizes the inevitable differences in the expression of that One Truth in different times and different places. Thus, a Traditionalist study of a specific cultural-historical study object, inevitably embedded in a certain time and place, always requires a contextual approach — an approach that respects and maintains the integrity of the Tradition that shaped it. The study object of *Alba Rosa* is the fate of the Western peoples during the Crisis of the Modern World — as illustrated by the Postmodern reality that is lived by the Dutch people. The Tradition that shaped the Western peoples is the Christian Tradition: in the case of the Dutch people, this is the specialized Tradition of Radical Protestantism — a particular Tradition it shares with the other 'guide nations' of Modernity: Great Britain and America. The author himself does not belong within the religious sphere of this Tradition, but he does belong within its cultural-historical sphere and he has directly experienced its religious sphere around himself throughout much of his life. Thus, the author is bound to observe the contemporary predicament of the Western peoples not only in the 'rear-view mirror' of Traditionalism but also through the lens of the Dutch Christian Tradition.

Tesi samanunga was edele unde scona
et omnium virtutum pleniter plena.

— *Munsterbilzen Evangelarium*

ORGANIZATION

Each of the 'Ten Traditionalist Essays' announced in the subtitle of *Alba Rosa* has a different theme, but these are all connected to each other. This section serves to explain this connection and the resulting organization of *Alba Rosa*. It also explains the relevance of the extra materials (the appendices and the study material).

The first chapter, 'The Harrowing of Hell', provides a Traditionalist evaluation of the Crisis of the Modern West at its present stage. It describes the present predicament of the Western peoples in terms of their recent psycho-historical development and puts it in the Traditionalist geopolitical perspective offered by (Neo-)Eurasianism. By elaborating on basic Traditionalist concepts, Chapter 1 also serves as a general 'introduction'.

The following chapter triad, Chapters 2 through 4, serves to illustrate specific aspects of the Crisis of the Modern West by analysing Dutch Postmodernity: these analyses are consistently contextualized to point out the relevance of the 'Dutch test case' for the Modern West as a whole. Chapter 2, 'The Crisis of the Modern West', offers a Traditionalist cultural-historical 'diagnosis' of Cultural Nihilist Postmodernity centred on Julius Evola's principle of the 'regression of the castes'. Chapter 3, 'The Dangers of Democracy', offers a specific political analysis and couches this analysis in terms of Nicolás Gómez Dávila critique of modern 'democracy'. Chapter 4, 'The Sword of Knowledge', investigates the historical origin of the Crisis of the Modern Netherlands on the basis of Julius Evola's principle of the 'treason of the clergy'.

The second chapter triad, Chapters 5 through 7, is aimed at a cultural-historical 'prognosis' for the further stages of the Crisis of the Modern West. Chapter 5, 'The Hamartiology of Modernity', clarifies the meta-historical and metaphysical *meaning* of the Crisis of the Modern West by couching it in the old Christian vocabulary of the Traditional West.

Chapter 6, 'The Living Dead', delves deeper into the core dynamics of the Crisis of the Modern West by analysing the phenomenon of 'social implosion' in terms of *Sunset*'s 'Archaeo-Futurist' double model of 'Vampirism-Narcissism'. Chapter 7, 'Shutdown', sketches the 'menu' of psycho-historical options open to the Western peoples as they approach the event horizon of Postmodernity, focussing in on the Traditionalist theme of the *mors triumphalis*.

The final chapter triad, Chapters 8 through 10, investigates the premises of a possible 'Archaeo-Futurist' rebirth of the Western peoples. In Traditionalist terminology, the synthetic fusion of archaic archetypes and futurist visions required for such rebirth would constitute a true 'Golden Dawn'. Chapter 8, 'The Archaeo-Futurist Revolution', sketches the philosophical foundations of the new patriotic-identitarian movement and its immunity to Cultural Nihilism by reviewing the key theses of Jason Jorjani's *Prometheus and Atlas*. Chapter 9, 'Twelve Rules for the Archaeo-Futurist Revolution', provides a Traditionalist recipe for the direction and control of a future patriotic-identitarian revolution, aimed at the re-institution and re-creation of Western civilization. Chapter 10, 'The White Rose', concludes *Alba Rosa* by providing an 'updated' version of the manifest of *Die Weisse Rose*; its subtitles are taken from relevant documents from the Dutch Heroic Age, but its contents are entirely relevant to all of the Western peoples.

Finally, *Alba Rosa* provides some extra materials. These materials are primarily meant for young people who wish to further investigate the various themes of *Alba Rosa*: they offer references and directions. Appendix A, 'Human Rights', elaborates on the Traditionalist critique of Modernist 'humanism' through a running commentary on the 'Universal Declaration of Human Rights'; this has been added to the English-language edition to compensate for the omission of an excerpt from *Sunset* that is included in the Dutch-language edition. Appendix B, 'Stultitiae Laus', provides Nietzsche's Classical Modern critique of the rationalist-scientist-nihilist worldview that ultimately became dominant in Postmodern Cultural Nihilism. The 'Study Material' provides basic study advice and

some elementary bibliography to allow young people easy access to the
materials relevant to the themes of *Alba Rosa.*

Irrespective of the organization outlined above, each of the ten chapters of *Alba Rosa* represents a self-contained essay, leaving the reader free
to read them in the order that he prefers.

> *(*) Bible citations are from the King James Version, Quran citations are from
> the Pickthall translation. The Holy Letters, all but first and second: these are
> the words, six and four, that should be read in the tongue of the SA.GAZ.*

> *(**) Despite its commitment to an accurate depiction of facts and a full at-
> tribution of intellectual rights, Alba Rosa is not a scientific treatise: reference
> notes have therefore been avoided. Instead, intellectual rights have been ac-
> knowledged by short bracketed references within the text itself. A few explan-
> atory notes have been added to Chapters 2 and 4, but these only serve to
> elucidate specifically Dutch themes.*

> *(***) The Glossary included in the 'Study Material' lists and translates all
> foreign phrases used throughout Alba Rosa (always indicated in italics).*

Disclaimer

As a Traditionalist critique of Postmodern Cultural Nihilism, *Alba Rosa*
covers a number of subjects that are presently subject to politically-cor-
rect taboo in Western Europe and the overseas Anglosphere. The key
themes of feminization, matriarchy, multiculturalism and ethnic replacement are effectively removed from public debate because any fundamental criticism of these processes constitutes a direct threat to the Cultural Nihilist ideology of *anti-Tradition* and *anti-identity*. The hostile elite
of the West has invested too deeply in its theory, and gone too far in its
practice, to ever turn back. The hostile elite is playing *va banque*; it is,
therefore, logical that the power of Western governments and media outlets is increasingly taking on totalitarian forms. The politically correct
consensus imposed by the mainstream media — recently strengthened by

various 'media laws' — is increasingly characterized by extremely selective news-gathering, slavish self-censorship and hysterical witch hunts. For the sake of their position and reputation, average academics, serious journalists and concerned citizens silently accept this development. Thus, fundamental critique is pushed to the margins of society: it is — still — the exclusive domain of 'political extremists' and the 'lunatic fringe'. Non-Cultural Nihilist thought, which necessarily includes the standard repertoire of Western philosophy, anthropology and cultural science, is quietly ignored and hushed up in the academia and media. Traditionalist thought was already removed from academic curricula and public discourse in the '60s, during the rise of Cultural Marxism — currently, the grand-inquisitors of the politically correct establishment have effectively declared it anathema. The same fate is now slowly being meted out to all other forms of thought originating with 'dead white men': the hostile elite has thus effectively pronounced a death sentence on Western civilization. Thus, every metapolitical statement based on Traditionalist thought now relates to the politically correct consensus of the Modern West as a glowing coal relates to a gunpowder keg. With *Alba Rosa*, it cannot be otherwise.

The genocidal totalitarian regimes of the 20th Centuries justified their inhuman repression by referring to their self-appointed historical missions and their supposedly democratic mandates. As the self-elected guardian of a supposedly 'optimal socio-political order', every totalitarian regime considers itself justified not only in using its institutional power for the political and judicial persecution of its opponents but also in enforcing its official ideology by means of indoctrination and manipulation. These practices take on the most perfected — most effective, most direct — form in the *politically correct totalitarian consensus* of Postmodern Cultural Nihilism. On the one hand, it rests on the motivating power (the 'carrot') of the political guidance systems of *Public Relations* (Edward Bernays, 1952) and *Manufactured Consent* (Herman & Chomsky, 1988). On the other hand, it rests on the correcting power (the 'stick') of the politically guided mechanisms of *social stigmatization* and *institutionalized psychiatry*. In its ideal form, the resulting totalitarian consensus constitutes a self-regulating mechanism that perpetuates itself by permanently well calibrated and highly deceptive fluctuations between formal (but repressive) tolerance and informal (but blanket) intolerance towards all forms of non-conformism.

Initially, the Soviet Union was on the vanguard of the development of the politically correct totalitarian consensus. Two of the corrective mechanisms developed by the Soviets are particularly significant: the concepts of 'counter-revolution' and 'political psychiatry'. During the Brezhnev years, the criteria for the judicial application of appropriate repressive measures — loss of civic rights, imprisonment, deportation, compulsory medication — were finally broadened to the point that over 20,000 political dissidents were locked up in asylums for the insane. The appropriate diagnosis of 'slow progressive schizophrenia' could even be made on the basis of 'mild symptoms' such as attempts at emigration, possession of forbidden books, participation in civil rights demonstrations and religious activities. Thus, social and psychological pathology was ascribed not merely to ideological, but also to intellectual and artistic 'deviations' from the 'party line'.

It was only after the fall of the Soviet Union that the 'Free West' would make up for its historical backlog. The development of an equivalent system of politically correct totalitarian consensus, tailored to fit Western societal conditions, was a function of the historical development of feminization (towards matriarchy) and xenification (towards ethnic replacement): the shift towards a dictatorship of a hybrid matriarchical-immigrant 'new proletariat' determined the form and intensity of the new totalitarian consensus. The institutionalized cognitive dissonance built into this new consensus requires an unprecedented level of intellectual and moral regression, to be finally followed by real-time 'idiocracy'; hence the accelerated phasing out of education and science. The 'alternative reality' aimed at has already been partially realized: corrupt party bosses are 'innovators', resentful feminists are 'power women', drug-dealing mafia bosses are 'investors', fanatical terrorists are 'unstable individuals', insolent asylum fraudsters are 'refugees' and criminal illegal aliens are 'dreamers'.

Sooner or later, everybody who does not conform to this absurd consensus ideology is associated with the ultimate stigmata of Cultural Nihilist neo-demonology: 'intolerance', 'sexism' and 'racism'. Primarily, these stigmata function as sub-rational-emotional markers in the feminized discourse that accompanies the matriarchy of the Postmodern West. In this regard, 'feeling terms' such as 'racism' can be understood as the Cultural Nihilist equivalent of the Bolshevik term 'counter-revolutionary'.

> 'Racism' is a term [now] usually only used by critics. Official definitions of 'racism' often state that the term should only be applied to the belief that some races are superior and on negative actions due to this. In practice it is often applied as a form of ad hominem on anyone believing in the existence of races or even on persons advocating restricting immigration, persons criticizing another culture or multiculturalism, persons supporting their own country/ ethnicity, etc. (Metapedia).

Such terms fit into the Orwellian concept of *Newspeak*: individuals tainted by them are per definition guilty of *crimethink*, a sin that defines them as *unpersons* in Cultural Nihilist utopia. The proto-totalitarian regime covers itself by stretching its maximally elastic 'anti-discrimination' laws to the point that rational debate concerning its key projects — matriarchical 'idiocracy', gender deconstruction, ethnic replacement — is no longer possible. Only a full internalization of politically correct cognitive dissonance (*blackwhite*, *double speak*) can still provide the goody-goody citizen with waterproof *crimestop*. The *Gutmensch* is born.

The Traditionalist cure for this psychopathological hijacking of the public debate is a rediscovery of the fundaments of Western civilization: a return to the indispensable hierarchical principle underpinning every authentic community. The first step to take is to rediscover the functionality of the classical principles of *Auctoritas*, *Nomos* and *Katechon*. Every authentic community is defined by *holistic vision* and *anagogic direction*: there, 'intolerance' and 'hate' have no place in the public sphere; they are mere signs of psychological immaturity in the private sphere. The Cultural Nihilist hostile elite *projects* such negative 'feeling terms' onto its enemies: it is, in fact, this elite *itself* that is characterized by structural resentment and irrational aversion towards everything that is more distinguished, more beautiful, more gifted and more humane than itself—which is nearly everything else in the world. From a Traditionalist perspective, a rational debate with the Cultural Nihilist hostile elite is therefore simply impossible: Traditionalism can only reject Cultural Nihilism and its total-itarian governance projects out of hand.

As is the case in every totalitarian governance project, the baseness and meanness of the Cultural Nihilist regime feed on the empty-headed-ness and hard-heartedness of its subjects. Thus, the regime fears authentic knowledge and authentic identity—their re-activation is the main task of the opposition. The hostile elite of the West has not yet reached its ultimate goal of totalitarian power; its proto-totalitarian regime still has redoubt-able enemies. These enemies, united in a growing patriotic-identitarian resistance, include all people who stand up to defend Western civilization.

Cet animal est très méchant; quand on l'attaque il se défend!

❧

CHAPTER ONE

The Harrowing of Hell

Ten Traditionalist Perspectives on Modern Eurasianism

PROLOGUE: THE BETRAYAL OF THE WEST

*A nation can survive its fools, and even its ambitious fools. But it cannot
survive treason from within. An enemy at the gates is less formidable, for he
is known and carries his banner openly. But the traitor moves amongst those
within the gate freely, his sly whispers rustling through all the alleys, heard
in the very halls of government itself. For the traitor appears not a traitor: he
speaks in accents familiar to his victims, and he wears their face and their
arguments, he appeals to the baseness that lies deep in the hearts of all men.
He rots the soul of a nation, he works secretly and unknown in the night to
undermine the pillars of the city, he infects the body politic so that it can no
longer resist.*

—MARCUS TULLIUS CICERO

URING THE 2017 GOLDEN DAWN CONFERENCE
in Rotterdam, Jared Taylor, the long-serving leader of the
American Renaissance Foundation, called German Chancellor
Merkel the 'greatest traitor of the West since Ephialtes'. Before addressing
the substance of this qualification, it is appropriate to consider its formal
aspect. The words chosen by Jared Taylor depart from two elementary

principles of the Western political debate: the notion of diplomatic etiquette and the notion of democratic legitimacy. The speaker implies that
diplomatic etiquette no longer applies to a legitimately elected democratic
leader when the democratic process results in the election of a traitor. The
question arises why a cautious speaker like Jared Taylor denies the political leader of Europe's most powerful country status and legitimacy. It is
clear that the times when good citizens would line the pavement and wave
their little flags for visiting foreign statesmen are over. But many in the
audience still needed some time to part with the old notions of 'friendly
heads of state' and 'democratic leadership'. They may be helped by a wise
aphorism: *It is shameful when a foolish youngster fails to guard his tongue,
but it is elevating when, after many years, a wise elder speaks out* (Nikolás
Gómez Dávila). Jared Taylor's words came as a relief to all those who have
long repressed their desperation about the fatal course which the Western
leaders have set for their peoples. This repressed sentiment is akin to the
desperation of the passengers of flight *United 93*, who on '9/11' finally decided to storm the cockpit. Now that the leadership of the West has turned
out to be a *hostile elite*, it cannot come as a surprise that the peoples of the
West are turning to emergency procedures. But for the young people of
the West it is not enough that they feel themselves to be finally understood
by an elder leader: they also need to understand the precise nature of the
treason involved. To understand this, they need insight into the worldview of the Western hostile elite and into the origins of this worldview:
this is the key to the Betrayal of the West.

Young Western people are now only familiar with authentic Traditional identities (ethnicity, class, community, family, vocation) and authentic Traditional values (religious duty, national honour, governmental responsibility, civic duty, civil behaviour) in a *negative* sense: they can now
only reconstruct these identities and values by *inverting* the experience
they have of their role models (politicians, teachers, idols, fathers). Instinctively all young Westerners know that they have been betrayed. Their
identities — ethnicity, class, gender, vocation — have been 'deconstructed'
in Cultural Nihilist programmes of globalization, mass immigration and

feminization. Their heritage — material assets, workers' rights, social security, education, culture — has been sacrificed to baby boomer privileges, neo-liberal deregulation and affirmative action priorities. Their future has been fatally compromised because the baby boomer hostile elite has delegated effective power to institutions that are located beyond the reach of democracy. Economic power has been ceded to a cartel of international banks and multinational corporations, abstractly represented as 'free market' and 'international competition'. Political power has been relinquished to a cartel of transnational institutions, abstractly represented as 'European Law' and 'international treaties'. Within these parameters, young Western people will never be able to come to grips with the issues that determine their future. The greatest of these issues are global climate change, technological transhumanism, ethnic replacement and social implosion. Within the present parameters of institutional power and public discourse even the most sincere attempts at reform — 'environmental sustainability', 'labour market reform', 'regulated immigration', 'social policy' — are doomed to degenerate into cynical political rhetoric. For young Western people acceptance of such political marginalization equals the acceptance of a legacy of unlimited liability: it would doom them to life-long debt slavery.

The only exit from this impasse is an intellectual counter-deconstruction of the entire Cultural Nihilist discourse. Here Traditionalist doctrine offers an escape route: Traditionalist doctrine exposes the historical fallacy of the Cultural Nihilist ideology: it exposes the intellectual and psychological roots of the Betrayal of the West. Only such a counter-deconstruction can open the way to preventing, combating and reversing the Decline of the West. The Decline of the West, dramatically realized in the great revolutions, world wars and civil wars of the 20th century, is a function of the clashing forces of Modernity and Tradition within and between the European peoples, embodied in different states and empires at different times. Western history has now deprived these antithetical forces of much of their impetus; the Postmodern socio-economic, cultural and geopolitical vacuum testifies to their 'mutual annihilation'. For the first time after a century-long downward slide, the possibility of an upward reversal now presents itself: the vicious circle of thesis and antithesis may be broken. A cultural and intellectual space is opening up for a *synthesis* — a synthesis of Modernity and Tradition that Traditionalist symbolism identifies as the 'Golden Dawn'. In theory, at least, this offers the European peoples, now facing the nadir of the Crisis of the Modern World, a possibility of re-inventing themselves and of re-conquering their place in the sun. History will not repeat this opportunity to surmount the Betrayal of the West: it is up to the young people of the West to grasp the significance of this last chance.

1. THE EURASIAN PROJECT

At last, it may be that Russia pronounces the final Word
of the great general harmony, of the final brotherly communion of all nations...

—FYODOR DOSTOYEVSKY

The Traditionalist discourse is the oldest and most reliable weapon available to the young people of the West in their struggle to deconstruct Cultural Nihilism, which in its turn is the foundational premise of the Decline and Betrayal of the West. About this discourse more will be said shortly. Except for a theoretical (intellectual, ideological) alternative to Cultural Nihilism, however, also a practical (geopolitical, socio-economic) alternative is needed. The theoretical discourse of Cultural Nihilism is implemented through a practical programme: the thalassocratic Atlanticism based on American superpower, better known as the 'New World Order' since 1991. The fall of the Soviet Union resulted in a unipolar geopolitical reality in which this New World Order was able to raise its Cultural Nihilist foundation myth to the status of a standard global discourse. Historically this new monopoly of Cultural Nihilism coincides with the intellectual closure of the Traditional School, founded by René

Guénon, Ananda Coomaraswamy and Frithjof Schuon and ending with Seyyed Hossein Nasr. This means that Traditionalist discourse has been sidelined and confined to the academic and esoteric margin. But the institutional marginalization and public near-invisibility of the Traditionalist discourse has also had a positive effect: it has cleansed this discourse of all residues of academic political correctness and tactical dialectical compromise. Traditionalism has been reduced to its core identities: *meta-historical* worldview, *metapolitical* discourse and *apolitical* hermeneutics. This makes Traditionalism a stable reference point for all those who seek to dismantle the New World Order: Traditionalism can serve as a *gauge* and a *measure*: it can serve to theoretically *evaluate* and *validate* practical alternatives.

During recent years the escalating crisis of Western Modernity has permanently alienated an entire generation of young Western people from the New World Order: its dominant discourse of Cultural Nihilism is increasingly experienced as totalitarian and anachronistic. This has resulted in the phenomenal growth of an 'alternative' and 'identitarian' movement, thus far undefined and uncoordinated. Thus far, the only philosophically coherent ideological model that has been formulated within this movement is Archaeo-Futurism. Thus far, this movement has failed to formulate a sustainable geopolitical strategy. Archaeo-Futurism however, does provide a possible point of departure through its affiliation with Eurasianism, i.e. the metapolitical discourse that privileges 'World Island'-based Tradition over 'Outer Isle'-based Modernity and finds its origins in the particular (Slavophile, Orthodox) Traditionalism at the core of the White Russian émigré movement. In the same manner in which Cultural Nihilism is practically implemented through thalassocratic Atlanticism, Archaeo-Futurism seeks an alternative to the New World Order by exploring Eurasianism. Thus, it is worth exploring the degree to which Eurasianism provides a realistic geopolitical strategy for the rising resistance movements of the West. In this regard, Traditionalism provides a useful research model because Eurasianism incorporates many Traditionalist ideas. A Traditionalist evaluation of Eurasianism can determine to what degree it can remedy the crisis of Western Modernity and whether it offers a viable alternative to the New World Order. It is important to determine to what degree Russo-centric Eurasianism is compatible with *Western* realities and to what degree it has geopolitical applicability to the *Western* peoples. For the sake of brevity, the 'West' will here be defined as that part of the European peoples that spent the entire 20th century outside the cultural-historical 'refrigerator' of Communism, and which was thus unremittingly exposed to the full force of Modernity. This 'West' includes the peoples of Western Europe and the overseas Anglosphere (which will here be defined to cover its Canadian-French and Afrikaans-Dutch appendices); these peoples have been hit hardest by Cultural Nihilism.

The following Traditionalist evaluation of Eurasianism aims at a cultural-historical 'diagnosis' of the Western peoples. This diagnosis should determine whether or not the Western peoples are at all able to undergo the 'therapy' of Eurasianism.

Every Traditionalist cultural-historical analysis is by definition *holistic*, and in this case, it requires a multidisciplinary approach for which the required assembly of instruments is far from complete. Even so, some basic outlines are already detectable. *Religiously*, the Cultural Nihilist discourse of the post-war baby boom generation — reaching absurdist extremes now that the hostile elite has discarded its mask — is a false doctrine of *subhuman (satanic) origin. Sociologically, it is a sub-rational modality of habitus. Psychologically*, it is an *egosyntonic syndrome* that excludes the possibility of objective self-analysis. Even these rudimentary outlines make it clear that it is only possible to speak of true 'betrayal' in a *retroactive sense*. The terms 'organized treason' and 'deliberate conspiracy' can only apply to the very highest echelons of the global hostile elite. This does not alter the historical liability of the hostile elite as a whole, but it does give an indication of the varying degrees of penalty applicable to its constituent parts. A future reckoning in terms of 'lessened responsibility' and 'limited accountability' will depend on the final historical balance of Cultural Nihilism, but if a minimum of Western civilization is salvaged from the wreckage, it is reasonable to expect that most of the hostile elite will end up in asylums for the insane and rehabilitation clinics rather than in prison cells or in front of firing squads. But irrespective of the manner in which the hostile elite is relegated to the dustbin of history, the question remains to what degree the Cultural Nihilist discourse has infected the masses of the European peoples. The ability of the European peoples to undergo a Eurasian 'therapy' ultimately depends on the degree to which they have absorbed and internalized Cultural Nihilism — and on the degree to which they have developed a natural resistance to it over the course of the last decennia. The result of the Betrayal of the West will depend on the answers to these questions. More concretely formulated, these questions are: how deep does the Betrayal of the West run — and why does it run so deep?

First and foremost, survival in the escalating Crisis of the Modern World — a crisis which is hitting the Western heart of Modernity first, deepest and hardest — demands a radical intellectual and existential shift. The first shift that is required is an irreversible transition from inner hyper-individualism and outer cosmopolitan universalism to inner community-identity and outer supra-national corporatism. Only on this basis can the European peoples be expected to achieve the *collective* will and the *collective* power that are required from them if they want to survive the approaching crisis of European history. The second shift that is required is a final abolition of reactionary hyper-nationalism. A hyper-nationalistic programme, such as that of the Third Reich, may result in spectacular gestures, but it is doomed to failure in the face of the quantitative resources of the New World Order. Eurasianism may provide a geopolitical framework for a collective approach: it is the logical central element of a 'boreal alliance' of all the European peoples. For the sake of brevity here the 'European peoples' will be defined in semi-linguistic terms as all peoples of Indo-European (Hellenic, Albanian, Romance, Celtic, Germanic, Baltic, Slavic, Armenian), Basque, Finno-Ugric and (North, South and East) Caucasian descent. Such a 'boreal alliance' obviously extends to the entire overseas Anglosphere and it finds its natural allies in the Indo-European peoples of West and Southern Asia, but it falls or stands with its geopolitically central element: Eurasianism. The realization of the Eurasian project depends entirely on the willingness and ability of the European peoples to proceed with the above-mentioned shifts. The historical Betrayal of the West is the root problem: the *inner* Cultural Nihilist betrayal opens the gate to the *outer* enemy. The Cultural Nihilist betrayal is effectuated by inner division: the strategy of *divide et impera* is operative *within* as well as *between* the European peoples. Within each people estates, classes, generations and genders are set up against each other through the 'deconstruction' of authentic identity and through the 'competitive' procedures of hyper-democracy. The European peoples are pitted against each other through manipulated historical 'rivalry' and through artificial diplomatic 'prestige'. This refined manipulation exploits the many psychohistorical traumas of the European peoples. The successful realization of the Eurasian project depends on a successful neutralization of these traumas.

The unity that the Eurasian project requires of the European peoples is only possible after a transparent historical analysis and a collectively cathartic 'therapy', focused on the debilitating traumas caused by the Second World War. A collective cultural-historical *Vergangenheitsbewältigung* and a psychohistorical settling of accounts are basic preconditions for snuffing out the Betrayal of the West. A fully validated Eurasianism requires an honest account of the Hellstorm that 20th century history brought upon the West. The unresolved past and the unrecognised injustice of this Hellstorm mean that the old divisions between the European peoples will continue into the 21st century. These fatal divisions are eagerly exploited by the great enemy of all European peoples: the global hostile elite of high finance, multinational corporations, Cultural Nihilist academia and *Social Justice Warrior* media. This global hostile elite has opened the gates of the West and is now inciting the non-European peoples to an ultimate all-out assault on the West. The inability to learn from the Hellstorm of 20th century history condemns the European peoples to a repetition in the 21st century: *Hellstorm 2.0*. Only learning the lessons of Hellstorm 1.0 offers them a chance to survive Hellstorm 2.0. History will not forgive the European peoples a second time.

2. HELLSTORM 1.0

Scipio, when he looked upon Carthage as it was utterly perishing
and in the last throes of its complete destruction,
is said to have shed tears and wept openly for his enemies.

—POLYBIUS

It is worth considering Jared Taylor's qualification of German Chancellor Merkel as the 'greatest traitor of the West since Ephialtes' from a Traditionalist perspective. Irrespective of the questionable notion that a woman can ever objectively experience herself as a 'traitor', the fundamental issue at stake is the true nature of the being and work of Merkel. These can only be grasped through a proper understanding of the German *Götterdämmerung* of 1945: Merkel personifies the posttraumatic schizophrenia of the human residue that remained on the territory of the former German state after the dissolution of German identity. Like all 'New Germans' born after *Stunde Null*, she is existentially conditioned by the deepest caesura known in Western history. *Stunde Null* is the historical 'black hole' that separates the hyper-identitarian Third Reich from the militantly nihilistic New World Order. Whereas Merkel's predecessor Helmut Kohl, sworn into the *Hitler Jugend* during the *Führergeburtstag* at Berchtesgaden, could still barely claim the *Gnade der späten Geburt*, but *Kohl's Mädchen* is already an entirely unsuspected product of the post-war regime. Whereas Kohl still had to cautiously steer a course between the pre-war generation and the post-war occupation, Merkel is already able to proceed full steam ahead towards the final destination of the 'Federal Republic': 'Anti-Germany'. This 'Anti-Germany' is the cultural-historical equivalent of a vanquished enemy that has been reduced to a castrated slave: a perfect exemplary warning in the service of the global New World Order. The direction of this project is explicitly expressed in the self-destructive discourse of the hostile elite: anti-nationalist political 'Europeanism', anti-identitarian social 'humanism' and anti-traditional cultural 'Americanism'. The final destination of the 'Anti-Germany' project can be deducted from statistical reality: economic tributary status (*Wiedergutmachung*, 'reparations', Euro-related sovereign debt liabilities, 'development aid', 'asylum facilities'), demographic sui-genocide (negative birth rates) and enforced *Umvolkung* (ethnic replacement through mass immigration). This Anti-German 'Federal Republic' is the deepening black hole at the heart of Europe, and the German Chancellor guards its psychohistorical 'event horizon'. There is a total taboo on everything that existed before *Stunde Null*, and the usurious mortgage of the past is eating up the German present as well as the German future. As in the 19th century, so again in the 21st century, the centrepiece of European civilization is Germany — but now in a perversely inverted manner. Bismarck's Second Reich was Europe's geopolitical heavy-weight, its guide in science and technology and its treasury of art and culture; now Merkel's 'Anti-Germany' is Europe's geopolitical dead heart, its heart of Cultural Nihilist darkness and its open door to terror and barbarity. Against this background, it is clear that stabilization of the black hole of 'Anti-Germany' is the urgent task of the Eurasian project: Germany is the engine of European Cultural Nihilism and the resulting geopolitical vacuum constitutes a fatal mortgage for Europe's present and future. Only an intrepid time travel across the event horizon of *Stunde Null* — a direct *Vergangenheitsbewältigung* — can cure the blind madness of German and European Cultural Nihilism. An immediate dismantling of the Cultural Nihilist 'state religion', with its central doctrines of Germany's people as a *negativ auserwähltes Volk* ('negatively chosen people') and of Germany's history as the *singulärste Schuld auf Erden* ('the world's uniquest debt') is an absolute precondition for the survival of European civilization (Rolf-Peter Sieferle, *Finis Germania*, 2017).

One of the elements that fell into the black hole of Germany's unresolved past was the wife of Merkel's predecessor Helmut Kohl, Hannelore Kohl: shortly before '9/11', she chose eternal sleep. Her personal history symbolizes the *Werdegang* of Merkel's 'Anti-Germany': her story gives a direct account of German history that renders superfluous many shelves of censored 'revisionist' history books. Until the day, in some distant future, when the assembled historians of European peoples decide to write down the Truth, nobody can know what was the true extent of the atrocities that have recently been reconstructed by writers such as Giles Mac-Donogh (*After the Reich*, 2007) and Thomas Goodrich (*Hellstorm*, 2010). But one thing is certain: they cannot be allowed to reignite the mutual cycles of hate and revenge that have drawn in the European peoples during the 20th century. The personal history of Hannelore Kohl knows no hatred and no revenge — only silent suffering and despairing death. In the hopeless final battles of the German *Götterdämmerung* she was one of the hundreds of thousands of German women and girls who had to empty the bitter cup of *totaler Krieg* till its last dregs; in 2001 she took the last sip of her own free will. The American air force had destroyed Leipzig and her parental house. The family was evacuated to the countryside, but was overtaken by the Red Army. Nobody has recorded how many soldiers outraged the twelve-year-old girl before she was 'thrown out of the window like a wheat bag'. Recorded posthumously was the broken life that resulted from those last hours before *Stunde Null*: the lifelong pain from spinal injury, the psychosomatic suffering that ended in extreme photophobia, the panic attacks around normal things such as the smell of garlic and alcohol — and the sound of the Russian language. The language of Pushkin and Tolstoy may have become unbearable because of the Soviet soldiers, but the Soviet generals let the soldiers do what they did and the Soviet politicians let them go unpunished. And then there were the German 'men' who 'survived': the German soldiers who did not fight to the death, the German generals who surrendered and the German politicians who went to parley with the enemy. After the *Wende* Helmut Kohl again went to parley — to redeem Hannelore's *Heimat*.

Nearly all European peoples suffered deeply during the 20th century. One day this suffering may be fully quantified and qualified, but it can never be justified. The two world wars, the great revolutions, the great civil wars, the Red and the Black Terror, the decolonization wars — all their victims demand appropriate remembrance and all their lessons must be learned. None of the European peoples is without reasons for hate and vengeance. But the European peoples can no longer afford to sit in judgment on each other if they want to survive the coming Crisis of the Modern World: divided they will fall, and only in unity can they remain standing. To resolve these hate and revenge complexes, it is useful to look at 20th century history in a new manner. Looking back across seven decades, one can see no longer an incoherent series of separate revolutions, wars and civil wars, but rather the outline of a single conflict. From a Traditionalist perspective this historical complex — the forty years between the First Russian Revolution of 1905 and the destruction of the Third German Empire in 1945 — appears as a single, comprehensive 'European Civil War' between the forces of Modernity and Tradition. The last phase of the conflict, otherwise knows as the 'Second World War', clearly shows its essential character as a *civil* war. In those years, millions of soldiers fought on the 'wrong side'. More than a million Soviet citizens fought against the Soviet government. More than fifty thousand Dutchmen fought for the Axis powers: between 1941 and 1945 more Dutch soldiers died on Soviet soil fighting *for* Germany than died during the 1940 Dutch campaign *against* Germany.

The author belongs to the small Dutch nation: he is not able and not allowed — nor does he want — to sit in judgment of the historical claims and questions of 'guilt' of the greater European nations. He can only see parallels in Dutch history: even the small Dutch nation, supposedly peacefully prospering between its dikes and windmills, has reasons for hate and revenge. Aside from the burden of four centuries of overseas (colonial, South African) history, the Dutch nation also carries the burden of 20th century European history. There is still latent hatred against Germany, which tried to quickly wrangle its way out of a two-front war by destroying Rotterdam (May 1940 — 900 dead) — five days of *Blitzkrieg* were followed by five years of terror, genocide and plunder. There is still latent resentment against America and England for the misdirected bombings of Nijmegen (February 1944 — 800 dead) and Bezuidenhout (March 1945 — 500 dead). But perhaps 'Nijmegen' and 'Bezuidenhout' allow the Dutch people a degree of empathy with the German people, who during the same years suffered Allied 'carpet bombings' on an incomparably larger scale. If the 56 bomber planes and 67 tons of bombs of 'Bezuidenhout' caused 500 dead, made 20,000 homeless and rendered large parts of The Hague uninhabitable for many years, then what was the effect of *800* bomber planes and *1.8 million* tons of bombs — during the first night of the Allied campaign against Hamburg alone (July 1943)? The chilling numbers of the German *Götterdämmerung* escape human comprehension: during the Second World War, more than 67 million tons of Allied bombs were dropped only on Berlin. Scientific analyses and statistics are useful and necessary, but they are wholly inadequate when it comes to measuring the depths of the tragic European Civil War: this measure can only be achieved by personal acts of witnessing, such as that of Hannelore Kohl.

Because, of all the Western people, the Russian people has suffered longest and most during the 'Western Civil War', it is fitting to also consult a Russian witness. Alexander Solzhenitsyn, an officer in the Red Army during the Soviet invasion of East Prussia, was arrested in February 1945 on charges of 'anti-Soviet propaganda'. During the following years of imprisonment and forced labour he wrote the long poem *Prussian Nights*; there he writes not only about the Russian revenge for Tannenberg, but also about the Russian war crimes that he witnessed in East Prussia. Solzhenitsyn's testimony proves that the Russian people is its own best judge. His words, implicitly dedicated to hundreds of thousands of Hannelores, accurately mirror the images of *Hellstorm 1.0* that have settled in the German psyche. Is it conceivable that these images — half-repressed, half whitewashed — unconsciously impel the German Chancellor, the childless matriarch of emasculated 'Anti-Germany', to the masochistic exercise of *Hellstorm 2.0*? Is this the self-enforced repetition of history in a perversely reversed 'role play'? Again, unpunished terror, plunder and mass rape — this time perpetrated by an intentionally encouraged invasion of 'refugees'. Again, the acceptance, the suppression and the impunity of the rape of the nation — this time by a *female* leader who stands up for the *perpetrators.* Instead of taking a poison capsule in a bunker, *Frau* Merkel ends up on a 'selfie' with the enemy. The real meaning of her infamous words *wir schaffen das* is this: *Deutschland ad acta legen.* Thus, she personifies the psychohistoric black hole in the heart of Europe, while Solzhenitsyn's words clarify its origin:

> *Zweiundzwanzig, Hoeringstrasse.*
> *It's not been burned, just looted, rifled.*
> *A moaning, by the walls half muffled:*
> *The mother's wounded, still alive.*
> *The little daughter's on the mattress,*
> *Dead. How many have been on it?*
> *A platoon, a company perhaps?*
> *A girl's been turned into a woman,*
> *A woman turned into a corpse.*
> *It's all come down to simple phrases:*
> *Do not forget! Do not forgive!*
> *Blood for blood! A tooth for a tooth!*

3. THE FALL OF THE WEST

vae victis!

Gli uomini e le rovine (1953) is the appropriate title of Evola's Traditionalist review of the Western Civil War. He points out the unifying factor of the converging elements of domestic revolution, civil war and international conflict: the meta-historical conflict between rising Modernity and declining Tradition, cutting straight through all the European peoples. Evola surveys the cultural-historical ruins that remain after the inevitable victory of Modernity and he warns the survivors of defeated Tradition against illusory political activism. This year sixty-five years will have passed since Evola's review; in the meantime, the ruins of the old West have been cleared physically and the heritage of the European civilization has been psychologically covered over by a radical Modernist 'Europe 2.0'. This 'Europe 2.0', implemented politically, monetarily and socially by the totalitarian EU superstate, has become the ideal laboratory of Modernity. Here the remnants of the European peoples are subjected to the most sadomasochistically bizarre forms of vivisection: demographic sui-genocide, ecocidal hyper-consumerism, militant secularism, ochlocratic hyper-democracy, institutional matriarchy and cultural oikophobia are the most poignant results of this historically unprecedented *Umwertung aller Werte*. The sheer scale aside, from a macro-historical perspective there is nothing new under the sun: this is the natural winding up of the legacy of the West. The universal patterns of defeat and downfall are self-evident. The fall of Carthage in 146 BC meant that men died in battle, that the city was destroyed, that the ground was salted and that the women and children were sold as slaves. The fall of Jerusalem in 70 AD meant that its Temple was destroyed, that its walls were torn down and that its inhabitants went into exile. The Fall of the West in 1945 meant that the victors could dispose of the land, the property and the people of much of the West — this is the ancient right of the victor, still incorporated in international law through the principles of *uti possidetis* and *ex factis ius oritur*.

But since that time the Fall of the West has also overtaken the 'victors' of 1945. For France and England, the pyrrhic victory of 1945 was merely a prelude to the final liquidation of their empire and their great power status. For Russia the dearly bought victory of 1945 was followed by an impossible — costly, prolonged, lonely — stand-off with the global power of the Anglo-Saxon thalassocracy, and the resulting economic bankruptcy was followed by the fire sale of the Soviet empire in 1991. After a short moment of euphoria, even the final remaining Western superpower, America, is now proving to be subject to the geopolitical laws of 'imperial overreach'. In spite of all its overblown rhetoric and saber-rattling, the American superpower has been fatally compromised. The overstretched American armed forces and the prohibitively expensive (inefficient, corrupt) military-industrial complex may still be able to execute short tactical interventions on behalf of the transnational interests of high finance, but the only true credibility they retain now rests solely on the all-or-nothing option of nuclear *Mutual Assured Destruction*. Astronomical debt and accelerated de-industrialization are sure symptoms of the implosion of American superpower. Thus, the official victors of 1945 have now effectively joined the official losers of 1945: they are now collectively subject to the historical mechanisms of the Fall of the West.

The themes and symptoms of the downfall of civilizations are universal. The cults and ideologies of Western Modernity are bankrupt: Italian and German Fascism was forcibly eradicated; Russian Communism and Western European Social Democracy have abolished themselves; Anglo-Saxon Neo-liberalism will die out with the baby boomers. Western property is being sold off everywhere: the Western colonial empires, including the Soviet empire, have been decolonized; the Western industries have been shipped overseas; the Western peoples have fallen into debt slavery through 'budget deficit' and 'consumer credit' and Western inner cities and artworks have been sold to Arab oil sheikhs and Asian business tycoons. Western women are being handed over collectively: West European girls are made available through the mechanisms of the 'dating site', the 'sex industry' and the 'grooming gang'; Russian women are flown over to the brothels and harems of the Near and the Far East; North American women are encouraged to 'interracial dating' by movie stars and marketing strategists. Western knowledge and culture are cancelled: education is 'internationalized'; science is 'valorised'; museums are 'commercialized'; art collections are 'privatized'. The public and ideological discourse of the European peoples is adjusted to these realities, it is calibrated to fit the final destination: the Fall of the West. This is the core functionality of Cultural Nihilism: it is a *slave discourse* — the self-destructive discourse of the cowards who survived the Fall of the West.

Psychohistorically, the Cultural Nihilist discourse can be explained by the collective post-traumatic stress syndromes of the defeated European peoples. The unmistakable symptoms can be understood as adaptive strategies at both the individual and the collective level. They vary from the standard symptoms of mental escapism (materialist focus, hedonistic consumption), cognitive dissonance (structural denial, irrational aggression) to collective 'Stockholm Syndrome' (*Social Justice Warrior* activism, oikophobic ideology) and acute masochistic depersonalization (sexual aberration, suicidal addiction). The public discourse of institutionalized schizophrenia is not merely aimed at repressing the traumatic past, but also at incorporating the equally traumatic present. This public discourse underpins the authority and policies of the hostile elite: it is the cornerstone of the Betrayal of the West. A discourse of demophobia and xenophilia represses the betrayal of nation and country. A discourse of feminism and 'gender neutrality' represses the betrayal of women and children. The Fall of the West and the Betrayal of the West necessarily complement each other: this is the double reality that the young people of the West have to face.

4. The Light of Traditionalism

Ich habe über viele Jahre um Licht und Sonne gekämpft — leider vergebens.
[Many years I have fought for light and sun — unfortunately to no avail.]

—Hannelore Kohl

Now that the Second World War is disappearing behind the event horizon of living memory, a new generation is facing the formidable challenge of deconstructing the mythological discourse of the old generation and reconstructing the censored facts. After the death of the war generation and the end of the victors' discourse, the young people of the West are confronted with an apparently impossible dilemma. On the one hand, they instinctively recognize the need to respect the sacrifices that their ancestors made for their peoples. On the other hand, they rationally recognize that the net result of these sacrifices has created a world that is now past its expiry date in every respect: not only materially (economically, ecologically), but also immaterially (socio-culturally, psychologically). The young generation, heirs to globalization and eurocracy, lacks not only a protected national home, but also a protective international order. The apparent impossibility of a realistic alternative is the most important reason for the persistence of the increasingly unbearable *Brave New Baby Boomer World*. But a cleansing of the Augean stables of Western ideology can no longer be postponed: the ideological and political delusions of the past seven decades must now end. A cleansing of the Cultural Nihilist legacy of the baby boomers will result in a political-philosophical *tabula rasa* on which a new generation can write new solutions for the formidable problems it is facing. The *realpolitik* combination of national identity and international reality, ideologically and politically sabotaged by the *baby boomer hostile elite*, must have the highest priority. The survival of the Western peoples during the approaching 'world state of emergency' depends on their ability to unify in the face of shared challenges and shared enemies.

On the one hand, young Western people are forced to re-invent their own ethnic, social, cultural and historical identities. The formation of a politically nationalist and socially conservative *génération identitaire* is a basic survival strategy in the poisonous aftermath of the fifty-years-long Cultural Nihilist 'harrowing of hell'. Above all, a reconsideration of authentic identity requires an exact inventory of the pathogenic legacy of the baby boomers. The toppling of the power structures of Cultural Nihilism — the neo-liberal regime of high finance, the hyper-democratic dictatorship of the consumer proletariat and the anti-nationalist tyranny of the New World Order (UN, IMF, NATO, EU) — requires the deconstruction of its founding discourse. The effective elimination of these *outer* structures is a *sine qua non* for the survival of the Western peoples and for the survival of all authentic forms of identity everywhere, but this elimination can only take place after an *inner* transformation.

On the other hand, young Western people are forced to find realistic alternative answers for the great international questions of the day. First, there is the irreversible heritage of a historically unprecedented interconnection between all peoples of the world: the precarious geopolitical balance between the nuclear states, the vulnerable machinery of economic globalization and the delicate 24/7 information culture of the World Wide Web; these are its most sensitive elements. Added to these questions are the threats posed by escalating global climate change, technological transhumanism, ethnic replacement and social implosion. The risks inherent in these converging processes and their complex interaction demand a high degree of supranational consciousness as well as a realistic practice of international *Realpolitik*. Young Western people cannot afford the luxury of regressive experiments with outdated ideologies (libertarianism, communism, fascism) and unrealistic ideals (national autarky, mono-ethnic purism, social paleoconservatism). That does not mean that everything within these ideologies and ideals must be rejected out of hand because they are too extreme by the standards of contemporary political correctness; it merely means that *they are not extreme enough* as remedies for the approaching world crisis. The realities of the approaching world crisis are such that they require an entirely new worldview, a worldview that sublimates and surmounts all preceding ideologies and deals. This new worldview — a new metapolitical discourse — can incorporate useful elements from preceding ideologies and realistic practices from preceding ideals, but what is truly required of the resulting synthesis is *synergic* value.

An effective solution to this dilemma — the combination of recovered national identities with a new international power balance — and a fundamental acceptance of a new metapolitical discourse are only possible after a correct assessment of the depth and urgency of the impending world crisis. The threats presently facing the Western peoples, separately and collectively, must be recognized for what they truly are: *existential* and *direct*. There is no longer any choice and there is no longer any time. Four specific threats are about to converge in a *Hellstorm 2.0* of apocalyptic proportions: *global climate change, technological transhumanism, ethnic replacement* and *social implosion*. Western mankind is facing the ultimate test of Western history without any protection. Without historical identity and communal solidarity, it is retreating from biological reproduction and cultural transmission: the results are fatal demographic collapse and self-hating cultural relativism. Without social and personal identity, it is withdrawing from civic duty and work ethics: the results are hyper-individualist 'disaster capitalism' and unrestrained hedonist materialism. Without sovereign states and ethnic solidarity, it is retreating from military duty and political responsibility: the results are 'open borders' and barbarian invasions. Without religion and a natural sense of justice, it is retreating from divine and human law: the results are collective narcissism and social implosion.

From a Traditionalist perspective the impending 'age of consequences' simply represents the historical final settlement of Western Modernity: Western humankind is approaching the terminal stage of a decades-long degenerative process. Escalating global climate change follows from de-naturalization and materialist hedonism. Escalating ethnic replacement follows from an exclusively materialist focus and a feminine anima. Escalating social chaos follows from matriarchal hyper-democracy and collective narcissism. The only way that the Western peoples can survive the existential threats of Hellstorm 2.0 is through a total mobilization of all disposable material and human resources, but these can only be effectively applied after a precise analysis of these threats. In Hellstorm 2.0 the four elements of global climate change, technological transhumanism, ethnic replacement and social implosion are intricately linked in a dynamic mechanism of bio-cultural feedback loops, much like a tropical cyclone is made up of the combined elements of hurricane wind, cloudburst and storm surge. A realistic approach to Hellstorm 2.0 demands a thorough study of this dynamic mechanism as well as a careful calibration of policy responses. Traditionalist thought can contribute to the study of the anticipated trajectory of Hellstorm 2.0 and the preparation of appropriate countermeasures. In the same manner in which a thorough meteorological analysis and an effective disaster plan can assist in coping with a superstorm, a Traditionalist analysis can assist in coping with Hellstorm 2.0.

Every authentically Traditionalist perspective is based on transcendental reference, giving it metapolitical validity. The supra-ideological transparency and the meta-historical deep perspective that Traditionalism offers can contribute to a collective, all-Western preparation for Hellstorm 2.0 — and to the defusing of those recent rivalries and those present conflicts of interest that prevent collective measures of self-defence against the greater threats of Hellstorm 2.0. A Traditionalist perspective teaches that the existential threats of climate change, transhumanism, ethnomorphosis and social atavism are the logical end results of the dynamic cultural-historical mechanism of Modernity, effectuated through the bio-cultural feedback loops of materialist-technological, socio-economic and epi-genetic adaptation. It should be noted that Traditionalism explicitly rejects exclusively materialist notions of evolutionism and determinism: this is why Traditionalism *never* defines authentic identities — ethnicity, caste, gender — in exclusively biological-physical terms (compare Evola's holistic definitions of ethnicity and gender). In the final analysis, Traditionalism assumes these identities as spiritual-mental and *biological-physical* conditions in equal measure — this is why the expression *bio-cultural feedback loops* is used here. At a sub-intellectual level, the feedback loops of Modernity are reflected in the socio-cultural processes of hyper-individual 'freedom', hyper-democratic 'equality' and hyper-materialist 'progress'. At an intellectual level they are reflected in the political-philosophical discourse of the 'Enlightenment': nihilist secularism, historical materialism and culture relativism. All conventional models of contemporary politics — above all the dominant neo-liberal model — are fully embedded in this Enlightenment discourse, and thus within the *immanently referential* worldview of Modernity. To think that politically correct contemporary ideologies can offer structural solutions to the catastrophes that follow from Modernity is logically absurd. An effective struggle against the plagues of Modernity is only possible after the deconstruction of the intellectual modalities imposed by Modernity. Traditionalism offers a *transcendentally referential* worldview that is larger than Modernity and that allows its catastrophes — its symptoms — to become rationally treatable.

Rational analysis and rational action, however, are only possible on the basis of authentic instinct and authentic intuition. An accurate assessment of the true depths of the approaching world crisis is therefore only possible on the basis of an accurate understanding of the *meaning* of Hellstorm 2.0. In this regard, Traditionalism is of inestimable value, because it is fully geared for the distillation of meta-historical *meaning* from historical phenomena. From a Traditionalist perspective meta-historical meaning follows directly from the degree to which macro-cosmic transcendental ideals are, or are not, reflected in micro-cosmic immanent reality. Traditionalism offers instruments with which to measure the discrepancy between these two. The instruments of Traditionalism set standard values in all spheres of human thought and action: in religion, politics, economics, social relations, culture and art. Traditionalism proceeds from the absolute polarities governing the human condition, symbolically expressed in binary identity oppositions: light-dark, heaven-earth, spirit-matter, soul-body, male-female. This implies that meta-historical meaning is embedded in a dual reality of (sub-human) biological evolution and devolution and (super-human) metaphysical ascent and descent. The contemporary hermeneutic value of Traditionalism rests on its ability to (partially) restore the human capacities for experience and knowledge, capacities which have been severely degraded by Modernity. By rephrasing universal polarities and binary oppositions in modern scientific terms and by projecting these terms onto the historic trajectory of modern 'progress' Traditionalist hermeneutics can dislodge the entire Modern *epistème*. Thus, Traditionalist hermeneutics allow renewed access to the meta-historical *meaning* of the approaching world crisis: it renders it again rationally accessible to modern humankind — at least in part. This meaning is inevitably lacking in the historical materialist categories of the Modern *epistème* because it resides mostly *above* the exclusively rationalist and utilitarian categories of Enlightenment thought. It is the task of critical thinkers to extend and supplement these categories. Classical Traditionalist concepts in this direction are René Guénon's *crise du monde moderne*, Carl Schmitt's *Ausnahmezustand* and Julius Evola's *regressione delle caste*. Recent alternative concepts are Peter Sloterdijk's *anti-genealogische Experiment der Moderne*, Guillaume Faye's *archéofuturisme* and Jason Jorjani's *world state of emergency*.

5. 'TAKE SHELTER'

And I looked, and behold a pale horse: and the name of him that sat on it was Death, and Hell followed with him.

—REVELATION 6:8

From a Traditionalist perspective, the full meta-historical meaning of the approaching world crisis unavoidably remains intellectually inaccessible and politically elusive as long as Modernity prevails as an existential modality. In this respect, Traditionalist thought can offer a solution because within the Traditionalist epistemological framework not only scientific insights, but also artistic reflection and religious prophecy have their rightful place.

In those instances in which rational comprehension fails in a *downward* direction, modern man must rely on the enigmatic cryptomnesic and hierophanic elements that sporadically assist him in the modern arts — to the extent that his existential condition *already* allows him to grasp their essential meaning. An example of contemporary art with direct relevance to the Hellstorm theme is the recent movie *Take Shelter* (Jeff Nichols, America, 2011). This movie can be interpreted as a symbolic expression of a collectively subconscious 'premonition' of the approaching Hellstorm 2.0 — a 'warning' of what will happen when contemporary man relies exclusively on modernist interpretation and defusing strategies.

In those instances that rational comprehension fails in an *upward* direction, modern man must rely on the ancient prophecies, which are creating increasingly sinister echoes in modern reality — to the extent that his existential condition *still allows* him to endure their essential meaning. By offering a synthesis of scientific insight, artistic reflection and religious prophecy the Traditionalist method offers a *holistic* approach to the Crisis of the Modern World: it renders the coming of Hellstorm 2.0 cultural-historically *meaningful* as well as psychohistorically *tangible*. Thus, an authentically

Traditionalist analysis is valuable in an effective metapolitical preparation for Hellstorm 2.0: it allows for a sharpening of intellectual analysis and a calibration of instinctive reaction.

6. 'HELTER SKELTER'

And [the angel] opened the bottomless pit; and there arose a smoke out of the pit,
as the smoke of a great furnace;
and the sun and air were darkened by reason of the smoke of the pit.

—REVELATION 9:2

On 19 November 2017, in California State Prison, Corcoran, occurred the death of Charles Manson, schizophrenic-paranoid cult leader, ritual mass-murderer and self-declared prophet of Helter Skelter. For young people this Sixties figure may be of limited historical interest—his pop idol status faded after he had spent half century in detention and after his feats of arms had been dwarfed by 'Jonestown' and 'Waco'. After the incorporation of 'slasher' pornification and 'senseless violence' in the standard discourse of the cultural mainstream, Manson's Helter Skelter may appear somewhat outdated and puny. Still, there are unexpected ways in which Manson remains an important icon of contemporary Western Modernity. Two aspects of the life and works of Manson are especially noteworthy: first his pioneering role in Sixties Counter Culture—the embryonic stage of Cultural Nihilism—and second his symbolic significance. In this sense, Manson represents an archetypal expression of the institutionalized schizophrenia and the collective narcissism that psychohistorically underpin the discourse of Cultural Nihilism. The culminating point of Manson's activism coincides with the high point of the Counter Culture movement (1967–69): these are the years in which the historical direction of baby boomer ideology was settled. Manson's Helter Skelter project represents not only a logically consistent and puritanically purified application of Cultural Nihilism, but also a serious attempt to realize the

Christian Apocalypse. His aim, a merciless race war and the destruction of the white race, was inspired by a schizophrenic combination of radical nihilism and religious inspiration (a sublimation of American racial guilt complexes, projected onto the Christian eschatological vision). His method, viz. the manipulation of inter-ethnic libido trajectories and sadomasochistic compensation mechanisms, realizes the ultimate malignant-narcissist 'freedom' of Modernity. His early 'propaganda of the deed' places Manson in the historical *avant garde* of Cultural Nihilism.

In the same manner that the terror of *Narodnaya Volya* provided the psychohistorical basis for the Red Revolution in Russia, so the Helter Skelter of Manson provides the psychohistorical basis for Hellstorm 2.0 in the West. In this regard, it is important to note that the 19th century Russian resolution of the psychohistorical discharge of Modernity, characterized by intellectual courage and literary inspiration, is still highly relevant to a correct diagnosis of 21st century Western realities. The radical nihilist programme of Chernyshevsky's *What Is to Be Done?* (1862) and Nechayev's *Catechism of a Revolutionary* (1869), psychologically elaborated in Dostoevsky's *Notes from the Underground* (1864) and *Demons* (1872), provide valuable insights into the psychohistorical dynamics of the same nihilism that feeds Hellstorm 2.0. But it is essential to note the structural inversion in the perpetrator-victim-beneficiary relation that takes place between the Russian nihilistic terror and the American Helter Skelter. During the terror of *Narodnaya Volya* a *real intelligentsia elite* (a) attacks the *political* exponents (b) of the traditionalist establishment to *lift up* (c) the *repressed* people (d) for the sake of *a secular ideological* programme (e). But during Helter Skelter, an *anti-intellectual hostile elite* (a') attacks the *cultural* exponents (b') of the modern establishment to *destroy* (c') the free people (d') for the sake of a *religious millenarian* programme (e'). The Russian nihilist terror involved a rationally coherent political programme aimed at social-economic emancipation, but the American Helter Skelter involves the sub-rational and atavistic realization of oikophobic-demophobic sui-genocide. Europe is located between the extremes of the Russian-Traditionalist and American-Modernist antipodes, in a sliding scale from the Intermarium (the East European inner circle) to the Atlantic Rim (the West European outer circle). The different psychohistorical positions of (parts of) Eastern and Western Europe with regard to the American-Atlantic and Russian-Eurasian antipodes is accurately reflected within the contemporary EU, which is witnessing a revolt of the moderately modernist Visegrad block against the extreme-modernist Brussels regime. It is important to remember that the soullessness of Merkel's 'Anti-Germany' is located exactly at the dead centre of this gravity field.

An accurate prognosis of the West's Hellstorm 2.0 can benefit from a forward projection of the psychohistorical trajectory that is implied by Manson's Helter Skelter programme. Although phrased in mythological terminology and based on visionary hallucination, Manson's programme contains a number of key concepts that can expose the psychohistorical dynamics behind the realities of contemporary Cultural Nihilism: the political programme of neo-liberal globalization, the totalitarian eurocracy and the neo-Kalergian *Umvolkung*. First, there is the *aim* of Helter Skelter: the destruction of its own (American) people, of its own (white) race and of its own (Western) civilization. These *explicit* aims of Helter Skelter are mirrored in the *implicit* aims of the political programmes of current Cultural Nihilism. Second, there is the *method* of Helter Skelter: genetic 'outcrossing' through exogamy (pattern: whites as wife-givers and non-whites as wife-takers), complemented by evolutionary 'cropping' through genocide (pattern: whites as φαρμακός and non-whites as *invidia*).

Again: these *explicit* strategies of Helter Skelter are mirrored in the *implicit* strategies of current Cultural Nihilism. Examples of implicit but effective strategies aimed at the exogamic exclusion of white males are economic demotion through xenophile and feminist 'affirmative action', social exclusion through matrifocal divorce and custody laws and cultural marginalization through matriarchal childrearing and educational practices. Examples of implicit but effective strategies aimed at white (sui-) genocide are ethnically selective natalist policies through culture-blind abortion and child support legislation, ethnic cleansing ('white flight') through culture-blind tolerance of criminality and harassment and — last but not least — ethnic replacement through mass immigration. The final stage of this dual exogamic-(sui-)genocidal strategy, implemented through hyper-democratic sanction, formal legalism and pathological-altruist indoctrination, will be *demographic inundation* — hastened where necessary through mass murder disguised as common criminality (as in South Africa). From a Traditionalist perspective these developments are necessary effects of the downward psychohistorical dynamics of Modernity, especially of *feminization* (cf. Chapter 6). The postmodern Western public discourse is now wholly dominated by irrational and unrestrained matriarchal impulses: emotional instability, out-group altruism, unstructured resentment and sadomasochist lasciviousness. Feminization is an essential element of the power of the Cultural Nihilist hostile elite: it is the basis of its *Helter Skelter 2.0* project. This foundation was laid at the same time that Manson dedicated himself to his Helter Skelter 1.0 project (1967–69). These were the glory years of 'second wave feminism': the formative years of the *baby boomer hostile elite* — including its most notorious *activist citizen*, Hillary Clinton.

Two aspects of the Helter Skelter 2.0 project are dangerous in a special manner. First, there is the emotional-subconscious and the irrational-implicit nature of its foundational discourse. This discourse excludes rational argumentation and thus creates a totalitarian consensus, guarded by the Never Sleeping Eye of the Orwellian New World Order, enforced by hordes of rabid *Social Justice Warriors* and covered by the 'international treaties', 'European law' and 'anti-discriminatory legislation' of the Western 'legal' order. Second, there is the slow-motion executive practice of the Helter Skelter 2.0 project, which is a multi-generational project relying on failing inter-generational cultural reproduction. The slower this executive practice, the more certain will be its result.

In the same way that the Manson Family of Biblically Elect had the illusion that they could survive Helter Skelter 1.0 in the 'bottomless pit', so the Cultural Nihilist hostile elite has the illusion that it can weather the coming Hellstorm in the well-deserved comfort of its gated communities. But in this respect it will be sorely mistaken: *quos Deus vult perdere, prius dementat.* In any real race war only one thing counts: the self-defined group. In the race war that the Helter Skelter 2.0 project contributes to Hellstorm 2.0, there will be only one real sanctuary: the living citadel of the ethnic group. The question arises, however, whether the Western peoples can still survive the downfall of their hostile elite in a historically recognizable form. To survive Hellstorm 2.0 the Western peoples will have to re-think the definition of what constitutes their 'own group' — what it still is and what it can be again. They will also have to consider the need for collective defence. The time has come for the Western peoples to consider the option of a shared Eurasian project.

7. THE EURASIAN CITADEL

A new name, its roots to antiquity tracing,
As great as Thermopylae, all fame embracing,
A name to wipe shame away, with its plain truth
Smashing to smithereens calumny's tooth.

—IVAN VAZOV

The preceding comparison of the Russian *Narodnaya Volya* and the American Helter Skelter has yielded a number of important Traditionalist benchmarks. These benchmarks clarify the acceleration of socio-cultural regression between mid-19th century and mid-20th century America: it is a regression which now threatens the existence of the entire Western world and by extension the entire modern world. But these benchmarks also clarify a cultural-historical law of 'inhibiting progress': the Crisis of the Modern World has hit 'backward' Russia earlier than 'progressive' America and this results in a limited historical 'immunity' for the Russian soul with regard to the impending Hellstorm 2.0. Here it is important to note the word *soul*: the *body* will remain susceptible to earthly destruction. — *And fear not them which kill the body, but are not able to kill the soul; but rather fear him which is able to destroy both soul and body in hell*

(Matthew 10:28). Historically, Russia was the last exile seat of the Roman Empire (the 'Third Rome') and the last refuge of the Orthodox religion; it is increasingly likely that it will also be the last citadel of Western civilization. The meta-historical fate of Russia is self-evident: geographically it covers the heart of the World Island and historically it has suffered the cruellest test of Modernity: *faute de mieux* it is the Last Katechon. Eurasianism translates this meta-historical reality into the geopolitical realm. From a Traditionalist perspective Eurasianism, therefore, has the potential to be more than a mere Russian geopolitical tactic: it could be a survival strategy for Western civilization as well. In terms of simple *Realpolitik* Eurasianism may be beneficial for Russia, but a truly *Traditionalist* Eurasianism will come at a high price for Russia. A Traditionalist Eurasianism will recognize Russia's high vocation as the Last Katechon, but this will also obligate Russia to fulfil the fullest Christian calling: self-sacrifice. If Russia accepts this vocation and if it is willing to pay this ransom, it must prepare for *total war* with Modernity. In this 'Last War of the World Island', which is also the ultimate Hellstorm of Western civilization, Russia will have to be the citadel of Western civilization. In this constellation, the Western peoples will eventually turn to Russia. Within these peoples, a Traditionalist intellectual re-armament will eventually lead to a Eurasian geopolitical orientation. This requires a radical shift in consciousness and an intellectual revolution — the taming of Atlantic Modernity and the destruction of thalassocratic geopolitics. This new course can only be expected from a new generation: the West's rising *génération identitaire*. The Eurasian Camelot must first be built in the hearts and souls of the young people of the West.

It is a well-known lesson of history that the sons must pay for the sins of the fathers, and this also holds true here: the young people of the West are forced to drink the poisonous cup of history to its bitter dregs. From a Traditionalist perspective it is inevitable that the survivors of the fall of a civilization are caught in the historical void of degenerated old visions and immature new ones. The young people of the West are forced to surmount the bankruptcy of the Western past and to accept the debt payments of the Western future. But existentially and intellectually they can fall back on the ultimate citadel of Western civilization: Traditionalism. Eurasianism is the only geopolitical project that remains compatible with Traditionalism; in theory, it can even topple the entire complex of Cultural Nihilism, thalassocratic-Atlantic Modernity and the New World Order. A Traditionalist Eurasianism is the only viable geopolitical project that may still prevent the West as a whole from committing the ritual suicide that the Helter Skelter 2.0 project of the Cultural Nihilist hostile elite has in store for them. In theory, this project offers opportunities for global and coherent strategies to cope with all aspects of this ritual suicide: ecocidal climate catastrophe, transhumanist extinction, sui-genocidal ethnomorphosis and social implosion. From a meta-historical perspective a Traditionalist Eurasianism is the only remaining option — the 'standard argument' — of the West in a collective sense: it is the last remaining collective strategy to cope with Hellstorm 2.0 and the Postmodern *age of consequences*. There are other options — arguments and scenarios — but these are not collective. Perhaps some of the Western peoples — or rather *parts* of these peoples — can still survive individually, but others cannot. Even if some potsherds can be preserved, the vase of Western civilization will be broken.

The modalities, ideas and ideologies of Western Modernity are finished. The three major political philosophies of Western Modernity — the First Political Philosophy of Liberalism, the Second Political Philosophy of Socialism and the Third Political Philosophy of Fascism — have passed under the horizon of Western history (Dugin, 2015). It is conceivable that some elements of these philosophies — to the extent that they have proven their historical value — may contribute to a synthetic Fourth Political Philosophy: in that case, the countless sacrifices that the European peoples have made to Modernity will not have been entirely in vain. Examples of such elements may be: a limited free market and limited civil rights (Liberalism), a public sector and workers' rights (Socialism) as well as organic corporatism and ecological holism (Fascism). A sped-up articulation of a Fourth Political Philosophy to cope with Hellstorm 2.0 is of the essence.

It is highly unlikely that the European peoples will be granted more than a brief respite before Hellstorm 2.0 hits them with full force — one or two generations at most. This is the proverbial quiet before the storm. A Fourth Political Philosophy informed by Traditionalism can serve as the intellectual and ideological foundation for a Traditionalist Eurasianism; together they can offer a citadel in which the European peoples can weather the impending fury of Hellstorm 2.0. But a realistic assessment of the trajectory and intensity of Hellstorm 2.0 is essential when deciding on the architecture of this foundation.

8. HELLSTORM 2.0

Aloft all hands, strike the top-masts and belay;
Yon angry setting sun and fierce-edged clouds
Declare the Typhon's coming.
Before it sweeps your decks, throw overboard
The dead and dying — ne'er heed their chains
Hope, Hope, fallacious Hope!
Where is thy market now?

—JOSEPH TURNER

Surviving the impending Hellstorm 2.0 and the resulting 'hour of the wolf' demands an accurate assessment of its four most dangerous elements, the 'Four Political Realities' of the Postmodern world. Despite the litany of diversions and assurances put out by Western governments, academia and media, it is now close to certain that the present trajectories of these four realities — global climate change, technological transhumanism, ethnical replacement, social chaos — are about to converge into a catastrophic end scenario. This imminent convergence of industrial ecocide, technocatastrophe, demographic inundation and social anarchy reflects not only the old Indo-European mythological motif of the *Götterdämmerung*, it also reflects the old Christian eschatological motif of the Apocalypse: *And the four angels were loosed, which were prepared for an hour, and a day, and a month, and a year, for to slay the third part of them* (Revelation 9:15). The survival of the European 'third part' of humankind demands not only a thorough analysis of the Four Political Realities, but also a sincere revaluation of these old motives. Any Eurasianism that transcends geopolitical opportunism will have to combine this analysis and this revaluation.

(1) *Global climate change* is the most elementary threat facing the European peoples. Some scientific scenarios are already predicting a full-scale climate catastrophe. It is as good as certain that the confidential files of the best-informed decision-makers contain disturbing scientific data and forecast models concerning anthropogenic climate change: the content of leaked reports and whistleblower testimonies indicates that numbers and projections leave little room for complacency. At the same time, escalating artistic visions of the 'climate question' indicate a subliminal but tangible societal unease: in 2004 *The Day After Tomorrow* still drew a romantic borderline at the Rio Grande, but in 2017 *Geostorm* already threatens with a straightforward *extinction level event*. It is as good as certain that neither scientists nor policymakers would benefit from publishing indigestible projections. In any case, Cultural Nihilist policy dictates that the immediate interests of the adults always prevail over the long-term interests of the children. Thus, it is quite possible that the baby boomers, in their role as all-consuming *avant garde*, have not merely initiated 'climate change', but that they have also deliberately instigated an authentic 'climate apocalypse'. In this regard, the life motto *après nous le déluge* takes on an entirely new meaning: it constitutes the baby boomer's position *par excellence*. At least those few people in the West that still take the Book of Revelation seriously can prepare themselves; for the great consumer masses, taking refuge in secularist escapism, there will be a very rude awakening.

The global reality of anthropogenic climate change demands a global response. The illusionary policy slogans of the Cultural Nihilist hostile elite — 'climate goals', 'emission ceilings', 'green strategies' — are long past their expiry dates. The delay tactics that the Atlantic New World

Order has implemented on behalf of the ecocidal multinationals are no longer tenable. The articulation of effective climate policy is a basic task of the Eurasian alternative. In the final analysis, the functionality of national infrastructure — from the Dutch dikes to the Russian railways on the Siberian permafrost — and the efficiency of national emergency systems — including the dams that protect London, Venice, Rotterdam and St. Petersburg — depend on global climate dynamics. National security policies are already directly influenced by changing climate patterns. Even now, changing precipitation patterns are forcing British and Dutch policymakers to adopt new agricultural and urban strategies. Even now, melting pole caps are forcing American and Russian policymakers to develop new energy and defence strategies. In this regard, an effective Eurasian climate strategy can be of inestimable value: it may preserve (some of) the boreal habitat of the European peoples. An effective push-back against outdated consumption patterns, as well as the accelerated development of new technology and infrastructure, would benefit from supra-democratic authority and supra-national coordination. The geographic depth, natural resources and technological know-how of Eurasia allow for collective strategies of unprecedented scope. The strategic profundity, economic autarky and technological prowess of a collectively operating Eurasia make it likely that the European peoples would survive even a climate catastrophe. A collective approach to new challenges — new settlement areas, new shipping routes, new business ventures — can even lead to unsuspected growth and prosperity. From a Traditionalist perspective a Eurasian climate strategy is not only valuable as a viable alternative to the ecocidal practices of neo-liberal globalization, but also as the basis for a new global ecological balance. The holistic ecological vision of Traditionalism stipulates a restoration of the original boreal biotope of the European peoples: a relatively sparsely populated region, with rich biodiversity and space for natural landscapes. In such a biotope, semi-autarkic urban centres, eco-technological infrastructure and pristine nature can be combined: it will be a place where culture and nature are once again in balance. The restoration of the boreal biotope and a re-arrangement of the Eurasian space are elementary preconditions for the physical, psychological and spiritual resurrection of the European peoples: access to wide spaces and pristine nature are basic conditions for the European peoples to flourish.

(2) *Technological transhumanism* is a much less known, but potentially equally serious threat. In the same way that global climate change constitutes an existential threat to the natural *habitat* of the European peoples, technological transhumanism constitutes an existential threat to their natural *essence*. The technological developments that stem from the materialist functionalism of Modernity are already pushing humanity across the threshold of a transhumanist future. Eugenic and reprogenetic technology is already a fact of life and moving in the direction of an 'algenetic' (alchemic-genetic) manipulation of basic biological characteristics such as phenotype, gender and intelligence. Scientific revolutions in cybernetics and bioinformatics are already creating biotechnological applications and artificial intelligence. Systematic studies of parapsychology and controlled experiments in psychotronics are already advancing 'scientific occultism'. Alarming artistic reflections of transhumanist developments are already commonplace in popular culture (Luc Besson's *Lucy*, 2014; Matthew Santoro's *Higher Power*, 2018). In combination with the escalating Cultural Nihilist deconstruction of all Traditional forms of human identity (ethnicity, gender, age) these developments are opening the apocalyptic perspective of a technological realization of the ideological projects ('postgenderism', 'posthumanism') and the narcissist 'alternative realities' ('ego-extension', 'ego-theism') of Postmodern Cultural Nihilism.

The uncontrolled development of transhumanist technologies under the Cultural Nihilist regime of the New World Order poses an existential threat in the most fundamental and essential sense of the word. This threat is most acute for the European peoples because these peoples are the primary target of the Cultural Nihilist hostile elite and because, as a whole, they are most directly exposed to modern technologies. The creation of a regulating framework for these technologies is, therefore, a basic task for an alternative Eurasian order. From a Traditionalist perspective, however, a Eurasian technostrategy needs to do more than impose *negatively* phrased regulating frameworks: it also needs to pursue *positively* phrased policy aims. The incorporation of the holistic vision of Traditionalism would provide a Eurasian technostrategy with guidelines for research and experiment: such guidelines guarantee respect for basic notions of human dignity and for Creation as a whole. Such respect will always be lacking within a framework of secular materialism: under the continued regime of the Cultural Nihilist hostile elite it is as good as certain that megalo-maniac 'sorcerer's apprentices' will eventually abuse modern technology.

(3) *Ethnic replacement* presently constitutes the acutest threat to West-ern civilization: even if the human race as a whole survives global climate change and technological transhumanism, then ethnic replacement will still mean that the European peoples will not be among the survivors. Eth-nic replacement — destruction of the European peoples and the creation of a new 'Eurasian-Negroid race of the future' (von Koudenhove-Kaler-gi) — is the real aim of the Helter Skelter 2.0 project of the Cultural Nihil-ist hostile elite. Its underlying logic is as clear as it is ruthless. The Europe-an peoples have proven to be historically incompatible with Modernity, as it is defined by Cultural Nihilism: this is why they have to be mixed with and replaced by more malleable — less intellectual, less demanding, less self-conscious — slave peoples. The European peoples are demographi-cally infertile under totalitarian dictatorship, they are economically un-productive in urban-hedonist stasis and they are politically unreliable in debt slavery. To the extent that the thoroughly beaten and deeply indoc-trinated Western survivors of the 20th century wars of annihilation and totalitarian experiments accept their fate — to the extent that they abolish themselves, mix themselves with mass-imported colonists or disappear in societal marginality — their diminishing presence may still be tolerat-ed. From a Social Darwinist perspective, their future is logically predict-able: it is a future of ecological marginalization and biological extinction. From this perspective such future is, in fact, an 'evolutionary necessity': the 'failed' aberrations of the human race are being replaced by 'better

adapted' varieties. With some luck, in the future the last remnants of the Western peoples may still be tolerated, much as the American Natives and the Australian Aborigines of today are still tolerated as shrinking cultural curiosities in remote reservations and slums, occasionally visited by a lost tourist or a bored anthropologist. It is much more likely, however, that the last remnants of the European peoples will be finished off by impatient and vengeful ex-colonial invaders from the Third World. Perhaps brave men may still hope for a heroic death, but there will be no Sparta to hear of their Thermopylae. But for beautiful girls there is no such hope: they will have to fully endure the sadistic revenge fantasies of the invaders. The 'grooming gangs' that flourish in the legal void of present-day ex-England are merely modest trial-runs for what history has in store for post-feminist European womanhood.

It is ironic that the 'best' ethnic replacement scenario is actually the 'Islamic scenario'. In spite of the loudly voiced concerns of Western nationalists and populists, the Islamic scenario at least allows the European peoples the opportunity of physical survival. Mass conversion to Islam — politically opportune or otherwise — at least offers the perspective of biological survival within a basic structure of social order. To be sure, the European survivors will experience life under a totalitarian theocracy, sustained by primitive collectivism, judicial cruelty and cultural levelling as a great setback in terms of civilization, but at least their physical continuation will still be an option. Much more drastic than the 'Islamic scenario' is what may be termed the 'African scenario'. A non-Islamic *Umvolkung* scenario is much less attractive, because it will lack all structure. In such a scenario the last Western peoples — islands of indigenous shipwrecked castaways in a sea of abject barbarity — will have to survive in an 'Africanized' Europe. Because most Western people would not survive a year of 'going native' in Kinshasa or downtown Johannesburg, it is necessary to briefly explain the words 'abject barbarity'. In the 'African scenario', the economy will founder in falling productivity, institutional corruption and unbridled nepotism. Infrastructure will crumble under demographic overload, technological incompetency and political disinterest. Public order will be crushed under failing law enforcement, ethnic violence and judicial chaos. In this scenario, 'political power' is a *contradictio in terminis*: every pretended governmental authority will have to bend to the reality of hyper-democratic idiocracy. Government officials will mobilize the hunger and resentment of the demographic majority against 'colour privilege', a 'privilege' that is inevitable due to well-established ethnic differentials in labour ethics, social structure and resource planning. The mass killing of the Belgian population in Lumumba's Congo, the legalized expropriation of the British population in Mugabe's Zimbabwe and the politically tolerated genocide of the Afrikaner population in Zuma's South Africa are only a foretaste of what awaits the European peoples in an 'African scenario'. Before Europe lets itself be colonized by Africa it would be useful for Europeans to inform themselves about the sadistic and bestial perversions that surrounded the much-lauded 'decolonization' of Africa. Perhaps the most frightening answer to the question of why young people in the West are not informed about these historical realities is that the malignant-narcissist hostile elite of the baby boomer generation actually — consciously or unconsciously — *wishes* to subject their children and grandchildren to these perversions and bestialities.

Halting and reversing the ethnic replacement must have high priority in the creation of an alternative Eurasian world order. The speed at which the Western peoples of the Atlantic littoral are being replaced is now so high that only a few decennia remain before these peoples will be minorities in their home nations. As long as the Cultural Nihilist ideology of the thalassocratic-Atlantic New World Order dominates public discourse throughout the West, any effective resistance against ethnic replacement is impossible. As long as the 'populist' and 'libertarian' patriotic resistance does not break with the political correctness discursive 'frame', and as long as they do not reject the hyper-democratic institutional 'frame', they are doomed to failure. Within the present parameters — the political practice of parliamentary democracy, the debate culture of the media cartel, the ideology of hyper-democracy — all attempts at a substantial reform of immigration policy will be futile. The 'long march through the institutions' is only suitable for Maoist 'fellow travellers': it corrupts, trivializes and vulgarizes. The only exit from this deadlock is a metapolitical revolution that deconstructs the Cultural Nihilist discourse and delegitimizes the Cultural Nihilist institutions. This implies a *top-down revolution*, inspired by higher authority and expressed in higher identity. A Traditionalist Eurasianism can offer both: it can offer the higher authority of authentic charisma as well as the higher identity of authentic community. In concrete terms, these are: *auctoritas* based on a historical *Ausnahmezustand* and *Volksgemeinschaft* based on historical affiliation. A Traditionalist Eurasianist project must be aimed at a metapolitical revolution that re-introduces these notions of authority and community.

(4) Even if the threats of global climate change, technological transhumanism and ethnic replacement can be averted, then still the European peoples face a fourth existential threat, viz. *social implosion*. Cultural Nihilism, with its poisonous combination of militant secularism, neo-liberal Darwinism and culture relativism, has a fatal effect on all authentic forms of religious, ethnic, social and cultural identity. The 'deconstruction' of these identities feeds the deluge of militant atheism, self-defeating oikophobia, atomizing anomie and collective narcissism that is rolling over the Western world. The visible increase of social chaos is simply the outer reflection of an invisible inner crisis of de-personification. The advance of social chaos may be greatest in America, which is the 'guiding light' of Western Modernity, but its symptoms are already visible throughout the entire West: hyper-democratic anarchy, ochlocratic mismanagement and idiocratic barbarism increasingly dominate the entire public space. The systematic deconstruction of all authentic forms of personal identity is *externally* institutionalized in matriarchic hyper-democracy, anti-nationalist legislation and xenophile 'affirmative action'. *Internally* it is realized through subconscious conditioning ('modern child rearing'), internalized cognitive dissonance ('modern education') and targeted subliminal manipulation ('modern media'). The result is a self-reinforcing cycle of collective degeneration and individual psychopathology — the logical

endpoint of this dynamic is social implosion. In the final analysis, it is this social pathology that is responsible for the existential threats of climate catastrophe, technological transhumanism and ethnic replacement. A healthy social organism does not destroy its own ecological niche, it does not experiment on its own vital organs and it does not tolerate parasitical hostile take-overs. From a Traditionalist perspective, the coming of Hellstorm 2.0 is a necessary evil: the ultimate test of Western civilization has the meta-historical meaning of a *purification* of the Western peoples. Perverted Cultural Nihilism and degenerate Modernity must die in the collective mind of the West before the heart of the European peoples can start to beat again. This purification demands nothing less than their spiritual re-birth. In this test, no exertion can be too demanding and no sacrifice can be too great. An essential teaching of the Western Tradition is the *mors triumphalis*: it stipulates that all those who commit themselves to the ultimate battle are certain of victory. A Traditionalist Eurasianism will have to practice this teaching.

A Traditionalist Europeanism will be able to direct the European peoples in the approaching *inner struggle*. At the heart of Traditionalism lies the *Sophia Perennis* and this Eternal Knowledge contains an irrepressible creative force: it is the power that lets the blind man again see the glorious dawn, that lets the crippled man rise again in youthful vigour, that re-ignites cold ashes into all-consuming fire. Thus, Traditionalist Eurasianism can lead the European people through Hellstorm 2.0 and guide them towards an unexpected resurrection. Provided it is led by a worthy Katechon and guided by Traditionalist values, Eurasianism has the power to resurrect authentic forms of identity in the European peoples: faith, ethnicity, estate, gender and vocation. This ability to reawaken the Western Tradition, still deeply buried under thick layers of theoretical treatises, political analyses and public debates, is of inestimable value. This secret fire, still smouldering deep in the bosom of time, has the power to burn down the entire titanic project of Cultural Nihilistic Modernity.

9. Across the Threshold of History

aut viam inveniam, aut faciam

In the face of the Four Political Realities of Hellstorm 2.0, young Western people cannot be altogether blamed for massively opting for escapism. But the remarkable lack of 'communal engagement' among post-baby-boomers is essentially due to the great fire sale of all forms of community and identity by the baby boomers: the criticism of the post-baby-boomers by the baby boomers is nothing more than a transparent outward projection of unsolvable inward guilt. Silently, the baby boomers are counting on the continued societal disengagement of the post-baby-boomers: such disengagement is an absolute precondition for the continued existence of the Cultural Nihilist New World Order. The Postmodern Western world is therefore fully geared to the propagation of escapism: except for the classic recipe of cognitive dissonance, nihilist materialism and soulless hedonism, there is now also a more accessible alternative: the *virtual reality* fantasy world of social media, gaming and infotainment. From a cultural-historical perspective these escapist facilities, plus a minimal level of material well-being, may be understood as a necessary 'bribe'.

The imminent self-abolishment of the historical ethnic communities of the West is a logical consequence of the baby boomers' collective conversion to Cultural Nihilism, but the self-abolishing process can only be fully completed after the biological end of the baby boomers themselves. From a bio-evolutionary (ethnic, cultural-adaptive) perspective the baby boomers are still a product of the historical ethnic communities of the West and as long as they are alive the main pillars of these communities need to be kept standing. Only after the biological end of the baby boomers can these pillars be finally discarded: nation-state, social hierarchy, church, academy, family. Until that time, a process of gradual reduction is necessary for the tactful and silent accomplishment of its ultimate aim. Until the final hour, the post-baby-boomers will be co-opted through a carefully calibrated combination of institutional pressure, intellectual deception and individual bribery. Thus, a significant number of post-baby-boomers have taken on the role of a *Sonderkommando*: they are assisting in the sui-genocidal process in return for a short respite and some small comfort. Thus, they are made to look away from the smoking chimneys, whose fires are fed with the shrinking remnants of Western civilization. This 'banality of evil' is a universal phenomenon: absolute evil is imperceptibly transformed into a daily routine. In all young people, conditioned in collective cognitive dissonance and adjusted to the 'inner exile' of escapism, the economic pressure of the 'labour market', the social pressure of 'political correctness' and the psychological pressure of the 'biological clock' eventually complete the process. After some years of social conformity not only the energy and beauty of youth fade, but also the instinct and integrity of youth; after a few years the youthful certainty that 'something is not right' is inevitably lost among the many compromises by which one disqualifies himself mentally and morally.

But young Western people should not entertain any illusion about the final destination of the self-abolishment project: the full menu of 'palliative care' will remain the exclusive preserve of the baby boomers. When the last baby boomer millionaire is finally disconnected from his respirator by his latest-import private nurse, the economic cake will be eaten. When the last baby boomer feminist leader finally hands over the keys of her ministerial safe to the first available ethnic replacement, the political farce ends. When the last baby boomer editor-in-chief finally turns off the light in the offices of the *Lügenpresse*, the last lights of Western civilization will be extinguished forever with it. Then, finally, the Betrayal of the West will sink in — but then it will be too late.

Western civilization is approaching its historical threshold and young Western people are facing a fork in the road: theirs is a choice between the wide road straight down into the abyss, and the narrow path straight up to self-renewal. Traditionalist Eurasianism can be this narrow path. The final prospect this path will command, far above Hellstorm 2.0, is a new future and a new *freedom* for the peoples of the West.

10. 'Za Vashu i Nashu Svobodu!'

Alle Gewebe der Tiranneien
Haut entzwei, und reisst euch los!
…Die Verwüstung, die Ruinen -
Nichts verhindre deinen Gang.

[All the webs of tyranny -
cut them down and free yourselves!
…The destruction, the ruins —
do not let them hinder you.]

—Johann Wolfgang von Goethe,
Des Epimenides Erwachen

Throughout the years, the old Russian revolutionary battle cry *za vashu i nashu svobodu* may have been abused by ruthless ideologues and opportunistic traitors, but its content indicates very precisely what an idealistic Eurasianism may fight for: 'for your and our freedom!' It expresses the essence of the common struggle of all European peoples for a shared ideal. It unites two elementary principles: respect for distinct identity and loyalty in a common fight. The fact that 'your' comes before 'our' means that so much *unites* 'us', that 'we' are willing to make *reciprocal sacrifices*. This battle cry summarizes and resolves the dilemma of the young people of the West: it conserves national identity, but it also announces a common struggle. It expresses the highest shared ideal of Western civilization: a confederation of related but sovereign peoples, defined by shared values and common enemies. The European peoples will only come together by their own sovereign choice. Only through a carefully calibrated Eurasianism can their confederation be achieved.

The battle cry 'for your and our freedom' is an invitation to many: aside from the peoples of Eurasia, it extends to the European peoples overseas—especially the nations of the overseas Anglosphere. In the final analysis, it invites all the European peoples to join in a great *boreal league*. Beyond this great alliance, it also invites strategic alliances with the Indo-European peoples of the Iranian and Indian worlds: these peoples may be considered as carriers of civilizations and geopolitical stabilizers in the deep south of the world. In its widest sense, it even anticipates the restoration of the high historical calling of the European peoples as the collective Katechon of the World: protectors, lawgivers, educators and benefactors of the southern and eastern peoples: this is their Higher Vocation and meta-historical destiny (cf. Chapter 4). From a Traditionalist perspective, this Higher Vocation is related to the mythical descent of the European peoples from immortal Hyperborea: their metaphysical exile on the World Island of Middle Earth implies a meta-historical leadership role with regard to all of humanity. This is the vocation of the Bringer of *Evangelion*, the Creator or *Nomos* and the Master of *Techne*. This notion is still preserved in the theme of 'the white man's burden'. In the Dark Age of Modernity this high calling has been inverted and perverted by slave-holding colonialism, thalassocratic imperialism and globalist exploitation. What the southern and eastern peoples truly resent in the European peoples, however, is not their original *vocation*, but their modern *degeneracy*. The southern and eastern peoples can only benefit from the European peoples' continued adherence to their original vocation: it is the source of spiritual freedom, scientific endeavour, just laws, liberating technology and soothing medicine.

From a Traditionalist perspective the Crisis of the Modern World has the meaning of a *purification* of the European peoples, 'designed' to make them return to their original vocation. The fact that, before they can return to their original vocation, the European peoples are made to fall back on their ancient ancestral homeland in the heart of the World Island is of great symbolic significance. This historic *retraite* and symbolic *penitence* are elementary preconditions for a restoration of the European vocation. In the final analysis, however, the battle cry 'for your and our freedom' already points towards an exalted final aim: a global *Pax Eurasiatica*.

From a Traditionalist perspective the final destiny of the Western peoples — either to dissolve in their psychohistoric nightmares, or to yet again witness a new Golden Dawn — entirely depends on their ability to re-affirm their own identities and interests before it is too late. From a Traditionalist perspective, however, real identities and interests are inextricably linked to an authentic vision of *destiny* — and there can be no authentic vision of destiny without transcendental reference. Thus, the highest Traditionalist perspective on the Eurasian project is necessarily a *vision*: a vision of unexpected resurrection. It is important to know that the Bolsheviks purposefully shorted the Russian battle cry *za vashu i nashu svobodu*: behind it can be found a longer Polish original, viz. *w Imię Boga: za naszą i waszą wolność*: 'In the Name of God: for your and our freedom!' May this incipit remind the European peoples that an authentic vision of the future can only be based on superhuman Divine Providence. May the young people of the West, wandering in the darkness of the Cultural Nihilist night, be granted the vision of a Golden Dawn. May they forget all that they have read here, if only they will remember this one thought of the old and wise Solzhenitsyn:

> Over a half-century ago, while I was still a child, I recall hearing a number of old people offer the following explanation for the great disasters that had befallen Russia: 'Men have forgotten God — that's why all this has happened.' Since then I have spent well-nigh fifty years working on the history of our revolution; in the process, I have read hundreds of books, collected hundreds of personal testimonies, and have already contributed eight volumes of my own toward the effort of clearing away the rubble left by that upheaval. But if I were asked today to formulate as concisely as possible the main cause of the ruinous revolution that swallowed up some sixty million of our people, I could not put it more accurately than to repeat: 'Men have forgotten God — that's why all this has happened.'

SUMMARY: TEN THESES

(1) The Betrayal of the West by its hostile elite can only be effectively countered by a fundamental deconstruction of its ideological discourse — Cultural Nihilism — and its foundational Modern (Enlightenment) *epistème*, characterized by nihilistic secularism, historical materialism and cultural relativism. Traditionalism triggers this deconstruction by exposing the historical shallowness of both: Traditionalism serves as a *gauge* and a *measure*.

(2) The geopolitical power of the Western hostile elite, structured in a thalassocratic-Atlantic 'New World Order', demands a viable alternative. Through an idealistically supranational and Traditionalist orientation Eurasianism can provide such an alternative.

(3) Given the emotional-subconscious and irrational-implicit nature of Postmodern Cultural Nihilism the Western people can only enter into a new Eurasian configuration after a thorough cultural-historical *Vergangenheitsbewältigung* and a complete resolution of their psychohistorical traumas.

(4) From a cultural-historical perspective, the self-destructive discourse of Cultural Nihilism is a *slave discourse*, befitting defeated and humiliated peoples. In the final analysis, the gradual decline of the Three Political Philosophies of Modernity reflects the collective defeat of all European peoples: Fascism was destroyed with the fall of the Third Reich, Socialism was discredited with the dissolution of the Soviet Union and Liberalism is already foundering with the rapid decline of American hegemony. Cultural Nihilism is the spiritual and intellectual void that follows the defeat of the European peoples.

(5) From a psychohistorical perspective, the self-loathing discourse of Cultural Nihilism is a *collective post-traumatic stress disorder*, befitting peoples that are abused and held hostage. In all Western peoples the collective symptoms of schizophrenic pathology and cognitive dissonance are self-evident, but they are deepest in that people which was most profoundly defeated:

the German people. The psychohistorical, cultural-historical and geopolitical void of contemporary 'Anti-Germany' is the 'black hole' of the West: this is why the real history of the Third Reich is subject to doctrinal taboo throughout the entire West.

(6) The recovery of Western national identities and Western geopolitical equilibrium depends on effective cultural-historical *Vergangenheitsbewältigung* and effective resolution of psychohistorical traumas. Until then, the Western patriotic opposition is reduced to ineffective 'cosmetic nationalism' and the Western hostile elite can continue to play off the European peoples against one another with ease.

(7) The trajectory of Western Cultural Nihilism is aimed at self-destruction: the Helter Skelter project of Charles Manson, which coincided with the formative phase of Cultural Nihilism, may be considered an archetypal expression of the Cultural Nihilistic programme of self-destruction: *exogamy* and *sui-genocide*. This programme is at the root of negative indigenous demography and ethnic replacement.

(8) In Russia the psychohistorical discharge of Modernity travelled a 'premature' trajectory: in Russia the mid-19th century terror of *Narodnaya Volya* relates to the early 20th century Red Plague in the same manner that the mid-20th century Helter Skelter relates to early 21st century Cultural Nihilism in the West. Thus, Russia has gained a degree of historical 'immunity' that allows it to fulfil the functions of the 'Last Katechon'; this will be the basis of an authentically Traditionalist Eurasianism.

(9) Any Eurasianism that aims to be both Traditionalist in orientation and viable in terms of *Realpolitik* will have to come to terms with the Four Political Realities of the contemporary West: global climate change, technological transhumanism, *ethnic replacement* and *social implosion*. A viable *Fourth Political Philosophy* will have to relate to these realities in a synthetic and synergic manner.

(10) Western acceptance of Traditionalist Eurasianism will depend on exorcizing Cultural Nihilist Modernity as an *existential modality*. This is the

greatest ordeal awaiting the West's *génération identitaire,* an ordeal during which it will look for the rise of a 'Last Katechon'.

CHAPTER TWO

The Crisis of the Modern West

A Traditionalist Diagnosis of Dutch Postmodernity

acquirit qui tuetur

THE DUTCH PREDICAMENT

OBSERVERS FROM THOSE REGIONS OF CHRISTEN-
dom that have still been spared the worst ravages of the fatal
autoimmune disease of 'Cultural Nihilism' may wonder at the
deafening silence that prevails across the dying nations of Western Europe
and the overseas Anglosphere. These nations are now about to taste the final
dregs of the bitter cup of Postmodern Cultural Nihilism — the fatal cocktail
of institutionalized atheism, 'disaster capitalism' and culture relativism that
full-blown Modernity has concocted for their peoples. Viewed from Russia
and the nations of Eastern Europe, which have only recently recovered from
the horror of the Red Plague and which are loudly and rightly reclaiming
their sovereign rights and cultural identities, the most unsettling feature of
the agony of the nations of Western Europe and the overseas Anglosphere
may be its awesome silence. The 'strange death' of these nations (Douglas
Murray, 2017) is outwardly characterized by the unfazed legalism of their
authorities, the detached 'political correctness' of their media and the apparently unreflecting fatalism of their people. To the extent that the silence

surrounding this contemporary Calvary is induced by the stoic acceptance of a fully deserved fate, it may seem historically justified. But to the extent that it ignores the undeserved suffering of many innocent people, this silence is inappropriate — this Calvary too has its unjustly condemned men, agonizing women and desperate bystanders. The innocent victims of Cultural Nihilism include not only those Westerners who suffer the daily horrors of endemic terrorism, mass-rape and violent crime. They also include the millions of indigenous Westerners who are becoming strangers in their own land, replaced by cruel colonists that take their possessions and their women. They also include the millions of Western men that are deprived of work by globalized neo-liberalism and institutionalized matriarchy, the millions of Western women that are deprived of marriage and motherhood by the enforced reversal of gender roles and the millions of Western children that are deprived of a proper family life and a proper education by the collapse of the entire social order. They are the innocent victims of the 'death by a thousand cuts' to which the 'leaders' of many Western countries have condemned their peoples. To all these victims, the historian owes a correct chronicle and a just judgment: he is compelled to speak out, even if the truth shatters many comfortable delusions.

Obviously, any modest voice speaking out from the small Dutch nation will tend to be drowned among the many voices speaking out from its three great neighbours; the small Dutch drama tends to be overshadowed by Britain's *Brexit* stand against EU tyranny, Germany's decision to proceed with accelerated *Umvolkung* and France's mad pursuit of nihilistic *laïcité* at all costs. The unobtrusively 'peaceful' public image of the Netherlands is further reinforced by a carefully staged appearance of prosperity and stability, aimed at attracting investors and tourists. The glittering material facade of international institutions, business centres and transport infrastructure, however, hides the socio-economic reality of a nation in existential crisis. A small elite of bureaucrats, business leaders and baby boomer retirees has monopolized the ability to live in prosperity and stability. For the large majority of Dutch people, day-to-day life is now marked by chronic economic insecurity, declining living standards, spiralling health care costs, imploding educational standards, effective mass illiteracy, constant terror threats, escalating ethnic tensions, disintegrating family structures and a nauseating public culture that approaches a real-time 'idiocracy'. This reality is silently ignored by self-censoring media, both at home and abroad.

In a sense, the Netherlands constitutes the perfect example of a successful Postmodern Cultural Nihilist dictatorship: it manages to outwardly project an idyllic vision of Postmodern 'progress' and 'freedom', in the same manner that the old Soviet Union managed to outwardly project an ideal image of a socialist 'workers' paradise'. But behind this facade, the Dutch people are facing the full historical force of Cultural Nihilism, in the same manner that behind the Soviet facade the Russian people were facing the full historical force of Bolshevism. And in the same manner that the Bolshevik facade was finally shattered in the East, so perhaps, one day, the Cultural Nihilist facade will be shattered in the West. For the West to return to anything resembling normalcy, however, alternative voices must be heard. The slavish silence of the West must end before the atrocious reality of Postmodern Cultural Nihilism can end. The strongest voice that can still speak up for the West is also its oldest voice: the voice of Tradition. It has been a long time since the voice of Tradition has been heard in the Netherlands — but no country should go silently into the night.

THE INTERNATIONAL DIMENSION

From a Traditionalist perspective, a nation that depends on other nations for its existence is no longer an authentic nation. In this sense, the modernist phenomenon of 'globalization', fostering inter-national interdependence, transnational institutions and cross-border migration, represents a quintessentially anti-Traditional subversion of the nation-state: it threatens the authority of the state as well as the identity of the nation. Historically, the Dutch nation-state has been a maritime, mercantile, colonial and imperial power: it was, in fact, one of the great Early Modern 'thalassocracies' that carried Western Modernity to the far ends of the Earth. In this sense, the

Netherlands now faces a ricochet effect: Postmodern 'globalization' represents a historical Nemesis to the direct heirs of Early Modernity's 'Protestant Ethnic' and Early Modernity's 'Spirit of Capitalism'. As in the case of other Western European nations, the Netherlands now faces the 'backlash' that inevitably results from the historical combination of two simultaneous processes: the *implosion* of formal colonial power and the *explosion* of informal transnational financial and business power. The former process results in the dissolution of ethnic cohesion through *centripetal* migration: long-term national identity is sacrificed to short-term economic interests. The latter process results in the dissolution of national sovereignty through *centrifugal* devolution: executive power is 'outsourced' to transnational institutions and non-state actors. After absorbing—but not *assimilating*—large numbers of migrants from its former colonies in the East and West Indies, the Netherlands continued to allow mass immigration for purely pragmatic economic reasons. Neo-liberal policies favour mass immigration because it allows for a larger 'labour reserve' (decreasing labour costs and workers' rights), a larger consumer basis (boosting business volumes and interest rates) and reliable electoral support ('new citizens' will vote for those who guarantee their continued 'citizenship'). After handing over customs control to the Benelux Union and defence responsibility to the NATO alliance, the Netherlands continued to cede more sovereign power to other transnational institutions: 'European law' takes precedence over Dutch law, 'Schengen borders' have replaced Dutch borders and a 'European currency' has replaced the Dutch currency. From a Traditionalist perspective, the Dutch state is on the point of disappearing as a sovereign state and the Dutch nation is on the point of disappearing as an authentic nation.

No other nation is obliged to help the Dutch nation in its present predicament; it is even dangerous and wrong to help those who do not want to help themselves. For its imminent disappearance the Dutch nation has only itself to blame. At most, other nations may one day soon be asked to show mercy to individual refugees seeking to escape the disasters facing the Netherlands. If they are not 'climate refugees' escaping the drowning cities of the Low Countries when the seas start to rise, then they may be the remnants of the indigenous population, escaping endemic terror, ethnic strife, social implosion and civil unrest — perhaps even civil war. All that these poor refugees may hope for is that other nations will view them as useful immigrants, remembering the old qualities of the Dutch people — productivity, self-reliance, intelligence and endurance. Before this comes to pass, however, it may be that other Western peoples can profit from the example of the Dutch predicament. Given the fact that other Western nations are now facing a somewhat similar predicament, a correct analysis of the mistakes of the Dutch nation may convince other nations to steer clear of the pitfalls that brought down the Netherlands. Such an analysis may still convince the relatively intact nation-states of Eastern Europe to resolutely defend their national sovereignty and national identity. With this in mind, it may be useful for foreign observers to study the preliminaries of the imminent 'Dutch doomsday'.

DUTCH DOOMSDAY

Although the Dutch word *noodgeval*, 'emergency', renders an aspect of the German word *Ernstfall*, 'case of seriousness', the reach of the Dutch is much more restricted: the precise content and grave severity of the German word cannot be easily translated into Dutch. Untranslatability always provides a reliable linguistic marker of the unique psychological qualities and spiritual peculiarities that characterize different peoples and cultures — even peoples and cultures that are so intimately related in ethnicity and history as the Dutch and German nations. Behind the solemn German word *Ernstfall* we can discern the profundity of German philosophy as well as the weight of German history. Even at its surface, we can discern the legal philosophy of *Nomos* and *Katechon* and the political practice of *Ausnahmezustand* and *Führerprinzip*. Behind the rational calculation of the Dutch word *noodgeval* we can discern the dispassionate sobriety of a typically Dutch sense of realism as well as the modest heroism of a typically Dutch resilience. Even at its surface, we can discern associations with a calculating 'insurance' culture (collective sea dike taxes, social security, limited liability) and a

dramatic history of *luctor et emergo*.[2] German culture is historically characterized by a collective commitment to structurally anticipate 'emergencies' through ideas and measures based on *Ernstfall* considerations. Thus,
German history is characterized by socio-economic harmony in peacetime
and political-military cohesiveness in wartime. Dutch culture is historically
characterized by a collective pragmatism and improvisation in dealing with
entirely unique 'emergencies'. Thus, Dutch history is characterized by institutionalized hyper-individualized socio-economic anarchy in peacetime
and short bursts of astounding collective heroism in wartime.[3]

The societal reality of the contemporary Western world, however, is such
that there is no longer any clear boundary between war and peace: the entire West is confronted with a rapidly escalating social-Darwinist 'civil war'
of unprecedented scope and depth. To the good old-fashioned capitalist war
of all against all are now added the new wars of young against old, women
against men and immigrant against native. Increasingly, these various new
forms of societal conflict tend to coalesce into one single 'permanent revolution' against all residual forms of social hierarchy and order. Those who
have joined the kleptocratic elite through lucrative 'privatization', globalized
'outsourcing' and financial malpractice can deprive the working poor of
their just wages. Those who 'immigrated' to the West through bureaucratic loopholes, 'investment schemes' and fraudulent 'asylum procedures' can
cheat their host nations out of their birthright. Those who nurture old black
and brown racial grudges against 'white privilege' can indulge in the sadistic humiliation of the women and children of the remnant Western natives
with virtual impunity. Those who disguise their cultural primitivism in the
pseudo-religious cloak of 'Islamism' can 'prove' the inferiority of the Christian message of peace by applying the label of 'holy war' to acts of barbaric
terrorism. Resentful feminists can 'deconstruct' manhood and its political

---

2 This is the motto of the Dutch province of Zeeland, referring to its constant struggle
   against the sea.

3 Commonly referred to as 'Dutch courage' by English participants in the Anglo-Dutch
   Wars.

derivates: honour, fidelity and honesty. Narcissist 'baby boomers' can fatally compromise the future and happiness of naive millennials. Only a few of the most drastic incidents of this near-global 'civil war' pass through political-ly-correct (self-)censorship: only occasionally does the international con-glomerate of *Lügenpresse* media report an incident of an illegal 'drone strike', a terror attack, a 'farm killing', a 'rapefugee' event, a 'grooming gang' or a rit-ualistic child murder. This new reality of 'permanent revolution' — the Post-modern equivalent of the Trotskyite 'no war, no peace' recipe — demands a thorough reflection on the permanent merger of enduring *Ernstfall* and incidental emergency. The structural lack of facilities to cope with *Ernstfall* conditions aggravates the permanent reality of continuous 'emergencies'.

Traditionalist concepts can contribute to a correct assessment of the acute social crisis facing the contemporary West. From a Traditionalist perspective, this crisis is a deeply tragic but entirely logical result of the failure of the *Ernst-fall* provisions of Western civilization. The militant secular nihilism, hyper-al-truistic culture relativism and warped historical-materialist world-view of the Western intellectual discourse are only compatible with the construction of secular and material *Ernstfall* provisions — and only to the extent that these are ideologically compatible with the neo-liberal model of the 'night-watchman state'. Only a few underpaid police officers are still left to investigate the alarm-ing proliferation of terrorist networks. Only a few overburdened soldiers are still left to deliver 'hit and run' pinpricks against the world's most dangerous totalitarian state and non-state actors. Only a few unsupported customs offi-cers are still left to occasionally pretend that Rotterdam Port and Amsterdam Airport are not the primary wholesale outlets for the world's greatest drugs cartels. These few hold-outs aside, the only *Ernstfall* provisions Holland has left are represented by material infrastructure — most sensationally the Zuid-erzee Works[4] and the Delta Works.[5] In the past, however, Holland also had a number of immaterial — institutional, socio-cultural — *Ernstfall* provisions that have been largely abolished in the course of Modernist 'progress', but

---

4 The dams, dikes and polders of a former inlet of the North Sea called the Zuiderzee.

5 The dams, levees and storm surge barriers around the Rhine-Meuse-Scheldt delta.

which were of even more vital importance for the continued existence of the
Dutch nation and people than its dikes and sluices. These were the *Ernstfall*
provisions that Holland inherited from the pre-modern world of Tradition,
the socio-political institutions and cultural-historical structures that created
and protected the border, ethnicity, language, values and culture of Holland
throughout the centuries. Monarchy, Nobility, Chivalric Order, Academy and
Guild were all among these *Ernstfall* provisions: these were the institutions
that Traditionalist thinkers have always considered as manifestations of the
Katechon, of the shield of civilization that protects every authentically Traditional community. A broken dike, a flooded polder, a ruined house — they
can be rebuilt. An extinct people, a forgotten language, a lost faith, a ruined
culture — they never return.

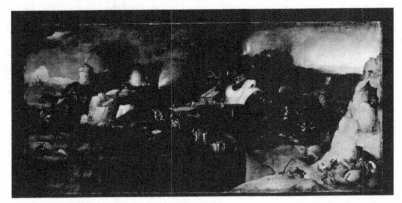

Ernstfall

Christ's Descent into Hell (student of Hieronymus Bosch, 2nd half 16th
century), Metropolitan Museum of Art New York. The apocalyptic visions of
the Bosch School date back to the great upheaval of the early Reformation in
the Netherlands, prefiguring the titanic struggle of the Dutch Eighty Years'
War against Spanish tyranny. The theme of this specific painting is divine
deliverance from a human-made hell: Adam and Eve can be seen kneeling as
they see the Saviour knocking down the gate of Hell.

MODERNITY: 'PROGRESS' & 'FREEDOM'

We have now sunk to a depth at which restatement of the obvious
is the first duty of intelligent men.
— GEORGE ORWELL

All those who refuse to be a nation and all those who wish to deposit religion and culture in the dustbin of history can rejoice in the fall of ancient *Ernstfall* provisions. For those who think in such a manner, there exists no 'loss of identity' and no 'oikophobia';[6] for them there is only scheduled 'progress' and commendable 'freedom'. This is the experiential bubble in which the Dutch social elite is living and in which the Dutch political regime is operating. For those whose inner orientation and natural habitus is defined by neo-liberal globalisation, anti-nationalist universalism and secular-cosmopolitan nihilism the advances of 'progress' are cause for joy: the 'homeopathic' dilution of ethnicity,[7] the 'internationalizing' reform of language, the 'deregulating' disruption of economic life, the 'deconstructing' subversion of religion and the 'emancipating' dissolution of social cohesion. These are the revolutionary processes of Modern 'progress' which create the existential vacuum of Modern 'freedom': the freedom to 'live' without a king who inspires fear and admiration, without a nobility that sets standards of public behaviour and good taste, without a church that requires piety and respectability, without an academy that demands knowledge and wisdom, without a husband who guards honour and virtue, without a father who decides on social boundaries and standards.[8]

---

6 A term recently introduced into Dutch public discourse by Thierry Baudet, leader of the new parliamentary party Forum for Democracy.

7 Terminology wrongfully ascribed to Thierry Baudet by the politically correct Dutch media.

8 An indirect reference to the title of the 1995 work *De verweesde samenleving*, 'An Orphaned Society', by assassinated Dutch patriotic leader Pim Fortuyn.

It is literally a borderless freedom — without constraints on materialism, without social norms, without cultural baggage, without moral duties and without pangs of conscience. It is not only the freedom of drug barons in fancy restaurants and pimps in fancy cars, but also that of smooth-talking politicians in custom-made suits[9] and bonus-grabbing bankers in stately mansions. It is the freedom to bury the law in bureaucratic 'governance' and to ridicule public justice in rigged 'debate'. It is the freedom to offer housing, healthcare, employment and subsidies to hundreds of thousands of fake 'refugees' and criminal asylum-seekers while hundreds of thousands of indigenous people are homeless, ill, unemployed or buried in ruinous debt. It is the freedom to hand over education and culture to unscrupulous 'financial managers' and resentful 'affirmative action' appointees at the expense of precious knowledge and irreplaceable heritage. It is the freedom to reserve scarce employment for bored feminists and incompetent *allochtonen*, or 'non-natives',[10] at the expense of unemployed bread-winners and potential heads of family. It is the freedom to quickly amass a fortune through drugs trade and prostitution and to reduce hard work and prudent thrift to laughable anachronisms. It is the freedom to kill unborn children and 'redundant' senior citizens for the sake of abstract illusions such as 'personal autonomy' and 'quality of life'. It is the freedom which gives a democratic 'right' to car ownership and air travel holidays, even if anthropogenic climate change has reduced former Dutch pastimes such as ice-skating and snowball fights to distant childhood memories. It is the freedom of 'parents' to build yet another holiday home when their children fund their education through ruinous student debts.[11] It is the freedom to indulge in fashionable abuse of your children or stepchildren with virtual impunity when serial monogamy and wife-swapping no longer suit your jaded appetites. It is the freedom to cheaply feed yourself

---

9 A reference to PM Mark Rutte, a.k.a. 'Mister Tefal'.

10 A politically correct euphemism for the non-ethnically Dutch residents of the Netherlands.

11 A reference to the new semi-American education funding system that came into full force in 2017.

on dead animals every day without having to think about the millions of innocent creatures that are ground into mincemeat by Holland's industrialized torture programme euphemistically known as the 'bio industry'.

This is the combined neo-liberal and cultural-Bolshevik freedom that allows Modernity's self-appointed *Uebermensch* to truly be 'himself', 'herself' or — according to the ironically accurate gender-neutral fashion — 'itself'. In that ultimate freedom the perfectly contented Postmodern consumer can finally withdraw into the undisturbed illusion of paradisiacal happiness: Friedrich Nietzsche's 'last man' has been finally realized in Holland, Western Modernity's true *gidsland*, or 'guiding nation'.[12] This is the freedom which beckons in the 'Orphaned Society' described by Pim Fortuyn and which is promised to the 'bastard children' described by Peter Sloterdijk. The baby boomers have been pioneering this freedom, the 'Canal District' people[13] are practising this freedom and 'Planet Section K'[14] is the guiding star leading to this freedom. Unlike that long-forgotten star of 2000 years ago, 'Planet Section K' does not shine for wise kings: instead, it lights the broad democratic road to the five-star inn of Postmodern 'self-redemption'. There stands the stable of the Modern Anti-Bethlehem, where everybody lives by bread alone, and the great prostitution of New Babylon, where nobody is disturbed by God or Law. There reigns the redeeming certainty that the struggle for a humane existence, the struggle for a dignified identity and the struggle against animalistic atavism are over for all time — simply because humanity has been replaced by the *Untermensch* reality of measureless materialism and heartless hedonism.

---

12 A reference to the 'progressive' pioneering role that Holland was supposed to play in the international arena during the 'Social Justice Warrior' government of PM Den Uyl between 1973–77.

13 A reference to the Social Justice Warrior elite inhabiting the fashionable inner city district of Amsterdam.

14 A term used by patriotic opposition leader Geert Wilders to indicate the fenced-off seats of the government in the House of Representative.

TRADITION: PALINGENESIA & ANAGOGICS

We sleep safe in our bed because rough men stand ready in the night to visit
violence on those who would do us harm.

— GEORGE ORWELL

Many Dutch people, however, still refuse to practice such bestiality and to live such beastly lives. There are still well-intentioned people who wish the Dutch people a different future. For all those who wish to stand up for the future of the Dutch people, it is vitally important that they be able to gauge the true depths of the *Ernstfall* facing the nation. They should recognize the unmistakable symptoms of René Guénon's *crise du monde moderne* and of Carl Schmitt's *Ausnahmezustand*. A number of recent politico-philosophical developments that have recently occurred in the wider Western world are relevant to the crisis facing Dutch society, and can help achieve a correct contextual assessment of that crisis. In recent years, a number of Western thinkers have taken the first cautious steps towards an intellectual *Bewältigung* of the escalating 'Crisis of the Modern World'. Peter Sloterdijk's *Die schrecklichen Kinder der Neuzeit*, Guillaume Faye's *Archéofuturisme* and Jason Jorjani's *World State of Emergency* contain a number of analyses and hypotheses that are directly relevant to this crisis. The recent rediscovery of older relevant material, exemplified by recent re-editions and reappraisals of the work of Oswald Spengler and Julius Evola, clearly indicate a general trend to a fundamental *Vergangenheitsbewältigung* throughout the Western world. The unofficial but very real 'state of emergency' that is prevailing throughout the West is already causing scattered incidents of metapolitical rearmament. These first centres of resistance cover a wide political spectrum, ranging from neo-liberal 'populism' (represented in the Netherlands by Geert Wilders' Party for Freedom) and libertarian 'renaissance' (represented in the Netherlands by Thierry Baudet's 'Forum for Democracy') to alt-right 'ethnonationalism' and old-right 'romanticism'. The ultimate weapon available to the West, however, is also its oldest weapon: its Traditionalist heritage. The Traditionalist 'Sword of Gnosis' is its weapon of last resort, to be drawn at the final hour: it can only be drawn from the stone of history by those who are aware of what is truly at stake.

The Dutch people are facing the abyss of historical oblivion. The young generation cannot ignore the double reality of true *Ernstfall* and acute emergency. True awareness of the existential crisis facing the Dutch people will force the young generation to urgently re-think the *Ernstfall* provisions with which this crisis can be overcome. So much time has passed since these provisions have been the subject of serious consideration, however, that it is necessary to first review their basic premises. What counts in any confrontation with an existential crisis is always the shortest way to safety and the first weapon at hand — this is true in the physical as well as the psychological sphere. Surviving a profound crisis requires the willingness to engage in total war — within and without. Confronted with an existential crisis a nation must rise above itself and re-invent itself. A nation's capacity for 'palingenesia' — self-renewal — rests on its ability to access the same agglomerate of impersonal and elementary powers that created it in the first place. This ability is both sub-human, because it rests on bio-evolutionary adaption, and super-human, because it rests on a transcendental reference. In older literature, the power agglomerate accessed is termed the 'nation's soul' and in ancient myths it is related to super-natural 'destiny'. In modern science this power agglomerate is described by means of abstract sociological and anthropological terminology. But this fact does not alter the experiential realities represented by the 'nation's soul' and its 'destiny'. All pre-modern communities, from the smallest jungle tribe to the greatest historical Imperium, are characterized by simultaneously sub-consciously and super-consciously real socio-political mechanisms and societal structures that foster biological and cultural continuity. These mechanisms and structures, which shield ethnicity, language, religion and culture from the wear and tear of history, are the *Ernstfall* provisions of the pre-modern world. Traditionalist symbolism expresses the dual nature of these *Ernstfall* provisions in the *double-edged sword*: it refers to a combined physical and spiritual power. At its highest level, this power creates the supra-national force of *Imperium*. When Imperium fails, power devolves to the next level — the level of the nation-state. What Jacob Needleman termed the 'Sword of Gnosis' refers to a power agglomerate of physical strength, intellectual discernment and spiritual insight. This combination grants the power of self-renewal not only to individuals and tribal communities but also to whole peoples and great states. This principle is symbolically represented in the mythologies surrounding magical swords such as *Gram* and *Excalibur*. The shining 'Sword of Knowledge' is always recovered or re-forged when disaster looms closest — in other words: when the ultimate *Ernstfall* must be faced.

Pre-modern life represents a single, continuous *Ernstfall*: the wolf eats the sheep, the boar eats the harvest, winter kills the elderly, childbed kills the baby, neighbouring tribes kidnap the girl, plundering bandits burn down the house and evil spirits possess the mind. The *Ernstfall* provisions of the pre-modern world are meant to deal with a permanent *theriomachy*, a never-ending 'animal struggle'. This existential war with a host of natural, human and spiritual enemies requires a permanent 'state of siege', a constant alertness and battle-readiness. This is the experiential reality that underpins all authentic forms of Traditional life. The world of Tradition is a black-and-white world of good and evil, light and darkness — it is a world that is lived by means of an uncompromising *Wehr- und Waffen-Instinkt* and which is guarded by guardians on both physical and spiritual walls. These guardians cannot make the least mistake: every lapse of attention, every doubt and every weakness of the guardians is fatal for the community. The guardian cannot confound a wolf for a sheep, a stranger for a friend, he cannot lose sight of the gate, he cannot be distracted by idle chatter, he cannot drink when others celebrate, he cannot let strangers talk to children and he cannot let strangers seduce girls. Self-discipline and self-sacrifice determine his thoughts and his behaviour. His vision must stay unclouded and his attention must be single-minded: his own people remain his own people, strangers remain strangers, women remain women, children remain children. Thus, strong, brave and wise people man the walls around vulnerable, sick and weak people. They protect the child, the woman, the old man — their function is institutionally and culturally anchored in their society. At the most primitive level, these people are the guardsmen who kill predators, the warriors who chase off enemies, the medicine men who heal the sick, the shamans who control the spirit world, the tribal elders who mete out justice and the chiefs who lead their people through the wilds of the world. At the most civilized level, these people are the dike-wardens who check the levees,[15] the knights who guard the border marches, the surgeons who cure bodies, the priests who cure minds, the magistrates who maintain the laws and the monarchs who maintain the peace. The archetypes of the world of Tradition are the anointed monarch, the born nobleman, the ordained priest, the oath-bound doctor and certified master craftsman.

The universally recurrent characteristics of the world of Tradition are: holistic integration, hierarchical organization and transcendental direction. All members of the community — tribe, nation — have their own particular place and each member has his or her own specific duties and rights. Place, duty and right reflect archetypal function: there are male roles and female roles, noble rights and civil rights, hereditary privileges and sacred offices. The direction of the world of Tradition is always anagogic: it looks upwards, it strives upwards, it is driven upwards. In the world of Tradition people are always *more* than themselves, even in their most mundane experiences. The expectant mother mirrors herself in the Mother of God, the beggar mirrors himself in the Poor Job, the dying man mirrors himself in the Martyred Saviour. The higher vocations are explicitly superhuman: the word of the Priest offers forgiveness, the sword of the Knight conquers the invader, the hand of the King grants healing. At their height, these archetypes reach heroic and holy transcendence. Even the stubborn clay and the down-to-earth people of the small

---

15 An ancient office still existing in the Netherlands, approximately equivalent in rank to a mayor or provincial King's Commissioner.

Netherlands have brought forth such greatness: Thomas à Kempis in lived mysticism, Desiderius Erasmus in philosophical scholarship, Willem Barentsz in daring discovery, Michiel de Ruyter in heroic sea wars, Rembrandt van Rijn in genius artistic vision. Throughout all the hierarchic layers of the world of Tradition rights and duties are always functional, imposing the heaviest burdens on the strongest shoulders. The ideals and ideas of the world of Tradition are superhuman for everybody — but they also grant superhuman strength.

Generation & De-generation of a People

If liberty means anything at all, it means the right to tell people
what they do no want to hear.
— George Orwell

From a Traditionalist perspective, peoples too have rights and duties, peoples too have superhuman ideals and peoples too have superhuman strength. A people conquers and defends a territory, a right to exist, a name and a reputation by collectively doing battle with natural challenges and human enemies. The resulting *landnám* may be limited to a few hectares of hunting grounds in a jungle or it may extend across thousands of miles to form a multi-continental Imperium.

The small Dutch nation represents a modest transitional form, ethnically based on the historical agglomerate of Germanic tribes that settled in the estuary swamps between Ems and Scheldt, slowly taking on its primordial shape over a number of centuries. The pressures of climate, geography and history moulded the specialist adaptations that determine Dutch identity — physically, psychologically and spiritually. This means physical survival of the dangerous tidal swamps, the storm floods and the atrocious weather. This means psychological tolerance of the endlessly flat horizon and the sunless winter. This means historical animosity against religious collectivism and political centralism. Swamp and *geest*[16] are cultivated as polder and garden.[17] Reed thickets and virgin forest are replaced by villages and cities. Domestic anarchy and foreign tyranny are replaced by law and autonomy. Superstition and witch hunts are replaced by science and humanism. The foreign Goliath — the Spanish world empire, the English naval challenge, the French Sun King — is defeated by the Dutch David.[18] The small Dutch nation has gained its sovereign place among the nations of Europe and the small Dutch state survives the 18th and 19th century social-Darwinist jungle war of nationalism and imperialism. The Netherlands survive the French Revolution, the European Revolution of 1848 and the First World War:[19] people and state absorb what is compatible, reject what is incompatible and survive what is pathogenic. Finally, however, the Second World War damages the roots of people and state. In the aftermath of the Second World War the first symptoms of fatal external and internal weakness appear: the Netherlands abandons its sovereign rights through the political-economic merger with Belgium and Luxembourg, the military pact with its wartime allies America and Britain and the retreat from the Dutch East Indies.[20]

---

16 Slightly raised dry and infertile landforms, usually adjoining the marshlands; the Dutch word *geest* is popularly associated with the homophone word for 'ghost'.

17 The famous Dutch flower fields, including the well-known tourist attraction *Keukenhof*, are concentrated in the transitional region between the sand of the dunes and the clay of the low-lying pastures.

18 References to, respectively, the Eighty Years' (or: Dutch Independence) War (1568–1648), the Second Anglo-Dutch War (1665–67) and the Franco-Dutch War (1672–78).

19 In the wake of the French Revolution the Netherlands were conquered by the First French Republic and annexed by Napoleon, but restored by the Vienna Congress. In 1848 a domestic constitutional compromise saved the Netherlands from revolution and civil war. During the First World War the Netherlands managed to maintain neutrality.

20 References to, respectively, the 1944 Benelux union, the 1949 NATO alliance and the 1949 independence of Indonesia. It should be noted that Indonesian independence was a result of pressure by Holland's 'ally' America. The Netherlands lost its New Guinea colony for the same reason in 1962.

After a short interlude of infrastructural modernization, mass emigration and cultural Americanization, starting from the mid-1960s the Netherlands suffers an identity crisis of unprecedented depth and scope. Thus far located on the historical margins of the Western mainstream, the Netherlands now finds itself in the political and economic vanguard of Western 'progress' and at the eye of the storm of Western Modernity. The Crisis of the Modern World hits the Netherlands with full force and the deluge of fully fledged Cultural Nihilism wipes out all the landmarks of identity and tradition. A heritage of centuries is squandered within the lifetime of just one generation — the 'baby boom' generation. Driven by unrestrained consumerism, hedonist narcissism and secular nihilism, the baby boomers build a megalomaniac new Tower of Babel. Traditional family farms are replaced by a grotesque 'bio industry' that sacrifices human health and animal welfare 'for a fistful of dollars'. Manufacture and industry are replaced by a 'service economy' and physical labour that cannot be 'exported' is delegated to foreign workers.[21] Honest trade and respectable banking, the traditional staples of Dutch enterprise, are replaced with the facilitation of industrial dumping, narcotics traffic, 'consumer credit' usury and money laundry through 'post-box firms'. The national currency is replaced by European 'monopoly money'. National borders are replaced by global 'free movement of goods and people'. 'International treaty obligations', 'European law', 'market mechanisms' and 'free trade competition' prevail over the most elementary notions of self-preservation, self-respect and moral responsibility.

Forced into a 'race to the bottom', Dutch workers are supposed to compete with Eastern European 'migrant labour'. Forced to implement the American commercial principles of 'internationalization' and 'valorization', Dutch universities and museums are reduced to a cultural desert. Within a few years, mass immigration causes the total Frisian population,

---

21 In 1964 and 1969 the borders were formally opened to Turkish and Moroccan 'guest labourers', many of whom were undesirables, who were deliberately 'exported' by their government.

indigenous since the time of the Roman Empire, to be outnumbered by Turkish and Moroccan residents.[22] Within a few decades, the legal fictions of 'citizenship education' and 'naturalization' allow for the mobilization of millions of 'new Dutch citizens' as consumers, 'labour reserve' and electoral reinforcement for the benefit of a tiny anti-national elite. Soon these *allochtonen*, fattened with 'targeted subsidies', pampered by 'affirmative action' and supported by 'anti-discriminatory' legislation, manage to massively infiltrate all levels of government, the security services, the institutes of higher learning and the public media. 'Child benefit' subsidies, 'family reunification' policies and 'refugee resettlement' programmes provide a continuous demographic reinforcement of legally enforced 'diversity'. Within a few years, monstrous ghettos are formed in the major cities of the country — breeding grounds for criminality, prostitution, extremism and terrorism. Within the lifetime of just one generation, the 'baby boom' generation, the country is heavily damaged — irreversibly damaged, as is silently hoped by the anti-national elite. All critics of globalization and mass-immigration are systematically persecuted and silenced, usually by means of politically correct witch hunts and public character assassination. Only a few exceptional talents are granted the privilege of straightforward martyrdom: the gifted spirit of Professor Fortuyn was expelled by a bullet.[23]

---

22 There are around 350,000 native speakers of Frisian, while the most conservative estimates put the numbers of Moroccan and Turkish residents at around 370,000 and 400,000 respectively.

23 A reference to the assassination of patriotic leader Pim Fortuyn on 6 May 2002, nine days before the parliamentary elections he was widely expected to win. The assassin was officially identified as a lone-wolf Social Justice Warrior, but various conspiracy theories continue to blame the Dutch political establishment for the conveniently timely elimination of the threat that Pim Fortuyn represented to the status quo. The Dutch people referred to him with the sobriquets of *Onze Pim*, or 'Our Pim', as well as by his academic title 'Professor'.

APPROACHES & CHOICES

In 2002, Professor Fortuyn wrote his last book — *De puinhopen van acht jaar paars,* 'The Ruins of Eight Years Purple'.[24] In that book, he was still able to prescribe a mild cure of democratic reforms and gradual political course corrections for his country. But even these moderate propositions were too much for the Dutch political elite: the elite opted for a *Flucht nach vorne.* Now, fifteen years later, the socio-political ruin that is the Netherlands requires a much deeper and larger archaeological project than Professor Fortuyn envisioned. A much longer gauging rod is needed to fully fathom the depths of the present crisis. The new generation will have to dig much deeper and cover a much larger terrain. It will have to reassess the fundamental notions of *Ernstfall* and emergency, because forty years of betrayal of the nation cannot be cured by a mere cosmetic operation. Perhaps deep in his heart Professor Fortuyn already suspected the true scope of the task ahead, because three weeks before he was killed he wrote in the re-edition of *De verweesde samenleving,* 'An Orphaned Society', that he had been granted the vision of Moses: after forty years in the desert the old prophet ascends a mountain to see the Promised Land. Professor Fortuyn is now allowed to rest from his heavy task, but there is no rest for the living. Now it is up to the new generation to reclaim the Promised Land and to take it back for its people. But this work can only be accomplished with superhuman strength: the pledge can only be redeemed through an unwavering trust in Divine Providence and a radical willingness to sacrifice comfort and egoism. Only Traditionalist wisdom can still rediscover the sources of this strength, this trust and this commitment. Only Traditionalist wisdom offers a degree of understanding that is sufficiently profound to truly appreciate the *Ernstfall* facing the nation.

---

24 The term 'purple' refers to the grand political coalition of 'red' social democrats and 'blue' neo-liberals that ruled the Netherlands from 1994 to 2002.

Traditionalist philosophy cannot offer ideological precepts and it cannot offer metaphysical hope — it certainly cannot offer a political programme. The only thing it can offer is a tested and proven formula for a clear-eyed reassessment of history. It can provide the intellectual and moral tabula rasa that is a prerequisite for an authentically effective form of metapolitical rearmament.

Various philosophico-scientific approaches are available to describe the generative and degenerative phenomena that create and destroy peoples and nations, i.e. their diachronic development and their synchronic identity. In the final analysis, all of these approaches are functional and they are complementary in relation to each other — even when a specific approach is preferred in certain settings of political correctness or when it is used to sustain certain power monopolies. The Modernist or 'historical-materialist' philosophico-scientific approach has become the preferred approach of institutionalized academic science. To the extent that this science is still sincerely practised, it focuses on material factors and utilitarian functionalities; these include genetic evolution, epigenetic tendencies, socio-geographical conditioning and socio-economic dynamics. The Traditionalist philosophico-scientific approach, on the other hand, focuses on immaterial factors and macro-cosmic functionalities — these include cultural-historical dynamics, psycho-history, meta-historical interpretation and transcendental references. From a Traditionalist philosophico-scientific perspective, the *Ernstfall* provisions of a given community are important reference points in describing the synchronic identity and diachronic development of that community; they allow for a diagnosis of the present sustainability and future trajectory of that community. The most important *Ernstfall* provisions that recur throughout Western and Dutch history are the Monarchy, the Nobility, the Church and the Academy. Thus, it is important to determine to what extent these old institutions — to the degree they still exist — can still be relevant as *Ernstfall* provisions in the context of the present Crisis of the Modern World. If they cannot, they will have to exit the stage of history in infamy. In that case, history may yet create entirely new institutions, suited to entirely new conditions: these new institutions will serve entirely new peoples and new nations — peoples and nations that will probably be radically redefined and historically unrecognizable. But if these old institutions recover their relevance to the present *Ernstfall*, they can provide the strongest shields and the best swords in a war of national rebirth. In that case, Western nations and peoples may yet survive in historically recognizable forms.

The fundamental issue at stake may be summarized in a single question: what is the contemporary *raison d'être* of these historical institutions? It is a question that the institutions of Academy, Church, Nobility and Monarchy must ask themselves — and it is also a question that only they themselves can answer. Can the Academy still be the Academy — and does it wish to be? Can it still return to the high task of substantive transmission of knowledge and fundamental research on behalf of nation and people? Or does it merely wish to generate comfortable tenures and hollow titles for resentful feminists, unscrupulous foreigners and corrupt management consultants? Can the Church still be the Church — and does it wish to be? Can it still return to the sacred task of spiritual defence and ministry on behalf of nation and people? Or does it merely wish to create a 'neo-spiritual' smoke-screen to cover self-appointed 'New Age' high priests, hypocritical sexual offenders and traitors who open the gates to criminal and illegal immigrants?[25] Can the Nobility still be the Nobility — and does it wish to be? Can it still return to the knightly calling to serve king and country in the military, at court, in diplomacy and in governance? Or does it merely wish to cover a cowardly love of ease with a beautiful old name? Can these old institutions reinvent themselves, and redefine themselves — where necessary with new people, new names and new ideas? Or do they wish to take their place in history's museum of curiosities? Can

---

25 A reference to the semi-legal assistance that the Dutch 'churches' render to fraudulent 'refugees' who have been refused asylum status, but whose continued residence is effectively 'tolerated' by the government. This practice is politically encouraged not only by the 'progressive' parliamentary block of Social Justice Warrior parties, but also by the 'Christian' parties of the present coalition government (the junior partners — CDA and CU).

these old institutions find a new role, befitting new conditions and new problems? Or do they wish to acquiesce in the pseudo-intellectual discourse of 'historical progress' propagated by the cultural-nihilist elite? In the latter case, they will disappear into the rubbish bin of history. At most, they will be reinvented — in a radically different form — by the people that they have betrayed.

There is one old institution that has not been questioned yet: the Monarchy. The reason for this omission is simple: in the Netherlands the Monarchy is beyond question; the Netherlands stands or falls with the House of Orange. A return to a 'republican stewardship' presided over by the House of Orange[26] is impossible: nobility can rise in title — from prince to king — but it cannot fall. This means that the Netherlands is either a Kingdom under the House of Orange, or nothing. The Dutch state and the Dutch people are both creations of William of Orange[27]: he is literally the 'father of the Dutch nation'. Whether one likes it or not, the conjoined destiny of the Dutch nation and the House of Orange is a fact, and it is a fact about which the real Dutch people do not tolerate disputation — in spite of all freemasonic fantasies, all republican rhetoric and all patrician envy.[28] The Orange Monarchy is the last line of defence and the strongest citadel of the Netherlands; it is the ultimate *Ernstfall* provision of the Dutch nation and people. Reverence and respect for the Orange Monarchy is not a matter of sentimental bigotry: it is first and foremost simple reverence and respect for the Dutch nation and the Dutch people. Second, it is the logical and inevitable consequence of any authentically Traditionalist approach to Dutch identity in terms of state and

---

26 A reference to the historically unique political system of the Dutch Republic (1581–1795), which was a non-monarchic confederacy of independent regions, each presided over by a stadtholder, a 'regency' office held by the House of Orange in a quasi-hereditary and quasi-permanent fashion.

27 William Count of Nassau-Dillenburg, Prince of Orange (1533–84), stadtholder of the provinces of Holland, Zeeland, Utrecht and Friesland and leader of the Dutch Revolt against Philip II of Spain.

28 In the Dutch context the term 'patrician' refers to the powerful merchants and bankers who tended to resent and fight the power of the House of Orange during the Dutch Republic.

nation. Third, it is a simple recognition of historical reality. The Kingdom of the Netherlands, as founded by the Vienna compromise of 1814, represents Dutch national sovereignty in the jungle of international geopolitics. The narrow-minded merchants, the independent gentleman farmers and the quarrelsome citizens inhabiting the Low Countries would never have survived the era of social-Darwinist nationalist and imperialist *Realpolitik* as a sovereign nation in the shape of a decentralized merchants' republic. The House of Orange, immensely rich *Uradel* with a redoubtable political and military reputation, not only continues to provide international prestige and diplomatic grandeur to a nation of *canards, canaux et canailles*,[29] but also continues to constitute a lofty symbol of national identity and historical continuity. Whereas the terror of 20th century hyper-democracy has reduced most Western heads of state to anonymous interim managers, the King of the Netherlands can still stand next to the Emperor of Japan on a footing of sovereign equality. Despite the hair-splitting of professional historians, the gossip of tabloid journalists and the ideological prejudice of bored intelligentsia, House of Orange is the Dutch nation and the Dutch nation is House of Orange.

PERSPECTIVE & SELF-ANALYSIS

In times of cultural drought the only remaining well is historical imagination.

— NICOLÁS GÓMEZ DÁVILA

If the tie between the House of Orange and the Dutch nation ever breaks it will not be because the House of Orange disappears, but because the Dutch nation disappears. By the time that a republican Rutte 'Regency' or a Pechtold 'Presidency' is announced,[30] the Netherlands will no longer

---

29 Voltaire's *bon mot* summary of his experiences with the Dutch Republic.

30 References to, respectively, Mark Rutte, PM on behalf of the extreme-neo-liberal VVD party and Alexander Pechtold, leader of the extreme-Europhile D66 party.

exist. Such figures will be mere caricature *landvoogden*, or 'district governors',[31] mercenary appointees of the international banking cartel and its Brussels politburo.[32] By that time, the 'Netherlands', overrun by a swarming mass of *métèques*, will be no more than a geographical expression. The 'Eurocratic scenario' — pseudo-autonomy as a lucrative colony under a Brussels superstate — may, in fact, turn out to be mere wishful thinking. In the long run, the 'Islamic scenario' is much more realistic: basic demographic calculation makes it likely that the future 'Netherlands' will simply turn into a *Sperrgebiet* of the 'Eurabian Caliphate'. The latter scenario holds little attraction — at least for the last non-convert natives. One of the last walls that separate the Netherlands from both of these scenarios is its Monarchy.

At this historic juncture, the choices that the old *Ernstfall* institutions of Monarchy, Nobility, Church and Academy will make for themselves and for the Netherlands are all-decisive. This means that refraining from choosing necessarily involves a choice: the choice to comfortably and carelessly enjoy a full bank account and a full stomach, but at the expense of the last remnants of common decency and self-respect. This also means that a choice for the road of least resistance has only one destination: degenerate and dishonourable oblivion. But when future historians will judge the imminent choices of these old institutions, they will also judge the choices of the nation that they were supposed to serve. The common people, effectively divided into what may be termed the Third, Fourth and Fifth Estates, are duty-bound to bear and maintain the *Ernstfall* institutions of this nation: the people should carry hierarchy and support its institutions. If the people fail in their duty, their institutions are left powerless. A people stands or falls as an organic whole: the head

---

31 The Dutch term *landvoogd* is historically associated with the 'Iron Duke' or 'Alva', the Grand Duke of Alba, who was appointed by Philip II of Spain to stamp out the Dutch Revolt through bloody repression.

32 It should be noted that to the Dutch people 'Brussels authority' is historically associated with totalitarian tyranny: Brussels was the administrative centre of Spanish power throughout most of the Dutch War of Independence.

does not work without the heart and the arm does not work without the lungs. Recognition of the need for unity, solidarity and cooperation — for a totalizing mobilization of the whole community in *Ernstfall* and emergency — is a fundamental principle of every authentic Traditionalist theory of statecraft. The holistic vision of Traditionalism teaches that such a mobilization is a fundamental prerequisite for the rebirth of a nation and a people. Only such a mobilization will allow the Dutch nation to rise from the ashes of Modernity. Above all else, the realization of this essentially timeless vision requires an inner re-generation: it requires a conscious and active rejection of the Modernist pretences of 'progress' and the Modernist illusions of 'freedom' — in other words, a total rejection of Modernist cultural-nihilism. This requires every member of the community — irrespective of formal rank, social status, educational qualification, gender and age — to look into the mirror and ask whether he or she can still see an authentic private destiny and whether he or she can still accept an authentic public role. The mirror of Traditionalism is merciless and it has some disagreeable lessons to teach to the Dutch people:

(1) The Third Estate — the 'Blue Book', the 'patricians', the *regenten*[33] — cannot separate itself from the nation by money and privilege: it cannot exist without the people. International investment portfolios and overseas real estate holdings are no substitutes for home and identity: even the richest bankers and the most cunning businessmen are still part of their people.

(2) The Fourth Estate — small and medium entrepreneurs, skilled workers, peasants, fishermen — should not imitate the riches and privileges of the patricians and the nobles. Hyper-materialist and immoral wishes are

---

33 All three terms cover approximately the same social class. The Dutch term *Blauwe Boekje*, or 'Blue Book', refers to an official publication of the genealogies of the non-noble Dutch elite. The Dutch term *regenten* refers to the semi-hereditary urban ruling class of the Dutch Republic. Some members of the old republican mercantile elite were ennobled during the 19th century. Those who were not think of themselves as co-equal with the nobility, especially as some branches of them are intermarried with the nobility. This sentiment, however, is not shared by anybody else.

inappropriate for an Estate that is called to productive labour and honourable family life. Ostentation and luxury are not appropriate for people who are called to hard work and simple responsibilities.

(3) The Fifth Estate — resident aliens — must accept a modest place and subservient role in the life of the host nation. Resident aliens should remember the generous hospitality of the host nation. Shared history gives certain groups — Israelites, Roma, West and East Indies ex-colonials, Afrikaners — the right to a permanent place in the Dutch nation, but not to full legal equality. 'Guest workers', 'migrant labour', 'refugees' and their descendants only have the right to temporary residence: those who no longer engage in productive labour and who no longer qualify for refugee status must return to their countries of origin. Those who are honest and honourable and who recognize the boundaries of common decency can count on a correct parting and a correct final settlement. Those who hold on to fictitious rights through bureaucratic fraud, legal tricks and criminal blackmail can ultimately expect an appropriate response. Those who are allowed to stay as members of the Fifth Estate will have to learn to live as guests. That means to maintain a respectful silence when the host nation discusses its own affairs and heritage — and to keep a respectful distance from the rights, property and people of the host nation.

(4) All groups must focus their effort and attention on the duties and responsibilities that they have been given by Providence. The First Estate, i.e. the Nobility, has been called to provide the soldiers, diplomats, courtiers, landlords and benefactors that serve the monarchy, the people and the country — without degenerating into rootless cosmopolitans. The Second Estate, i.e. the Church, has been called to provide priests, deacons, teachers, nurses and social workers — not for illegal aliens, but for its own nation. The Third Estate, i.e. the patricians, has been called to sensibly and prudently maintain a financial and industrial framework that creates wealth for all — without becoming an 'expat' community in its own country. The Fourth Estate, i.e. the working people, has been called to be productive in professional vocation and to be faithful in family life — not only for the present generation and the present time but also for the next generation and for the future of the nation. The Fifth Estate, i.e. the resident aliens, has been called to remain faithful to

its alien roots with maximum autonomy according to the principle of 'sphere sovereignty'[34] — without being a burden on the host nation.

(5) All individuals must limit their effort and attention to the duties and responsibilities that they have been given by Providence. Bankers and businessmen have a right to enjoy the fruits of their ingenuity and their entrepreneurial ventures — but not to exploit the common people or to interfere in affairs of state. Scientists, artists, entertainers and sportsmen have a right to use their God-given talents and to appropriate public recognition — but not to financial excess and not to interference with public policy. Women have the right to marriage and motherhood — but not to simultaneous experiments in terms of private relations and paid employment. Men have a right to respect as breadwinners and heads of the family — and they must be allowed to be both — but not to abandon work and family commitments at will. Older people have a right to economic security, proper healthcare and the gratitude of the community — but not to a disproportionate share of national wealth and not to excess luxuries at the expense of young people who still have to start their own lives.

(6) Hyper-democracy, in which everybody is allowed and forced to participate in decision-making, is incompatible with the great variety of collective identities and individual destinies that co-exist within every great people. To remedy the disaster of hyper-democracy it will be necessary to limit the democratic process to appropriate spheres of self-regulating sovereign groups and to limit the democratic franchise according to direct interest, proven competency and effective financial contribution. It is unjust to give religious majorities the 'democratic right' to decide about the behaviour and conscious of minorities that have a different worldview. It is unjust to give a mass of lazy spongers the 'democratic right' to decide how many taxes hard-working people should pay to keep them in idleness. It is unjust to 'democratically' force hard-working men who have to feed and clothe their families to pay for

---

34 The concept of *soevereiniteit in eigen kring*, or 'sphere sovereignty', stipulates differentiated authority and responsibility. It is important in Neo-Calvinist thought and it was important in the policies of Dutch statesman Abraham Kuyper.

the irresponsible partner and parenthood choices of confused and dissolute women. It is unjust to give a mass of envious foreigners the 'democratic right' to decide which rights they have in relation to indigenous people whose ancestors have built the nation. It is unjust to give a mass of brainless consumers the 'democratic right' to decide about the future of the global ecosystem and about the fate of millions of innocent animals.

(7) Only the simultaneous and full application of the Traditionalist principles of holistic integration, hierarchic organization and transcendental direction can prepare the Dutch people for the *Ernstfall* and emergency of the present Crisis of the Modern World. The fatal 'progress' of hyper-democratic Modernity and the destructive 'freedom' of Postmodern cultural-nihilism can only be exorcized by an honest look in the harsh mirror of Traditionalism. This same Traditionalism, however, also offers the glorious perspective of a national rebirth — a rebirth that can grow from the natural solidarity, the inner strength and the common sense which Divine Providence has granted the Dutch people in ample measure.

If the old institutions and the traditional qualities of the Dutch nation prove themselves unequal to the modern challenges of inter-ethnic struggle, intercultural conflict and interreligious competition, then the nation as a whole simply does not deserve to survive the impending Crisis of the Modern World. In that case, the forces of nature and history must run their course and the Dutch nation must disappear in the great tides of the world. If it must be so, may Divine Providence return our land to the sea — may the waves mercifully cover the moral cowardliness, the political treason, the social injustice and the cultural dirt of the 'last Netherlands'. If it must be so, may Divine Providence grant our people an honourable seaman's grave, worthy of our noble ancestors.

❦

CHAPTER THREE

The Dangers of Democracy

A Warning from Dutch History

*dedicated to 'Forum for Democracy' — because another false dawn
is too tiring*

POSTMODERN DEMOCRACY:
THE DUTCH TEST CASE

*Democracy can stimulate the human power drive
without providing any actual power.*

— MENCIUS MOLDBUG

ROM A TRADITIONALIST PERSPECTIVE, THE IN-
cidents of Modern 'democratic politics' — elections, appoint-
ments, debates — are simply staged spectacles in an entirely
predictable *théâtre de l'absurde*, merely meant to maintain a politically
correct illusion of 'popular consent'. To a certain extent, however, they
may be 'diagnostically' significant: specific political incidents may be indic-
ative of general, long-term developments in the socio-cultural pathology

of which Postmodern 'democracy' is merely a symptom. Thus, from a Traditionalist perspective, the rise of the so-called 'populist' movement throughout the Postmodern West is an interesting development, because it contains elements of a(n imprecisely articulated) neo-identitarian and neo-authoritarian reaction against Cultural Nihilist 'standard democracy' (as defined by its aims of neo-liberal globalism, militant secularism, social deconstruction and anti-nationalist culture relativism). In Latin America, populism is associated with the 'pink tide', personified by its 'three musketeers': Hugo Chávez (elected president of Venezuela in 1999), Lula da Silva (elected president of Brazil in 2003) and Evo Morales (elected president of Bolivia in 2006). In Eastern Europe, populism is associated with (nationalist, communitarian, socially conservative) 'illiberal democracy', as in Vladimir Putin's Russia, Viktor Orbán's Hungary and Miloš Zeman's Czech Republic. In Western Europe, populism is associated with the rise of 'Eurosceptic' and 'anti-immigration' parties, such as the *Front National* in France, the *Freiheitliche Partei Oesterreichs* in Austria and the *Partij voor de Vrijheid* in the Netherlands. Throughout Western Europe and the overseas Anglosphere, the rise of the populist movement is primarily fuelled by growing indigenous discontent with the accelerated enforcement of the pet projects of Cultural Nihilist hostile elite: *ethnic replacement* (mass immigration, selective natalism, affirmative action) and *neo-liberal 'shock therapy'* (de-industrialization, deregulation, privatisation). Overall, the populist movement forms a substantial threat to the global dominance of the transnational *hostile elite*.

At its provisional height, this populist movement led to unexpected anti-globalist victories in the British EU membership referendum and the American presidential election of 2016. After the British vote for 'Brexit' and the American vote for Trump, it was widely thought that the momentum of the populist-patriotic surge in the Anglo-Saxon world might be replicated in continental Europe in an election series scheduled for 2017. Three of these elections were generally regarded as key stepping stones: these were, in increasing order of significance, the Dutch general elections in March, the French presidential elections in May and the German federal election in September. The first of these, the Dutch general elections of 15 March, were widely considered as a key indicator of the 'political mood' in continental Europe: its outcome was widely felt to be a reliable indicator of the outcome of the upcoming elections in France and Germany, the twin pillars of the EU project. With hindsight, this analysis was proven correct: the marginal electoral victory of the Cultural Nihilist hostile elite in the Netherlands was closely replicated in France and Germany. Thus, an analysis of the Dutch parliamentary elections of 2017 may help to explain the relative 'immunity', thus far, of continental Western Europe to the spread of populism. The preceding chapter has described Cultural Nihilism's general socio-cultural configuration in the Postmodern Netherlands; this chapter will describe its precise political configuration and its significance as an important test case of Postmodern 'democracy'.

Geopolitically and historically, the Netherlands is situated right in the heart of the Cultural Nihilist 'European project', which is aimed at the abolition of national sovereignty (Monnet's 'European federation') and the creation of an ethnic 'melting pot' (Kalergi's 'Eurasian-Negroid race of the future'). Thus, its geopolitical and socio-economic policies are bound to reflect — positively or negatively — those of its three great neighbours, Britain, France and Germany. 'Brexit' leaves the Netherlands without its traditional British strategic ally in the EU: this weakens the Netherlands stance against the Franco-German extreme-integrationist axis. The result of its 2017 parliamentary elections scuttled the Netherlands' hope of following Britain and exiting the EU: this leaves the Netherlands at the mercy of an ever more radical Eurocratic tyranny. Writing in 2018, the results are already visible: increased tributary payments (more 'contributions' to make up for 'Brexit' and new 'funds' to shore up the 'Euro'), further mass-immigration (new 'proportional asylum quota' and more 'obligatory family reunification') and diminished civil rights (new censorship through new 'hate speech' and 'fake news' legislation). An analysis of the Dutch parliamentary elections of 2017 will help to explain how Postmodern 'democracy' allows such obviously self-destructive policies to be implemented 'in the name of the people'. This Dutch 'test case' illustrates the utter incompatibility of Postmodern 'democracy' with the fundamental self-interest and self-preservation of the peoples of Western Europe.

An analysis of the Dutch parliamentary elections of 2017 will help to explain how Postmodern 'democracy' allows such obviously self-destructive policies to be implemented 'in the name of the people' throughout Western Europe. The results of the Swedish *Riksdag* elections of September 2018 illustrate this point: they clearly indicate an overall tendency towards politically fatal 'Dutchification' and stagnation.[35] Thus, the Dutch 'test case' of 2017 proves the utter incompatibility of Postmodern 'democracy' with the fundamental self-interest and self-preservation of the peoples of Western Europe.

THE DUTCH ELECTION RESULTS — CHART

chambre introuvable

The following chart allows foreign observers a quick overview of the new Dutch political reality after the elections of 15 March 2017: it shows the power relations in the 150-seat Dutch House of Representatives (*Tweede Kamer*). It should be remembered that these election results represent a significant distortion of true popular sentiment: nearly 20% of the increasingly disappointed and apathetic electorate did not participate and there were considerable 'irregularities' in the manual counting process. Given the slim parliamentary power margin of the resulting Dutch government these factors are important. Above and beyond this, it should be remembered that during the last decades, particularly lax 'naturalization' procedures have added up to two million voters to the electorate: these new 'citizens' inevitably strengthen the vote for the parties that guarantee their continued 'citizenship', i.e. principally the SJW and liberal parties. Note: in the table below, the governmental block, which is still led by PM

---

35 Cf. www.theguardian.com/world/2018/sep/10/swedish-election-highlights-decline-of-europes-main-parties.

Mark Rutte (*VVD*) but now includes no less than four parties with a combined majority of only one seat, is indicated in **bold**; the patriotic block, which now includes the Party for Freedom (*PVV*, led by Geert Wilders) and Forum for Democracy (*FVD*, led by Thierry Baudet) is indicated in *italics*.

Block	*Seats*	Changes since 2012	*Party*	*Core electorate*	*Seats*	Changes since 2012
Government	*76*	+ 5	**VVD**	**Liberal-Business**	*33*	- 8
			D66	**Liberal-Nihilist**	*19*	+ 7
			CDA	**Christian-Bourgeois**	*19*	+ 6
			CU	**Christian-Progressive**	*5*	0
Conservatives	3	0	SGP	Christian-Conservative	3	0
SJWs	49	- 12	GL	Green-Nihilist	14	+ 10
			SP	Socialist	14	- 1
			PVDA	Pseudo-Socialist	9	- 27
			PVDD	Animal Rights	5	+ 3
			50PLUS	Pensioner Rights	4	+ 2
			DENK	Minority Rights	3	+ 1
Patriots	*22*	+ 7	*PVV*	*Libertarian-Populist*	*20*	+ 5
			FVD	*Libertarian-Intellectual*	*2*	+ 2

THE DUTCH ELECTION RESULTS — COMMENTARY

Some comments are useful for foreign observers to navigate the political landscape resulting from the 2017 election:

(1) Despite the government coalition's narrow majority, it is unlikely to be affected by dissent. The leaders of all three junior coalition partners have opted to take their seats in parliament to enforce internal party discipline. The

government can also rely on the 'faithful opposition' of the Christian-Conservative SGP, which tends to put political stability above political principle.

(2) Following the demographic decline of the baby boomers, the political tendency among native Dutch population is towards a decline of the Social Justice Warrior parties. The loss of these parties generally translates into the gain of the patriotic parties.

(3) The native Dutch population is increasingly polarized into two diametrically opposed groups: the wealthy 'elite' and entrepreneurial wannabe elite (together perhaps about 20% of the population), which favours the liberal parties, and the increasingly marginalized 'common people', who favour the patriotic parties.

(4) The rapid demographic rise of a non-native electorate, accentuated through accelerated 'immigration' and 'naturalization' procedures, translates into an electoral strengthening of the governing liberal parties: the non-native electorate now views them as the guarantors of continued non-native privilege. This factor also increasingly delegitimizes the 'democratic mandate' claimed by the political elite.

(5) The decline of the classical Social Justice Warrior parties has led some of their non-native supporters to form their own party: DENK. This new party, de facto controlled by the Turkish government, is the first independent non-native parliamentary party in the Western world.

(6) Domestically, the current socio-economic trajectory suggests a general trend towards further political polarization — and further devolution of power to ethnicity-based interest groups. On the one hand, the wealthy native elite will combine with the new non-native electorate in supporting the pro-globalist, pro-European, pro-business liberals. On the other hand, the marginalized native 'common people' will increasingly support the patriotic parties. The simple mathematics of demographic development, however, 'democratically' dooms the patriotic cause of the native people.

(7) Internationally, the 2017 elections condemn the Netherlands to continued adherence to popularly discredited 'superstate' structures such as EU,

Schengen, the euro and NATO, further exposing the country to mass immigration, international crime and labour outsourcing — and implicating it in continued globalist agendas of military aggression and economic imperialism. Given the electoral trajectory mentioned under point (6), only a drastic political realignment of its economically and politically dominant neighbour, Germany, can allow the Netherlands to escape from its nearly seventy-year-long diplomatic servitude.

THE DUTCH ELECTION RESULTS — PROGNOSIS

In terms of the patriotic and identitarian cause, the only glimmer of hope visible in the murky wake of the incompetently fraudulent, foreign-manipulated and journalistically rigged elections of 15 March 2017 is the meteoric rise of the Forum for Democracy, appearing practically out of nowhere on the parliamentary scene. Forum for Democracy reaches beyond the bland libertarian populism and the facile anti-Islamic rhetoric of its older patriotic fellow-traveller, the Freedom Party: Forum for Democracy addresses a wider identitarian agenda and aims at more fundamental political reforms. But it should be noted that Dutch parliamentary history is full of such false dawns — embers of consciousness and resistance in the ashes of the national body politic. Many good political beginnings and many sincere political start-ups have been smothered by organizational infiltration, media manipulation, violent intimidation and good old-fashioned bribery. To the extent that such embers were not snuffed out in their early development, they were slowly choked by the poisonous fumes of parliamentarianism and institutionalization. To the extent that ambitious newcomers are not stopped in their tracks by procedural formalities and bureaucratic resistance, they tend to be eventually co-opted into the Dutch governing elite.

Forum for Democracy is media-savvy and its two dashing parliamentary representatives have made a good start, but they need to remember the true meaning of 'parliamentarianism' and the true nature of 'democracy'.

Concerning 'parliamentarianism', they would be well advised to remember the words of their illustrious rebel predecessor: Ferdinand Domela Nieuwenhuis. Nieuwenhuis not only considered the phenomenon of the 'parliament' to be best expressed in the portmanteau of the two French words *parler* and *mentir*, 'speaking' and 'lying', but also stated that the Dutch parliament was 'the most disgusting in the civilized world'. As they attempt to cross the mudflats of the Dutch political landscape, the parliamentarians of Forum for Democracy would also be well advised to learn the lessons of Dutch history — and to study the more fundamental lessons of Traditionalist political philosophy concerning the actual meaning of 'democracy'.

BEYOND DEMOCRACY: LESSONS OF DUTCH HISTORY

In a strange way, the present Dutch political landscape reflects the challenging Dutch natural landscape, characterized by dangerous tidal sea arms, ever-shifting river beds and uninhabitable marshlands. Many times throughout history this vulnerable lowland country, taken from the sea by the hard work of many generations, has been re-invaded by the sea: this long battle against the elements is the greatest Dutch national epos. But now even greater dangers threaten the Netherlands. Never before has the Dutch political landscape been invaded by hostile elements as it has been during the last decennia. Anti-national neo-liberalism has destroyed much of the Netherlands' industries and trades, anti-national secular nihilism has undermined its churches and families, anti-national cultural bolshevism has hijacked its arts and sciences and anti-national multicultural activism has abolished its borders and sovereign rights. The present Dutch political landscape is now splintered in an unprecedented manner — it is now wholly dominated by irrational forces of hyper-democracy. The resulting political fragmentation inevitably strengthens the power of the Cultural Nihilist hostile elite: *divide et impera*. Before the patriotic and identitarian opposition can hope to loosen the Cultural Nihilist stranglehold on the body politic, it will have to understand how this situation has come about. It will have to learn the lessons of Dutch history:

First: the tight-fisted, narrow-minded and cold-hearted Pharisees who have been banking, trading and scheming in the Netherlands for many centuries, will never voluntarily hand over true power. They will rather cut the dykes, open the sluices and give the land back to the sea than to hand it over to those who actually want what is good for the Dutch people — economic justice, social equilibrium and national honour. They will rather see the land disappear, the people drown and the culture swept away than to hand over power to those who actually want what is best for the nation.

Second: the liberal-Capitalist, secular-nihilist and anti-national politicians who have been 'governing' the Netherlands for many decades, will never voluntarily hand over the state apparatus — least of all democratically. When their rival is not worn down, corrupted and co-opted, they will simply resort to murder — as in the case of Professor Fortuyn. They will say that it is more 'convenient that one man dies for the people'.

Third: foreign models, resources and auxiliaries — even the most generous and most noble — will not prevail against the stubborn mental diseases bred by the toxic swamp of native 'democracy'. The fever-ridden swamps of the Netherlands not only became the graveyard of the mighty Spanish Empire, but they also put a full stop to many mighty armies — as happened with the French in 1672, the Russians in 1799 and the British in 1809. The native swamp of democracy must be drained first.

Let the brave little knights of Forum for Democracy remember that the many will-o'-the-wisps of the Dutch political 'Dead Marshes' have led astray — and killed — greater men than themselves. Brighter lights than theirs have been extinguished in the Dutch political swamp. They should realize that theirs is a hazardous quest.

THE DANGERS OF DEMOCRACY — FREELY INSPIRED BY NICOLÁS GÓMEZ DÁVILA

THE SIGNPOSTS OF DEMOCRACY:

The word 'democracy' never indicates a political fact: it merely indicates a metaphysical perversion.

✳

Life is hierarchic: only death is democratic.

✳

Man can only be free in a hierarchical society, because it is the only one where he feels the urge to be free.

THE SHOALS OF DEMOCRACY:

The legitimacy of power does not depend on its origins but on its goals.

✳

A free society is not a society that has the right to choose its ruler, but a society that chooses as its ruler the one who has the authentic right to rule.

✳

The number of votes on which a government is based is not the measure of its legitimacy, but rather of its mediocrity.

✳

A democratic parliament is not the place for debate, but the place where collectivist absolutism issues its proclamations.

✳

It is not worth listening to representatives who do not represent eternal values.

THE GUIDES OF DEMOCRACY:

Slowly by slowly, the library of history transfers the thinkers of democracy from the political section to the psychiatric section.

*

There is irredeemable meanness in the proponents of democracy: they are the dedicated accomplices of a phenomenon that kills everything good and beautiful.

*

Democratic politicians are the condensation of the stupidity of the rabble.

*

If we see an intelligent man becoming a politician we feel the same as when we see a beautiful girl becoming a nun.

*

Advocates of true democracy will sacrifice even their personal interests to their social resentments, but only after they have sacrificed the interests of the people.

THE FELLOW TRAVELLERS OF DEMOCRACY:

The rabble never rises up against despotism: it rises up against bad food.

*

The rabble does not vote for cures, but for anaesthesia.

*

The rabble is only seduced by prostituted ideas.

THE TRAFFIC RULES OF DEMOCRACY:

The basic postulate of democracy: the law is the consciousness of the citizen.

*

Under the aegis of democracy, the law is not feared by real criminals, but only by those who are falsely accused.

THE DESTINATIONS OF DEMOCRACY:

The democratic society of the future: slavery without masters.

✳

Society becomes a combination of prison and asylum once the democratic happiness of the citizen becomes the aim of its rulers.

✳

A true political role for the rabble always ends in a hellish apocalypse.

RESOLUTIONS:

Every cultured person has the duty to be intolerant: tolerance proves the end of authentic culture.

✳

When dialogue is the only way out, the situation is hopeless.

✳

Surrender to the majority only becomes an option once we are out of ammunition.

(*) *Note that the Traditionalist critique of Modern 'democracy' provided in this chapter is supplemented by a Traditionalist critique of Modern 'human rights' in Appendix A.*

❧

CHAPTER FOUR

The Sword of Knowledge

Think not that I am come to send peace on earth:
I came not to send peace, but a sword.

— MATTHEW 10:34

ETHNIC VOCATION

As individuals have a vocation, so peoples have a vocation:
they either radiate this vocation or are left infertile and obscure
according to whether they obey it or resist it.

— POPE PIUS XII

IN TRADITIONALIST THEORY, ALL FORMS OF AU-
thentic identity, including religion, ethnicity, caste and gender, appear as 'vocations': they have the role of immanent and micro-cosmic 'callings' that reflect transcendental and macro-cosmic ideals. From
a Traditionalist perspective, therefore, the birth of individual human
beings in specific physical, geographical, historical and cultural settings
is never a 'coincidence': rather, it is considered a 'destiny' that involves

specific privileges and specific limitations, specific duties and specific rights. To the extent that the individual is capable of understanding and coming to terms with the exoteric and esoteric meanings of this destiny, he experiences his life in terms of a 'calling'. On an individual level, the obvious categories of 'biological calling' (race, gender, age) and 'cultural calling' (ethnicity, caste, heritage) are augmented by highly personalized categories that combine physical, intellectual, moral and spiritual aptitudes: these are the additional dimensions of 'calling' that are commonly referred to as 'talents'. The resulting specific 'admixtures' create so great a spectrum of individual variety, that each single human being can, theoretically, be considered 'unique' — worthy of a unique name and a unique place in the world. In the world of Tradition, however, this 'uniqueness' of individuals was *not* what counted: what counted was the extent to which individuals were capable of reproducing on a micro-cosmic level — i.e. *in* their *personae* — the macro-cosmic ideals that underpinned their overall vocations. This pursuit of vocation and its implicit 'drive to destiny' account for the anonymous and archetypal quality of the ancient world of Tradition — for its imperious grandeur, sublime art and impersonal detachment. In the world of Tradition humanity always attempted to mould and conform itself according to ideal 'models'. These archetypal models — 'King', 'Warrior', 'Priest', 'Father', 'Mother', 'Husband', 'Wife' — were essentially *superhuman* ideals. In terms of Modern psychoanalysis these models generally match Jung's *archetypal images* — 'unconscious' mediators of a hidden *unus mundus*. Modern mankind is now so far removed from these archetypes, and from the Transcendental Sphere that they reflect, that it even doubts whether they ever really existed. But despite their excision from the physical world and their suppression in the psychological, they continue to haunt Modern mankind in occasional flashes of numinous experience — dreams, visions and portents.

In the world of Tradition the realization of these ideal models required a deliberate dissolution of 'self' and a strenuous stylization of 'personality'. The 'de-personalization' involved in this archetypal conformity accounts for phenomena such as the regnal name of the king (assumption of sacred office), the accolade of the knight (passage to noble status), the tonsure of the monk (renunciation of worldly aspirations). Obviously, the extent to which individuals actually achieved their personal vocation fluctuated, but the superhuman ideal that this vocation referred to did not. In other words: the *standard* of vocation was always immutable. This standard was guaranteed by the holistic quality and anagogic direction that characterize all Traditional communities: 'individuality' and 'personality' were always inextricably linked to communal functionality as well as transcendental purpose. It is the gradual departure from this standard, this functionality and this purpose that defines 'Modernity'. Thus, Modern 'history' and Modern 'progress' are basically descriptions of the loss of all substantive forms of vocation. From a Traditionalist perspective, authentic identity can be defined as conformity to substantive vocation; failure to conform to substantive vocation therefore equals loss of authentic identity. Thus, Modernity can be defined as *failure of vocation* and *loss of identity*: in this sense, Modernity is nothing more than the *negation* of Tradition.

In the world of Tradition the concrete collective identity of 'a people' — (an ethnicity) was always an agglomerate of concrete identities: religious identity, genetic identity and linguistic identity were its essential components. Shared spiritual experience, shared genealogical heritage and shared linguistic medium defined the boundaries of ethnicity. To a certain extent, these boundaries were permeable: Traditional ethnicities were *bio-cultural organisms* that had to be able to grow, diminish and adapt according to changing circumstances. They had to be able to absorb, reject and change new religious ideas, new genetic elements and new linguistic concepts according to their needs. Thus, the boundaries of Traditional ethnicity were flexible — but not infinitely so. Strong ethnicities were always characterized by strong boundaries, and the strongest ethnicities, the ones that endured longest, were those that had the strongest boundaries. This is illustrated by the fact that the oldest surviving historical ethnicity, the Jewish ethnicity, has very high 'boundary walls': the prolonged and steep process of 'conversion to Judaism' constitutes, in fact, a carefully screened programme of ethnic assimilation: 'absorption within the Jewish people' would be a more accurate term. Within the boundaries of the Traditional ethnicity 'peoples' are defined by — and literally enclosed within — *highly specialized existential modalities*. Within these modalities, individuals live the life of their people, and 'peoplehood' is alive in them. In Modern philosophical terms, the boundaries of these modalities match Heidegger's *specialized time* (the protective temporal horizon of *Kulturkreisen*) in *specialized space* (the protective spatial horizon of *Blut und Boden*), a theme that will be explored in more detail in Chapter 8.

Whenever individuals exit the existential modalities of their people, without being ritually 'transferred' to another people through strictly formalized exchange procedures (marriage, adoption), they become *outcasts*: they literally become 'nobodies'. An archetypal expression of the resultant 'loss of soul' is found in the Biblical account of the Curse of Cain: *And now art thou cursed from the earth, which hath opened her mouth to receive thy brother's blood from thy hand; When thou tillest the ground, it shall not henceforth yield unto thee her strength; a fugitive and a vagabond shalt thou be in the earth* (Genesis 4:11–12). In the world of Tradition, the loss of ethnic identity meant a fate worse than death itself, as is reflected in the lament of Cain: *And Cain said unto the Lord, My punishment is greater than I can bear. Behold, thou hast driven me out this day from the face of the earth; and from thy face shall I be hid; and I shall be a fugitive and a vagabond in the earth; and it shall come to pass, that every one that findeth me shall slay me* (Genesis: 4:13–14). Thus, the dissolution of ethnic identity under the aegis of Modern 'progress' effectively places Modern men under the Curse of Cain: as they are reduced to atomized individuals without a past and without a future, without a home and without a name, they become 'lost souls', condemned to wander the Earth without rest and without destination. On these lost souls the meaning of 'Ethnic Vocation' is inevitably lost. Under the shade of this 'loss of soul', it is the duty of well-intentioned educators to point out to young people the great loss they will incur when they abandon their Ethnic Vocation.

ETHNIC VOCATION
IN THE POSTMODERN WEST

And Cain went out from the presence of the Lord,
and dwelt in the land of Nod, on the east of Eden.

— GENESIS 4:16

Within the framework of the Postmodern ideology of Cultural Nihilism, Ethnic Vocation is a taboo subject: the merest hint that ethnic identity might have a 'higher meaning' — as is inevitably implied by the term 'vocation' — is bound to raise a formidable barrage of slander and abuse. The standard Cultural Nihilist reaction to any rational discussion of the subjects of historical ethnicity and national identity includes accusations of 'racism' and 'nationalism', terms that in Western public discourse are inextricably associated with the unresolved traumas of the 20th century history of the Western peoples. These literally senseless accusations are obviously aimed at repressing any reminder of the highly 'inconvenient truth' of the doubly bio-evolutionary and cultural-historical reality of ethnicity. Cultural Nihilist doctrine is simply incompatible with rational discussion of this reality. Inevitably, the Cultural Nihilist hostile elite inhabits a hermetically closed mental bubble, which allows it to remain in permanent denial. It is up to the new *génération identitaire* of the Postmodern West to exit and explode this bubble, to reclaim its legitimate inheritance and to recover its Ethnic Vocation.

The 'Western peoples' can be pragmatically defined as the indigenous peoples inhabiting the European continent to the west of the religious divide imposed by the 1054 Great Schism line (roughly the present EU and EEA, excluding Romania, Bulgaria, Greece and Cyprus) plus their overseas settlements (the worldwide Anglosphere, parts of Latin America and South Africa). By this approximate definition, they include at least four dozen ethnicities, all of which have their own specialized Ethnic Vocations. These Ethnic Vocations, however, do have certain features in common. Despite substantial historical admixtures and some extreme variations, these features include (1) a *shared physical phenotype* (the 'Caucasian Race'), (2) a *shared religious Tradition* (the Catholic/Protestant *res publica christiana*) and (3) a *shared linguistic heritage* (the Indo-European language family). From a Traditionalist perspective, these three 'criteria' are neither rigidly materialist nor rigidly reductionist: 'phenotype' refers to *model physical expression* rather than to 'racial purity', 'religion' refers to *model spiritual experience* rather than to theological dogma and 'language' refers to *model creative ability* rather than to linguistic exclusivity. In this regard, it is important to emphasize the historically *hybrid* phenotypic, religious and linguistic roots of Western civilization: the origins of this civilization are to be found in *Völkerwanderung*, which resulted in continent-wide phenotypic admixture, *Evangelization*, which resulted in an effective fusion of Christianity with Paganism, and *Romanization*, which resulted in the imposition of Classical standards on all Western forms of intellectual and artistic expression. Furthermore, the three criteria of phenotype, religion and language are neither totally exclusive nor totally exhaustive: they leave a considerable space for 'anomalies', in the form of deductions, compromises and additions. Most prominently these anomalies include: (1) considerable genetic fluidity in some overseas settlements (most importantly in Latin America north of the Tropic of Capricorn), (2) some religious fluidity in the old borderlands with Orthodoxy and Islam (most importantly in the Ukraine and the Balkans) and (3) specific linguistic exceptions (most importantly the Finno-Ugric peoples). According to a maximally 'inclusive' definition, this means that at least some of the non-Caucasian populations of Latin America and some of the non-Christian populations of the Balkans may be identified as 'Western'. An objective standard of 'Western identity' may be the *Voluntary 2:1 Standard*, which revolves around the aforementioned three markers of ethnicity (phenotype, religion and language): if the large majority of a given people share two of these three markers, that people may be considered 'Western', *provided it wishes to explicitly identify itself as such.* In this regard, the *voluntary* character of Western identity is crucial, because the authenticity of this identity depends on a combination of interior experience (an interior sense of Western identity) and external assimilation (a sense of shared destiny with other Western peoples). This voluntary aspect reflects the core mechanism of Ethnic Vocation, viz. the immanent effectuation of a transcendentally defined *act of will.*

Some examples will serve to illustrate the use of this Voluntary 2:1 Standard. By this standard, the Finno-Ugrian peoples of Finland, Estonia and Hungary as well as the Bosnian and Albanian peoples of Muslim faith, all of them historically, consciously and intentionally embedded within Western civilization, *are* Westerners. By this same Voluntary 2:1 Standard, however, the Israelites and Roma populations living in Western countries *are not* Westerners: despite considerable overlaps (phenotype and language in case of most Israelites, religion and language in case of most Roma), they self-identify as non-Western and this self-identification should be respected. These people have distinct historical rights as long-term residents, but they basically remain 'guests' by their own wish.

Finally, it is of fundamental importance to stress that a consistent application of the Voluntary 2:1 Standard should induce extreme caution regarding the actual 'Western' identity of many contemporary 'Westerners'. Under the aegis of Postmodern Cultural Nihilism, many 'Westerners' emphatically *reject* their own historical identity: they are vehemently opposed to any sense of self in term of historical phenotype, historical religion and historical language. They positively seek phenotypic deconstruction through compulsory 'colour blindness', religious deconstruction through militant atheism, and linguistic deconstruction through obligatory cosmopolitanism. This is already resulting in large-scale *métissage*, public-sphere *laïcité* and run-away *créolisation* in the European heartland of Western civilization. Arguably, the Traditional ideals of the Caucasian phenotype are currently much more prized outside the West, than in the West itself: the Iranian and Indian peoples are currently more preoccupied with phenotypic heritage ('Aryan ancestry', 'caste purity'), than are their much more 'purely' preserved Caucasian 'relatives' in the West. Similarly, the Traditional ideals of Christian spirituality are currently much more prized in the churches of the Christian East, than in those of the Christian West: the Orthodox and Monophysite Churches are currently going through major revivals, while the Catholic and Protestant Churches have reached a stage of terminal decline. Specific Postmodern phenomena of political, social-economic and cultural 'globalization', such as neo-Kalergian 'Eurocracy', neo-liberal 'open borders' and 'internationalized' academia, may be considered as reliable indicators of the degree of institutionalized oikophobia that has been made possible by the systematic rejection of historical Western identity by contemporary 'Westerners'. From a Traditionalist perspective, the collective identities of the non-Western 'migrants' that are currently colonizing the Western heartland — populations that are socio-culturally primitive, but demographically viable — are much more authentic than the improvised and disposable hyper-individual 'identities' of these ethnically 'deconstructed' ex-Westerners.

As stated earlier: it is now up to the new *génération identitaire* of the Postmodern West to undo the ethnic 'deconstruction' perpetrated by the baby boomers, and to reclaim its legitimate inheritance through a rediscovery of Ethnic Vocation. In the European context, simplistically 'racist' or 'ethno-nationalist' agendas will not suffice in this regard. These agendas are exclusively rationalist-materialist constructs that might have some relevance in the context of specific ethnic conflicts in the overseas West, such as America and South Africa, but they are entirely inadequate in terms of European metapolitical discourse and European identity politics. For the European identitarian movement, racial self-awareness and ethno-nationalist self-defence constitute, at most, last-ditch 'fall back' positions. But before that desperate ultimate stance is forced upon the European peoples, the reaffirmation of their own specialized Ethnic Vocations — preservation of their own specific historical identities — will inevitably have priority. That said, the fact that Europe's different peoples share a substantial degree of common identity gives them good cause to pragmatically ally against an enemy they now all share: the transnational Cultural Nihilist hostile elite of the West. The clear and imminent danger of ethnic replacement that now emanates from the hostile elite requires a maximal degree of inter-national cooperation and coordination.

On a political level, an appropriate response to this danger could be a *confederative league*, i.e. a pragmatic alliance that leaves intact the full sovereignty of each state and nation while temporarily directing their joint resources at the common enemy. In this regard, the old Polish and Russian revolutionary slogan 'for our freedom and yours' points to historical precedents for the preservation of separate identities during a common struggle. On a metapolitical level, an appropriate sense of *shared fate* can be found in the Traditionalist concept of *meta-historical destiny*. Traditionalist authorities such as Julius Evola teach that the collective destiny of the Western peoples is determined by their shared privileged (superhuman, 'Hyperborean') ancestry and (noble, 'Aryan') lineage. This meta-historical vision is scientifically mirrored in sustained research into shared linguistic roots (Anquetil Duperron), shared social structure (George Dumézil) and shared worldviews (Max Müller). In Europe, scientific research into the origin, identity and destiny of the Indo-European peoples was negatively affected by National Socialist abuse of the key term 'Aryan'. In Asia, this research, which received much of its impetus from the work of Bal Gangadhar Tilak, has meanwhile continued apace. Recently, European researchers have finally shed the politically correct taboo on ethnic identity and origin as legitimate subjects of scientific inquiry, but it will take a new generation of thinkers, scholars and artists to fully re-appropriate these subjects for Western philosophy, science and literature. But the present Western *génération identitaire* does not need to wait for this faraway moment: ethnic identity surpasses a mere intellectual grasp of facts: it is an experiential reality that can be directly re-appropriated simply by being re-lived.

HIGHER CALLING

For my thoughts are not your thoughts, neither are your ways my ways,
saith the LORD. For as the heavens are higher then the earth,
so are my ways higher than your ways, and my thoughts than your thoughts.

— ISAIAH 55:8–9

The Traditionalist concept of meta-historical destiny may be elaborated above and beyond the specific trajectories of specific peoples (i.e. their Ethnic Vocations): groups of peoples may also share a historically determined experiential reality of a higher order, a shared 'Higher Calling'. Thus, Modern history shows that the Western peoples as a group share the 'Higher Vocation' of *Katechon of the World*: the Western peoples are collectively fated to be the protectors, lawgivers, educators and benefactors of the Southern and Eastern peoples. Collectively they are the Bringer of *Evangelion*, the Creator of *Nomos* and the Master of *Techne*. Essentially, this Higher Calling is beyond the full grasp of the human intellect; essentially, it is *superhuman*. However, even the most basic knowledge of world history and even the most rudimentary understanding of the world of today illustrate that this Higher Vocation is also a tangible *reality*. Only the Western peoples' continued adherence to this Higher Vocation assures the other peoples of the world of the gains of Western civilization: spiritual freedom, scientific endeavour, earthly justice, liberating technology and soothing medicine. The specific Ethic Vocation of each specific Western people may be considered as a partial and special — historically and geographically conditioned — reflection of that shared Higher Vocation.

Because each of the Western peoples — however small — has its own role — however modest — within this Higher Vocation, the author will now limit himself to discussing the specific Ethnic Vocation of his own small people: the Dutch people. Perhaps other peoples may benefit from a discussion of the fate of the Dutch people under the aegis of Cultural Nihilism, because this unfolding fate may hold the key to understanding the future fate of the Western people as a whole. The Dutch people is un- doubtedly among the *most modern* of the Western peoples; it only took shape under the impact of full-blown Modernity (Early Capitalism, Age of Discovery, Post-Renaissance Humanism, Radical Reformation). Ever since its rise to nationhood the Netherlands has retained a distinctly 'pro- gressive' cultural-historical 'edge', as evidenced in its pioneering role in hyper-capitalist experimentation, technological innovation and extrem- ist hyper-secularism. In this sense, the Netherlands is an intrinsic part of the *avant garde* of Modernity, alongside other typically 'Protestant Ethic' nations such as Switzerland, Britain and America. Thus, the Netherlands may very well serve as a cultural-historical 'test case', offering a preview of what may be in store for the rest of Western civilization.

The third chapter already described this 'test case' — the Postmodern predicament of the Netherlands as a 'lesson of history' — and this fourth chapter will investigate the special Ethnic Vocation of the Netherlands as the necessary background to this lesson. Because no comprehensive cul- tural-historical summary is possible within the limited framework of *Alba Rosa*, this third chapter will focus on the single most important element of the Ethnic Vocation of the Netherlands: Radical Protestantism. This chapter will show not only how this particular element forms the neces- sary background to the Crisis of the Modern Netherlands, but also how a correct grasp of its meaning can help overcome this crisis. Because Radi- cal Protestantism is a vital element within Western Modernity in general, this analysis can also be valuable in the international identitarian search for metapolitical formulae to remedy the Crisis of the Modern West.

Τὸ Κατέχον

And now ye know what withholdeth that he might be revealed in his time.
For the mystery of iniquity doth already work: only he who now letteth will
let, until he be taken out of the way. And then shall that Wicked be revealed,
whom the Lord shall consume with the spirit of his mouth, and shall destroy
with the brightness of his coming.

                                   — 2 THESSALONIANS 2:6–8.

In its original outline, this chapter was written as a contribution to a Russian research project named *Katehon*. Every linguistically educated Bible student knows what this very special term refers to. But because Scripture is read less and less, this paragraph is introduced by the translation of the relevant verses. At the same time, this introductory Word indicates the concept that is the focus of this chapter. It is important to state this focus explicitly to those who still intend to be Christians in a newly paganized world.

Those few Christians who have remained faithful when the Dutch people descended into apostasy should know that they are not alone: even outside the persecuted Church and outside their *Behouden Huys*[36] there are still people who have not fallen into idolatry. Perhaps these remaining faithful, wandering in the new spiritual desert of the Modern Netherlands, are re-living the experience of the prophet of Tishbe: *...and he requested for himself that he might die; and said, It is enough; now, O Lord, take away my life for I am not better than my fathers* (1 Kings 19:4). But these faithful should know that they are not alone — that there are still others, invisible and hidden. Twenty-eight centuries ago the sorely tested

---

36 An allusion to the *Behouden Huys*, or 'Safe House', the improvised shelter in which the expedition of Dutch polar explorer Willem Barentsz, which attempted to reach East Asia through the Northeast Passage around Siberia, survived the arctic winter season of 1596–97 on the northern tip of Russian Nova Zembla.

prophet was moved to return to the place where the Law, forgotten and reviled in his day, had first been given, thinking he was the only one who had remained faithful to it. His lonely quest, however, did not result in a resigned repeal of the Law by the Lawgiver, but rather in a mission that would return the People to their Covenant. Reverently covering his face with his mantle, the prophet is given a remarkable message: *Yet I have left me seven thousand in Israel, all knees which have not bowed unto Baal, and every mouth which hath not kissed him* (1 Kings 19:18).

The Dutch people can mirror themselves in this ancient lesson: the Katechon has not yet been removed, the Law is still standing and there are still many who are conscious of the Dutch Vocation. Despite the reality of apostasy, deviously presented as 'progress' in the 'politically correct' media, there are still many people who have not bent to the idol of nihilistic secularism and who have not kissed the feet of the golden calf of materialistic hedonism. In the politically correct lying press all those who raise their voices against the neo-liberal demolishers' regime that hides under the mantle of pseudo-Christianity[37] are depicted as primitive 'populists'.[38] In the make-believe 'public debate' all those who use their heads and hearts to combat the Cultural Marxist consensus prevailing within the academic and intellectual establishment are depicted as guilty of 'hate speech'.[39] But all those who dedicate their honest and modest work to the preservation of the endangered heritage of their ancestors — authentic doctrine, authentic knowledge, authentic identity — deserve recognition of their effort and respect for their courage. It is their unbowed stance

---

37 A reference to the 'Rutte III' coalition government of Liberal and Christian Democrat parties that was installed in 2017. An overview of the Dutch political landscape at the time of writing is found in Chapter 3.

38 In the present Dutch context the term 'populist', pejoratively used by the state-sponsored media, is mainly used to refer to the PVV 'Freedom Partij' of Geert Wilders.

39 A reference to the *caoutchouc artikel*, or 'rubbery article', 137d of the Dutch Penal Code, which has been used to arbitrarily persecute members of the patriotic political opposition, most recently Geert Wilders, leader of the PVV 'Freedom Party'.

and their honest witnessing that are helping to preserve a remnant of this heritage (Daniel 3). Many of them are finding themselves outside of the Church, unwittingly and innocently, because they were not instructed in the Faith, neither by their family nor by their teachers. The remaining authentically Christian churches are correct to maintain a proper distance from the political world and to maintain various degrees of quarantine with regard to *all that is in the world* (1 John 2: 15). But this should not extend to reckless otherworldliness regarding their responsibility for their flock: these churches would be well advised to heed the fact that outside of their walls there are still many people who refuse to bow to literally *foreign* idols — people who deserve their support. Many people outside these churches still experience the *foreign-imposed* idolatry of 'globalizing' neo-liberalism, 'pan-European' anti-nationalism and nihilistic 'culture relativism' as a literally *alien* cult. Where knowledge of Scripture and experience of grace are lacking, philosophy and ideology serve as weapons against this alien cult. To the extent that such philosophies and ideologies are compatible with authentic scriptural knowledge and divine inspiration, these churches would do well to make a careful study of those extra-ecclesiastical discourses that are opposed to the dominant system of idolatry.

It is of vital importance that all responsible Dutchmen of good will unite and take counsel in the face of the approaching Crisis of the Modern Netherlands. It is essential that church-going Dutchmen look at their non-practising comrades from this perspective. There is no reason to take offence at superficially 'heathen' terminology if the underlying analysis and intention objectively conform to the 'standards and values'[40] upheld by the Church, i.e. if they objectively translate and foster eternal Truth. The Katechon is more than the Church only: it can be in everybody that

---

40 A reference to the slogan *normen en waarden*, which was introduced into the Dutch political debate by Minister of Economic Affairs Herman Heinsbroek (member of the party of the assassinated patriotic leader Pim Fortuyn) in 2002. It was subsequently appropriated as a pseudo-conservative propaganda ploy by Christian Democratic PM Jan Peter Balkenende.

sincerely seeks, hears and knows that Truth. *The wind bloweth where it listeth, and thou hearest the sound thereof, but canst not tell whence it cometh, and whither it goeth; so is every one that is born of the Spirit* (John 3:8). All Dutchmen who are sincerely concerned for the future of their people should realize the following: flexibility of mind and fundamental reorientation are absolute preconditions for surviving and overcoming the Crisis of the Modern Netherlands.

This chapter serves to contribute to this reorientation and offers church-going Dutchmen the opportunity to learn about one specific anti-secular, but non-ecclesiastical discourse: the Traditionalist discourse. In terms of this discourse, i.e. of Traditionalist epistemology and hermeneutics, the authentically Christian churches represent remnants of the authentic Christian Tradition. From a Traditionalist perspective, the Modern world still counts several authentic Traditions — above all the five great world religions; but these Traditions, now all marked by various degrees of historical 'wear and tear' as the result of the storm of Modernity, are not interchangeable at will. God's Creation is characterized by near infinite physical variety — variety in climate, terrain, plant life, animal life, human life — and human understanding of God and Creation conforms to this variety. In every human collective (people, tribe, lineage) and in every human individual (man, woman, young, old, rich, poor) this understanding is expressed in different ways in accordance with this variety. From a Traditionalist perspective, Dutch religious forms and Dutch religious experiences represent a precious heritage: they represent special 'adaptations' and 'applications' of God's Master Plan that are specifically suited to this country and this people. Against this background, Dutch Protestantism can be understood as a historically necessary archetype: it constitutes an essentially Dutch expression of the authentic Christian Tradition. Thus, the Protestant churches — to the extent that they can still call themselves authentically Christian — should be aware of their high responsibility as the executive force of the Christian Tradition for their people. Thus, they are required

to 'accept their responsibility'.[41] Their responsibility is nothing less than
the responsibility to act as Katechon to their country and their people — and the Katechon does not carry only a shield, but also a sword.

In Traditionalist symbolism every authentic Tradition may be represented as the 'Sword of Knowledge'. This image is also found in the first
vision of the last book of the Bible: *and out of his mouth went a sharp two-
edged sword* (Revelation 1:16). It is with this vision in mind that this chapter calls upon the authentically Christian churches to redefine their role
in the approaching Dutch *Ernstfall*, the Crisis of the Modern Netherlands.
This life-threatening crisis justifies sharp words: the Sword of Knowledge
must remain sharp.

THE DUTCH VOCATION

> *Ye are the salt of the earth: but if the salt have lost his savour, wherewith shall
> it be salted? it is thenceforth good for nothing, but to be cast out, and to be
> trodden under foot of men.*
>
> — MATTHEW 5:13

To accurately fathom the depths of the Crisis of the Modern Netherlands
it is necessary to grasp the roots of the original *immaterial* roots of Dutch
national identity. In Traditionalist terminology, this refers to the *transcendental referent* of the immanent phenomenon of 'the Netherlands'. In
religious terms, this refers to the *Dutch Vocation*. Revisiting this referent

---

41 A reference to the Dutch phrase *zijn verantwoordelijkheid nemen*, or 'to accept one's
responsibility', which has the popular connotation of a deeply private awareness
of one's duty in life, distinctly reminiscent of the Calvinist notion of constantly
facing Divine Judgment in an intensely private manner. In dominant Dutch neo-
liberal discourse, this phrase has been twisted to the point of perversely justifying
a neo-Capitalist break with the ancient Dutch traditions of social inclusiveness and
solidarity. The abuse of this phrase by Christian Democrat politicians to justify neo-
liberal policies indicates the degree to which they have betrayed their historical trust.

inevitably implies reconsidering a motif that is essentially incompatible with Modernity: the motif of the Netherlands' Christian heritage. From a Traditionalist perspective, Christianity is merely one of multiple authentic religious Traditions and there exist multiple forms of (more or less) authentic Christianity. But this 'relatively relativist' perspective does not in any way diminish the intrinsic value of each authentic religious Tradition: this perspective is a hermeneutic instrument and does not affect religious identity as such. As stated earlier: authentic Traditions are never exchangeable at will. Human intellectual and experiential capability, whether individually or collectively defined, may exceed specific forms of identity, but they never eliminate identity. The historical identity of the Netherlands is inextricably bound up with Christianity: the original Vocation of the Dutch people as *a whole* stands or falls with its Christian identity — irrespective of the different roles of individuals within the national collective. The Christian Tradition emphasizes the role of different ethnic identities until the end of time: it is written that the angel will cast the devil into the abyss *'that he should deceive the nations no more'* until the end of the Thousand Year Reign (Revelation 20:3). Thus, it is clear that, within the realm of worldly affairs, respect for *ethnic* identity remains of vital concern for Christians on a collective as well as individual level. A premature and ideologically motivated 'universal brotherhood of all peoples' — an essential 'article of faith' of secular-nihilist Modernity, such as represented by Socialism and Liberalism — is not only contrary to every form of rational political practice, but also to every authentic form of authentic Christian religious experience.

Despite the profound effects of anti-Christian Modernity, the specific Vocation of the Dutch people *in a collective sense* therefore retains an undiminished Christian character. Under this Christian identity it is possible to discern the substrate identities of Indo-European ethnicity and nature-worshipping spirituality, but these substrate identities are no longer specifically *Dutch*: at most they can be defined as 'Germanic' and 'ex-pagan' and, as such, they are necessarily shared with other 'Germanic' and 'ex-pagan' peoples. To fall back on such substrate identities involves an atavist regression into a pre-Dutch *Urzeit* — a phenomenon that became temporarily visible during the Nazi-German occupation, when the specifically Dutch and Christian identities were pealed away. More specifically the Vocation of the Dutch People is inextricably moulded by the 16th century Radical Protestant vision of a new Chosen People, purified by history, dedicated to unblemished adoration and shielded by Divine Providence in a new Holy Land. The preceding *Devotio Moderna*, with its ideals of interior devotion and personalized Imitation of Christ,[42] can be understood as a necessary precondition for this Protestant vision. In this sense, the Reformation could never truly break the historical continuity of the Christian Tradition: there can only be one true Church, even if its members cannot agree on its worldly reflection. From a Traditionalist perspective, there is much to 'criticize' in the historical role and effect of the Protestant Reformation; the theses of Max Weber's *Die protestantische Ethik und der Geist des Kapitalismus* (1905) are merely faint reflections of the more fundamental criticism of the Traditional School. When textual critique of the Holy Books ends in secular 'deconstruction', when worldly sanctification ends in hedonistic materialism and when personal justification ends in narcissist individualism, then Protestantism may be said to be the frozen water that cracks the Rock of Saint Peter. But it is not the water that causes the split: Protestantism is merely the ultimate distillation of the Christian Well. It is the Wintertime of Modernity that determines its work.

The unique 16th century *Res Publica Christiana* between Ems and Scheldt,[43] experiencing itself as a providential miracle in a world of spiritual darkness and political tyranny, was deeply moulded by the

---

42 A reference to the famous devotional book *De Imitatione Christi* by Thomas à Kempis (1380?–1471). He was born in present-day Germany but worked and lived in the Low Countries and is one of the best known members of the Modern Devotion revival movements.

43 A reference to the Ems and Scheldt Rivers, which became the 'natural boundaries' of the Dutch Republic during its Eighty Years' War of independence against the mighty Hapsburg Empire.

Protestant vision. From a Traditionalist perspective, it is important to note that, while Protestantism is inextricably linked to Modernity, it also constitutes an ultimate and desperate attempt to realize the Christian vision during the rapid onset of the Dark Age of Modernity. It represents a sublime attempt to realize a *City upon a Hill* (Matthew 5:14), even after the total loss of ancient institutions, ancient communities and ancient certainties. It represents an iconoclastic *Flucht nach vorne* — into Modernity — and at the same time a purist retreat into the core experience of the Christian Tradition: redemption and resurrection. In this sense, the Dutch people is a quintessentially *Modern* people: it has its origin on the threshold of Modernity and it is characterized by a radical incorporation of Modernity in its 'spiritual sense'. The historical radicalism of this incorporation may be gauged by its 'choice' for the most radical form of Protestantism: Calvinism. The collective archetype of the Dutch people bears the indelible stamp of this historical 'choice'. This means that the capacity of the Dutch people to adapt to Modernity is very great: it experiences itself as Modern and it is able to 'live' Modernity as a natural existential mode, instead of merely 'submitting' to it in a passive manner. This has 'advantages' and 'disadvantages'. The Dutch peoples share these 'advantages' and 'disadvantages' with other Radical Protestant peoples: it is possible to discern a 'shared destiny', especially with the Anglo-Saxon 'fellow thalassocracies'. An evident advantage is a considerable socio-economic adaptability, resulting in social malleability and economic prosperity. An evident disadvantage is a permanent cultural-historical instability, resulting in low social cohesion and weak ethical standards. This specific combination allows the Dutch people to endure an exceptional degree of anarchy, capitalism and Darwinism, but it also renders it particularly vulnerable to the Modern plagues of political hyper-democracy, social hyper-individualism and Cultural Nihilist secularism.

But there are borders to the Dutch adaptability to Modernism, simply because there are borders to the definition of the Dutch Vocation and to the malleability of the Dutch society. Across these borders, this Vocation fades away and this society disappears. A re-appraisal of the pre-Modern roots of the Netherlands and a reconsideration of its Christian heritage are essential in determining these borders. This re-appraisal and this reconsideration permit a rediscovery of the simultaneously old-Christian and classic-Protestant ideals of worldly sanctity, socio-ethical transparency and a self-effacing work ethic. The Dutch Vocation expresses these ideals in a number of extremely stylized forms. In the physical landscape, there is a heroic attempt at near-restoration of the earthly paradise through incessant, self-denying labour: this is visible in a magical landscape of straightened water courses, symmetrically arranged enchanted flowers and exquisitely designed miniature gardens. In the psychological landscape, there is a nearly superhuman attempt at a collective, self-denying Imitation of Christ through the systematic cultivation of conscientiousness and self-control: this results in communities where front doors no longer need locks and where lost wallets return to their owners without their contents being touched. In the personal landscape, the work ethic is fully internalized, nearly to the extent of changing Adam's condemnation to hard labour into a blessing. The solemn vows of monasticism are nearly entirely internalized in unprecedented degrees of thrift, taciturnity, charity and volunteer labour. A constant awareness of God's presence is sublimely incorporated in scientific objectivity, artistic contemplation and spiritual silence.

Until deep into the 20th century, the Dutch people raised themselves up in conformity to this Vocation — until Modernity swept over the nation in the Second World War: this is the point at which the Dutch Vocation was overtaken by Modernity. Modernity subsequently attacks the Dutch soul through its two characteristic weaknesses — weaknesses that inevitably accompany its two characteristic hyper-Christian features. When self-denial and interior retreat are no longer aimed in a Christian-anagogic direction, they are liable to hypertrophy into senseless self-abasement and slavish servility. These excesses are latently present in all the Christian peoples of Europe, but most strongly in Protestant peoples because in them the authority of Traditional Katechon institutions (Monarchy, Church, Nobility, Academy) is per definition weaker. These two potential weaknesses render the Dutch people very vulnerable to exploitation by the Cultural Nihilist hostile elite, especially through *ethnic replacement*, i.e. the replacement of the Dutch people through gradual but constant mass immigration. This is the historical background to the perversely sadomasochistic fatalism and the perversely servile docility with which the indigenous Dutch population reacts to effective colonization in its own homeland. This collective ricochet psychopathy can only be effectively combated if it is understood in its proper context of the hyper-Christian and post-Christian perversion of the Dutch Vocation. Thus, a proper re-appraisal of the authentic Dutch Vocation as a Christian nation and a proper re-evaluation of the authentic Christian doctrine are the keys to the solution of the Dutch 'ethnic question'.

GER TSEDEK & GER TOSHAV

But he answered and said,
It is not meet to take the children's bread,
and to cast it to dogs.
— MATTHEW 15:26

As stated in Chapter 2, it was only Professor Fortuyn's sacrifice that firmly established the Dutch 'ethnic question' as the number one item on the Dutch political agenda. Earlier attempts by political parties such as the 'Centre party' (*Centrum Partij* 1980–86) and the 'Centre Democrats' (*Centrum Democraten* 1984–2002) to openly address the issues of 'immigration' and 'social integration'[44] had been successfully suppressed by a

---

44 A reference to *integratie*, a specifically Dutch ethnic policy model of enforced 'cultural fusion' and manipulated 'acculturation' based on the culture relativist ideology of 'multiculturalism'. This Modernist ideology of anti-identitarian 'multiculturalism' should be carefully distinguished from the sociological phenomenon of multi-ethnic coexistence in Traditional supranational states, which was always characterized by strict ethnic separation (e.g. the Ottoman 'millet system').

combination of *agent provocateur* infiltration, witch hunt journalism and violent 'Antifa' intimidation. Professor Fortuyn paid for his brave patriotism with his life: the Dutch people recognized this sacrifice by honouring him as the second greatest personality of Dutch history — just behind William the Silent, Father of the Nation.[45] The memory of his sacrifice effectively obliges all subsequent Dutch thinkers to continue adding to his legacy until the Dutch ethnic question is solved in a sensible — and *timely* — fashion. All throughout his life, Professor Fortuyn struggled with the identity problems that are characteristic of Modernity, both in the public and in the private sphere,[46] but he was not a heathen; his trust in Divine Providence remains in plain view even in the most 'worldly' of his writings. He accurately regarded the Church as a failing institution and he attempted to find secular remedies for the failures of the Church. The single most dramatic failure of the Dutch Church — here abstractly defined as the Dutch remnant of authentic Christianity — is its inability to teach and guide the Dutch people in its relation with other peoples, inside and outside the border of the Kingdom.

This inability must be sought in its Modern teachers, not in its Traditional teachings. Its Modern teachers have inflated the doctrines of Christian *caritas* and *humanitas* to a premature and absurd degree of universality. Thus, they have fed the pathological altruism that has brought about the betrayal of the Dutch Vocation. They have diverted the moral authority and material means of the Church from their own country and their own people. For decennia now, they have supported an 'open borders' policy that runs counter to the fundamental identity and the fundamental interest of their own country and their own people. They have failed to distinguish between what is own and what is foreign; they have failed to distinguish between their own people and foreign sojourners.

---

45 A reference to the 2004 public poll *De Grootste Nederlander*, or 'The Greatest Dutchman', organized by the Dutch public broadcaster *KRO*. It followed the format of the BBC's 'Greatest Briton'.

46 A reference to his controversial personal stance on religious and sexual identity; Professor Fortuyn was am openly gay recalcitrant Catholic.

Thus, they have failed in their duty as Katechon. They have taken an undeserved and unlawful advance payment on the borderless and universal Kingdom of Heaven that only God Himself may declare. They have far exceeded their modest worldly remit, which is limited to authority over *their own* country and *their own* people. They have committed the grievous sin of *superbia* and they still lack the courage to turn to *penitentia*. They do not understand that in Heaven the *ba'al teshuvah* — the 'master of repentance' — is superior to those that have always remained pious, despite the clear Message of Scripture: *I say unto you, that likewise joy shall be in heaven over one sinner that repenteth, more than over ninety and nine just persons, which need no repentance* (Luke 15:7).

It is the task of those theologians and authorities who have remained faithful to Tradition to cleanse the Church from the evil of Modernity. Nobody outside the Church is permitted to lecture them. But what is permitted for outsiders is to point out the urgency of the task — and to warn when the boundaries of permissible human failure are reached. When the Church transgresses the boundary between censurable shortcomings and unreasonable stubbornness by continuing to promote mass immigration and to support illegal aliens, then she finally becomes an accomplice of the destructive policies of the anti-national elite; then she becomes a part of this elite.

Ethnic Vocation — and the future of any people — entirely depends on the coherence of a double physical and psychological identity. This reality is best illustrated in the ancient People of the Covenant: the People of Israel has managed to retain its identity longer than any other historical people and the key to its preservation can be found in its adherence to its Law regarding aliens. The spiritual leaders of the Dutch people would do well to learn from the Law that has protected and preserved the People of Israel for millennia. At the most elementary level, this requires the understanding and application of the two legal principles of *Ger Toshav*, the 'resident alien', and the *Ger Tsedek*, the 'righteous alien'. The first notion refers to adherence to basic legislation by all aliens with legal residence in the ancient Land of Israel. In the context of the Modern Netherlands — and

that of many other Modern Western nations — this notion can be applied
to all strangers who wish to (continue to) legally reside in the Netherlands
as strangers, i.e. as alien residents keeping their own identity. The second
notion refers to the voluntary acceptance of the whole Law of Israel, spiritually expressed as 'conversion' to Judaism. In the context of the Modern
Netherlands, this notion can be applied to all strangers who sincerely wish
to become part of the Dutch people. Thus, in an unexpected manner, the
Israelite *halacha* provides a transcendentally inspired legal model that can
contribute to a solution of the seemingly unsolvable Dutch ethnic question.

Approaching this question from the perspective of the *halacha*, a
Dutch *Ger Toshav* would be the following: an alien with residence rights
and legal protection who retains his own ethnic identity, including his
legal nationality. In this regard, it is important to distinguish between *judicial* and *authentic* (or 'natural') nationality: the former refers to mere
administrative *citizenship* and the latter refers to real *ethnicity*. Real ethnic
identity has two complementary components: (1) the identity which the
individual *himself* subscribes to and (2) the identity which *others* ascribe
to him. Authentic identity requires that there is a match between subjec-
tively experienced identity and collectively recognized identity. Authentic
identity requires a high degree of collectively experienced historical continuity: it requires an actually or intentionally shared history reaching back
to the oldest roots of ethnicity — and to Ethnic Vocation.

In this sense, the so-called 'Dutch nationality' of the large majority of
'new Dutch citizens' — those immigrants who have gotten hold of a Dutch
passport during the last decennia — is no more than a *legal fiction*: they
are effectively 'fake Dutch'. This legal fiction — the personalized equivalent of a 'mailbox company' — may suit the anti-national hostile elite (as
labour reserve, consumer mass and electoral support base), but it also involves a great risk. This legal fiction allows a large population of opportunistic 'migrants' undeserved access to national resources — and to profit
from a 'double nationality'. Scripture teaches that *No servant can serve two
masters: for either he will hate the one, and love the other; or else he will
hold to the one, and despise the other* (Luke 16:13). The obvious injustice of

ignoring this ancient wisdom is compounded by a demoralizing effect on the indigenous Dutch people. They see that random strangers gain easy access to rights and facilities for which they themselves — and generations of their ancestors — have made great sacrifices. They also see that entirely maladjusted 'guests' think themselves suitable to participate in debates and decisions regarding the house and property of their host nation. Consciously or unconsciously, these observations colour the behaviour and attitude of indigenous Dutch people: they do not truly accept the 'new citizens' as compatriots because they do not recognize themselves in them. But they will recognize themselves in the ancient history of the persecuted People of the Covenant:

> Neither have our kings, our princes, our priests, nor our fathers, kept the law, nor hearkened unto thy commandments and thy testimonies, wherewith thou didst testify against them. For they have not served thee in their kingdom, and in thy great goodness that thou gavest them, and in the large and fat land, which thou gavest before them, neither turned they from their wicked works. Behold, we are servants this day, and for the land that thou gavest unto our fathers to eat the fruit thereof and the good thereof, behold, we are servants in it. And it yieldeth much increase unto the kings whom thou hast set over us because of our sins: and they also have dominion over our bodies, and over our cattle, at their pleasure, and we are in great distress (Nehemiah 9:34–37).

It is against this background that the much discussed phenomenon of 'silent discrimination' may be understood: it explains the passive but stubborn negativity of the indigenous Dutch people that many 'new citizens' complain about. This phenomenon proves that legal fictions such as 'citizenship education'[47] and 'naturalization' are simply no substitute

---

47 A reference to the procedure of *inburgering*, or 'citizenship education', a legal requirement for 'naturalization' as a tool of the policy of *integratie*, or 'cultural fusion'. The entirely fictitious nature of *inburgering*, compounded by a structural failure to implement its requirements and a plethora of legal 'exemption', may be gauged from simple statistics: after completion of the *inburgering* programme, most of its participants still fail to speak the Dutch language, still fail to obtain gainful employment and still fail to abide by basic Dutch behavioural norms.

for authentic identity — irrespective of the obligatory politically correct discourse of the supposed 'universal equality' of all of humanity. In this sense, the anti-national hostile elite victimizes its 'new citizen' population in the same way that it victimizes the indigenous population: the 'new citizens' are first given the sweet-tasting tranquillizer of entering a utopia of 'equality', but then wake up to the bitter reality of their unchanged ethnic identity.

The alternative would be to offer these 'fake Dutch' the option of obtaining authentic *Ger Toshav* status in the Netherlands: not taking on a *fictitious* 'Dutch' nationality but retaining their own *authentic* nationality and being recognized as such. This would mean full *sphere sovereignty* for each legally recognized foreign community, with its own family law, its own education, its own health care, its own social security and its own political autonomy. *Suum cuique* — to the degree that this sphere sovereignty is compatible with minimum standards of Dutch public life and that it does not impose undue burdens on the Dutch indigenous people. As long as these resident aliens respect the Dutch law and abstain from unacceptable habits (the death penalty, corporal punishment, wife beating, public butchery, animal cruelty, etc.) and as long as they provide for their own expenses they can be allowed to stay on indefinitely. By and large, they can be allowed to shape their lives according to their own preferences through their self-governance, their administrative organization, their own taxes, their own schools and their own medical facilities — as long as they do not intrude into Dutch politics and Dutch governance, and as long as they do not burden the Dutch taxpayer. In return for a modest tax, they will be domestically protected by Dutch law enforcement and they will be free to travel internationally with a Dutch travel document as Dutch *citizens* without being Dutch *nationals*.

Under the new dispensation most 'new citizens' would qualify for *Ger Toshav* status, provided they legally commit themselves, with the caveat that, as soon as they fail to live up to their contractual obligations (through e.g. terror, criminality, political activism), they will be deported without further ado. For good reason, Scripture states: *Let favour be shewed to the wicked, yet will he not learn righteousness: in the land of up-rightness will he deal unjustly, and he will not behold the majesty of the Lord* (Isaiah 26:10). But it is likely that under the new dispensation many 'new citizens' would themselves wish to leave, because, as soon as they are disconnected from Dutch subsidies and benefits, they will be forced to fend for themselves. The ultimate responsibility for social security will revert back to the ethnic community, which will be required by law to create a social network that conforms to basic Dutch standards of decency, i.e. no structural homelessness, no deep poverty and no unattended sicknesses. Under this new dispensation recourse to criminal behaviour will also be impossible: the full costs of criminality against the indigenous population will be charged against the community to which the criminal belongs. This will create a self-regulating modality in which there is no room for 'free riders', sponging, fraud and criminality. To speed up the departure of undesirable elements it is advisable to institute a universally accessible, temporary repatriation programme, which will give all 'new citizens' the possibility to give up residence voluntarily in return for a small life-long stipend and basic travel facilities. Investing in a repatriation programme of small inducements will pay off in the long run, because it benefits society through long-term reductions in the cost of law enforcement, legal procedures and damage control.

For those foreigners who sincerely seek to truly become Dutch, i.e. to *assimilate* in a credible manner, there will always be the option of applying for *Ger Tsedek* status. For good reason, Scripture states: *Open ye the gates, that the righteous nation which keepeth the truth may enter in* (Isaiah 26:2). In this regard, however, high requirements are essential: only those who have proven themselves as a *Ger Toshav* can apply for recognition as *Ger Tsedek* — the first status can be a prerequisite for the second status. The actual assimilation process can reflect the heavy Israelite *giyur*, or 'conversion', process and can include elements such as an official sponsor (e.g. a Christian Church, an indigenous community, an academic authority), guarantees (e.g. a security clearance, a background check, a surety payment) and a personalized multi-year commitment. Logical commitments can include elements such as a thoroughly tested Christian or humanist identity, a public renunciation of all other religions, a high-level language exam, the official adoption of a traditional Dutch name and an official oath of allegiance.

The Biblical concepts of *Ger Toshav* and *Ger Tsedek* are primarily valuable as solutions for the current Dutch ethnic question: they can regulate the status of the *present* alien population. Above and beyond this, it will be necessary to instate credible defences against *future* mass immigration. This means that *Ger Toshav* status should be restricted to those aliens who are presently residing in the Netherlands, i.e. to those who presently hold a paper 'Dutch nationality' or a permanent residence permit. Above and beyond this, only *temporary* guest workers and *temporary* asylum seekers can be accepted: guest workers only through sponsorship by accredited private employers and asylum seekers only through invitation by accredited private charities. Future guest workers and asylum seekers will have to be selected and screened in their countries of origin and employers and charities will bear the full financial and legal responsibility for them. They will all have to reapply for residence permits every year so that their status can be reviewed and they will be excluded from applying for *Ger Toshav* and *Ger Tsedek* status: before they come to the Netherlands, they will be explicitly told that they can never be more than temporary guests there. To discourage undue hopes, residency guest workers will not be allowed to own real estate and they will have to leave when they have children during their stay in the Netherlands. To discourage false expectations, the earnings of refugees will be kept in savings accounts until their departure and they will have to stay in especially supervised facilities. *Dura lex, sed lex.* Cross-border marriage and family reunification will remain the privileges of the indigenous people. *Quod licet Iovi, non licet bovi.*

It will be up to sharp-minded legal experts to create a fitting contemporary framework for the Biblical concepts of *Ger Toshav* and *Ger Tsedek*, but it is up to the wise teachers of the Church to point out to them the ultimate *purpose* of these concepts: the preservation of the Dutch people — and of the Dutch Vocation. All *chassidei 'umot ha-'ōlam*, all 'pious people of the world', are called to study the Law and to learn from it so that they can prosper in the world according to their own Vocation. If the Dutch Church recognizes the Law as its standard then it is obliged to make clear decisions — before it is too late.

POSTSCRIPT: FROM THE 'AMĪDAH

Attah chonen le-adam da'at u-melammed le-enosh binah:
chone-nu me-Itkha de'ah binah ve-haskel.
Barukh Attah Adonai chonen had-da'at!

[You bestow wisdom on man and teach insight to the human being:
Bestow on us from Yourself wisdom, insight and discernment.
Blessed are You, Lord, Who bestows wisdom!]

CHAPTER FIVE

The Hamartiology
of Modernity

THE REAR-VIEW MIRROR OF TRADITIONALISM

The gates of hell are open night and day;
Smooth the descent, and easy is the way:
But to return, and view the cheerful skies,
In this the task and mighty labor lies.

— VIRGIL, *THE AENEID*
BOOK VI (DRYDEN TRANSLATION)

A TRADITIONALIST CULTURAL-HISTORICAL IN-
terpretation of Western Modernity, as initiated by the book *The
Sunset of Tradition*, has two specific benefits for those young
Western people who are seeking viable alternatives to the bankrupt Cultural Nihilist worldview of the baby boom generation.

First, Traditionalist hermeneutics are characterized by a structurally
holistic methodology: it puts the lived human reality of Modernity and
the characteristic pathology of Modernity into perspective by studying
them at several levels simultaneously. Thus, the typically Modernist

phenomenon of 'hyper-democracy' is clarified as the result of multiple, simultaneous cultural-historical developments: the bio-evolutionary development of urban-industrial (over)populations, the sociological development of the 'regression of the castes', the political development of totalitarian collectivism and the psycho-historical development of collective narcissism. The holistic approach of Traditionalism offers an alternative to the mono-causal approach of the Historical Materialist worldview that underpins Cultural Nihilist ideologies such as social-Darwinist neo-liberalism and Cultural Marxism.

Second, Traditionalist hermeneutics is characterized by an automatic distillation of *meta-historical meaning*: by placing the objective material reality and the subjective human experience of Modernity in a coherent historical context, they gain relative meaning. Superficially unrelated Modern existential crises (industrial ecocide, cannibalistic hyper-capitalism, social atomization, existentialist philosophy, deconstructive art) regain their essential meaning through a simple description in terms of historical synchronicity and their collective opposition to preceding historical realities. Traditionalism summarizes this description as the 'Crisis of the Modern World' and it interprets Cultural Nihilism as an inevitable phase of this crisis. Thus, Cultural Nihilism is stripped of its mythological status as 'progress'. Instead, it is recognized in its essential meta-historical role as a psycho-historical 'weapon of mass destruction', utilized against all forms of authentic identity and operating through denial, abolition and inversion.

Apart from its own coherent hermeneutics, Traditionalism offers a coherent system of archetypal symbolism: it preserves theoretical knowledge of Traditional symbolic systems so that one day they can be practically re-activated. Forms of re-activation (metamorphosis, palingenesia, resurrection) are possible at all levels and in all dimensions: individually and collectively, esoterically and exoterically, physically and psychologically. At the lowest individual level, such reactivation can take the form of strictly personalized 'rebirth' (conversion, redemption, transfiguration); at the highest collective level, it can take the form of a re-commencement of history (a Renaissance, a Thousand Year Imperium, a Golden Dawn).

A self-surpassing resurrection of Western civilization from the ashes of Cultural Nihilist Modernity is only possible by a *re-experiencing* of archetypal Western symbolism: the re-conquest of Western identity is only possible by *re-living* those symbols that characterize authentic Western identity. Chapter 4 already mentioned some of the core symbols of the collective 'Higher Vocation' of the Western peoples: Bringer of *Evangelion*, Creator of *Nomos* and Master of *Techne*. But these core symbols are merely abstract reflections of the *macro-cosmic ideals* of Western identity: they lack *micro-cosmic reality* if Western men deny them in themselves. Realization of this collective Higher Vocation (of the Western peoples as a collective) as well as realization of separate Ethnic Vocations (of each separate Western people as a specific 'incarnation' of that Higher Vocation) demands a minimal degree of individual exposure to transcendental experience: a minimal degree of 'soulfulness', 'inspiration' and 'rapture'. In accordance with the dualistic Western spiritual identity of pagan nature worship and Christian self-transcendence, pre-Modern Western man was doubly exposed to such experience. First, by this predominantly agricultural existence, he was intimately linked in spirit to his boreal biotope, characterized by mythically archaic half-nature half-culture landscapes and by a tyrannical seasonal cycle that demanded constant forward thinking. Second, deeply internalized ethics and highly sublimated awareness of salvation made him experience himself as an intrinsic part of the Christian Church: he *incorporated* ecclesiastical doctrine because he himself *personified* the Church. Western man only lost his access to these transcendental experiences after his final transition into de-naturalized urbanity (the Industrial Revolution) and de-institutionalized religiosity (the Protestant Reformation).

To return to what was lost — or rather, to find a new road to an old destination — means this: recognizing what was lost, comprehending why it was lost and redeeming it. The first stop on this journey back to authentic identity and vocation is 'taking stock' — making an inventory of the spiritual losses suffered by Western man after his surrender to Modernity. The most obvious 'accounting method' for making such an inventory is the application of the standard spiritual measure of Western civilization: the Christian measure. In this regard, the question of whether or not the Christian measure is the best conceivable measure — whether or not it is intrinsically 'superior' in comparison with other religious traditions — is entirely irrelevant. The same applies to the question of whether or not Westerners still 'feel' Christian. The Christian heritage of Western civilization is still its heart and even if Western people take on another faith, they will still have to find a way of incorporating this heritage if they want to retain their identity. Even if substantial sections of the Western peoples 'convert' to Islam in the near future — an alternative that is highly preferable to certain destruction through Cultural Nihilist social implosion — their Christian heritage must have a prominent place within a new 'Euro-Islam'. In the Balkans and on the Black Sea littoral there are already many examples of Islamic cultural forms that are calibrated to incorporate Western civilization and Christian heritage (the Bektashi in Albania, the Naqshbandi in Bosnia). There, Christian heritage is fully expressed by interpretations and experiences of Islam that are spiritually and intellectually far superior to the atavistic forms of Islam found in primitive non-Western peoples. There, it is even possible to discern a synthetic sublimation that truly *unifies* the three Abrahamic religions. It is only such a sublimation that can rise above pure Christianity: thus, such a vision may be a future — effectively millennialist — vocation, but it is still very far removed from current reality (cf. Seyyed Hossein Nasr, 1975). The current reality is that what now calls itself 'Islamic' is far less civilized than what still calls itself 'Christian', for the simple reason that the peoples that carry Islam are largely far less civilized than the peoples that are still called Christian.

For now, however, the psycho-historical inventory of contemporary Western civilization that is here aimed at can only proceed from its psycho-historical standard condition, and that standard condition is Christian. Thus, this chapter must emphasize the importance of Christian spiritual inventory; it will measure some of the characteristic features of Western Modernity by the measure of the old Christian catechism. It should be noted, however, that Traditionalism itself cannot provide such a spiritual inventory: Traditionalism is merely the Guardian of Tradition — of all authentic Traditions — and it is not Tradition *in and of itself.* Traditionalism can merely point out the way back — the way up, back to an authentic Tradition. From a Traditionalist perspective, all authentic Traditions may be understood as specific reflections of the *Sophia Perennis* and the *Empyrean,* all of them equally precious, but never freely interchangeable. Individual 'lost sheep' from the scattered Western herd may find shelter and salvation elsewhere through religious conversion or esoteric mysticism. But for the Western herd as a whole, there is only one obvious road to a self-surpassing resurrection: the road to the *Seven Storey Mountain* of Christianity (Thomas Merton, 1948).

'THE SEVEN STORY MOUNTAIN'

The failure of Christianity is Christian doctrine.
— NICOLÁS GÓMEZ DÁVILA

In the author's recent book *Sunset,* the genesis of Modernity is analysed from different cultural-historical perspectives without the assumption of a hierarchical priority between the simultaneous and mutually reinforcing transformative processes that are the central themes within these different perspectives. In a radical departure from academic consensus historiography, which is entirely based in Historical Materialism, no causal priority is assumed for processes of political and social-economic transformation over processes of religious and psycho-social transformation. In accordance with its Traditionalist perspective, *Sunset* recognizes only one form of 'determinism', viz. the hierarchical priority of the macro-cosmic transcendental sphere over the micro-cosmic immanent sphere. Traditionalism, proceeding from the principle of the *(philo)Sophia Perennis*, assumes all immanent phenomena that are observable in the earthly realm to be — direct or indirect, positive or negative — reflections of the transcendental realities of the heavenly sphere. Thus, all the various transformation processes that are characteristic of the Modern Age (capitalist-monopolist accumulation in the economic sphere, the regression of the castes in the social sphere, totalitarian collectivism in the political sphere etcetera) appear as *mere* symptoms of a single meta-historical reality, viz. 'Modernity', defined as the inevitable inversion of 'Tradition' during the Dark Age (the Christian End Times, the Hindu Kali Yuga).

From this perspective, Modernity, and the unprecedented damage it is inflicting on the human and natural world, gains meta-historical *meaning*. The 'demonic' slavery, exploitation and destruction of humanity and nature — of the Earth itself — are not merely historical 'collateral damage' and cosmic 'coincidence'. In terms of ontological categorization, the damage suffered by humanity and nature are the *affection* (the subjective *paschein*) that accompanies the *substance* (the objective *ousia*) of Modernity. The damage suffered is the substantive *time content* of the Dark Age and it determines the *ontological experience* of Modern man, either passively or actively, as the perpetrator of Modernity or as its victim. Approaching the chronological trajectory of the Dark Age, each authentic Tradition — each authentic religious Tradition — interprets this ontological experience in its own manner, fitting it into its particular doctrines and rituals. In terms of an eschatological 'solution', each of the three Abrahamic religions has articulated its own particular themes, according to its particular bio-evolutionary and cultural-historical context: Judaism emphasizes 'Exile', Christianity emphasizes 'Redemption' and Islam emphasizes 'Submission'. Thus, each of these religions articulates a specific *metaphysical* 'answer' to the *meta-historical* 'problem' of Modernity, answers that 'fit' to the peoples that have cultural-historically associated themselves with these religions. In the face of the approaching culmination of Modernity — the 'Crisis of Modernity' — the Western peoples now experience a deep existential crisis, which can be traced back to a failure of the Christian 'answer' to Modernity. Thus, the psycho-historical inventory-taking that necessarily precedes the 'psycho-therapy' of the Western peoples must proceed from a Christian standard measure.

In old-fashioned Christian terminology, this matches the examination of conscience that must precede the act of contrition in the sacrament of confession. From a cultural-historical perspective, it can be said that the Christian identity of the Western people constitutes a major 'handicap' in their ability to face Modernity. Western civilization is empathically 'individualistic' in the sense that Christianity requires a permanent individual 'self-renewal'. Unbreakable self-assertiveness and unshakeable self-confidence, derived from an Eternal Covenant, allow Israelites to thrive even in external exile and persecution; these are entirely lacking in Christianity, which requires permanent self-investigation and self-transformation. Self-absorbed fatalism and self-evident directedness, derived from a stylized-recapitulating contractual simplicity, allow Muslims to thrive even in urban-hedonistic tribulation and temptation — these are entirely lacking in Christianity, which requires self-sacrifice and self-conquest.

A statement of these Christian 'handicaps' also indicates the final frontier of the 'therapeutic' functionality of any Traditionalist cultural-historical diagnosis of the Crisis of the Modern West: such a diagnosis can point Western man to the right road, but he himself will have to walk this mysteriously impossible road, as a pilgrim and a penitent. Before Western civilization can *collectively* overcome this crisis, every Western man will have to *privately* subtract himself from it. If the orthodox Israelite and the faithful Muslim can simply *live* his beliefs, the truthful Christian is forced to *re-create* them. Such a Christian life demands a *counter-temporal*, vertical self-renewal that is particularly difficult during the time-obsessed Dark Age, much more difficult than the *inner-temporal*, horizontal self-realization that is required from the Israelite and the Muslim. From this perspective, it is no surprise Western man has historically been the first to abandon Tradition — and that the plagues of Modernity have struck the West first and hardest. At this point of pilgrimage in the Night Land of Modernity, Traditionalism cannot *lead* Western man, it can only *remind* him of his old Christian vocation and of his old Christian catechism. What Divine Providence has decreed as the final destiny of Western man inevitably escapes a mere cultural-historical analysis, but that there will be a relation between original vocation and final destiny is self-evident. In the words of Thomas Altizer: *If one has been given a history in which God is present, then one must respond, whether positively or negatively, or both, to the name of God, if only as a means of making one's history one's own. If all those who ignore history become its victims, then it should also be realized that whoever ignores the God of our history becomes the victim of God.* Thus, this chapter can only conclude by symbolically pointing to the old Christian catechism — and to the direct relationship between the typical symptoms of Modern Age and the Seven Cardinal Sins of the Christian Tradition.

'Se7en'

And now I cry to You as the Prodigal
— Orthodox Great Lent Hymn

Even in present Postmodern reality, fully dominated by Cultural Nihilism and entirely characterized by the militant-secular rejection of all authentic forms of religious ethics, Western culture is still pervaded by an indeterminate and uneasy feeling of 'discontent'. In this regard, Modern art takes on the function of an 'artistic prosthesis' for the amputated religious consciences of Western man. Artistic emphasis on the exploration of absurd, grotesque and deviant motives points to a collective 'bad consciousness'. For Western man, now living in atavistic collectivism, the archaic religious and deeply Christian personal motives of crime and punishment, conscience and enlightenment, remorse and confession are presently accessible only through the Modern arts, strictly defined as 'leisure time' entertainment. These arts, defined as 'fictitious visions' and 'non-committing expressions', are the last free space for (semi-)religious experience in the public domain. Only the arts are still allowed — within certain limitation — to concern themselves with old religious notions such as absolute Truth and absolute Evil, mainly through their (largely negative) projections on marginal social phenomena such as extreme psychopathy ('horror') and paranormal perception ('science fiction'). The increasing preoccupation of young people with elaborate artistic fantasy themes — and their increasing escape into 'virtual realities' — can be explained, at least in part, by the fact that the rest of the public domain no longer offers space for substantial religious or spiritual discourse.

This 'demotion' of the Western religious and spiritual discourse, its relegation to the artistic domain, is a reliable indicator of the acceleration of the decline of Western civilization. In this regard, structuralist anthropological analyses of particular Modern works of art can offer valuable insights — but such analyses fall outside the scope of *Alba Rosa*. But to conclude this chapter on the *hamartiology*, the 'study of sin', of Modernity, it is deemed useful to point to the occasional reappearance of purely Christian teachings in Postmodern art. An example of such a reappearance is the movie *Se7en* (David Fincher, 1995), in which a Postmodern re-examination of the classic 'seven cardinal sins' of the Christian catechism is expressed in the horror of 'forced contrition'. To the extent that religious doctrine and spiritual discipline have failed, the movie points to the only remaining possibility for the resolution of the old sins: 'hellish purification' in *this world* (for a theological exploration of this theme, cf. Altizer, 1970). *Se7en* artistically expresses a realistic final scenario for the Crisis of the Modern World: a worldly realization of the otherworldly hell of Christianity; it tells the viewer to think again about the ancient wisdom of his forgotten catechism.

The Seven Cardinal Sins (Saint Gregory the Great)

Latin	English	Demon	Symbol	Modern symptom	Remedy
Gula	Gluttony	Beelzebub	pig	Consumerism	Temperance
Luxuria	Lust	Asmodeus	goat	Sexualization	Chastity
Avaritia	Greed	Mammon	money	Materialism	Charity
Ira	Anger	Satan	lion	Totalitarianism	Patience
Acedia	Sloth	Belfagor	snail	Anomie	Diligence
Invidia	Envy	Leviathan	snake	Narcissism	Gratitude
Superbia	Pride	Lucifer	peacock	Enlightenment	Humility

The Seven Social Sins (Frederick Lewis Donaldson)

Social sin	Modern symptom	Remedy
Wealth without work	< Consumerism	economic corporatism & capital controls
Pleasure without conscience	< Sexualization	religious sacraments & social control
Commerce without morality	< Totalitarianism	fair trade standards & strong competition laws
Politics without principle	< Imperialism	organic hierarchy & compartmentalized governance
Religion without sacrifice	< Anomie	religious affiliation & institutionalized charity
Knowledge without character	< Narcissism	vocational discernment & educational discipline
Science without humility	< Enlightenment	bio-ethical codes & limits on scientific authority

'CRIME & PUNISHMENT'

The Modern world shall not be punished: it is the punishment.

— NICOLÁS GÓMEZ-DÁVILA

In the Book of Exodus, the Bible relates what can happen to a people when its rulers purposefully and stubbornly persist in their sins. An enigmatic Divine judgment announces the impending effects of Providence on the Egyptian slave masters of the People of the Covenant: *And I will harden Pharaoh's heart, and multiply my signs and my wonders in the land of Egypt. But Pharaoh shall not hearken unto you, that I may lay my hand upon Egypt, and bring forth mine armies, and my people, the children of Israel, out of the land of Egypt by great judgments. And the Egyptians shall know that I am the Lord, when I stretch out mine hand upon Egypt, and bring out the children of Israel from among them* (Exodus 7:3-5). This Divine pronouncement proves that the following Ten Plagues of Egypt are meant to provide *insight* into Divine Providence. In other words: those unwilling to learn must suffer. In this regard, it is important to note that the multilayered and complex symbolism of the Ten Plagues has a meaning that is not merely *abstract*, as an illustration of the metaphysical theme of 'crime and punishment', but also *concrete*, as a practical warning.

From this perspective, it is important that Modern Western people study the Hamartiology of Modernity. Knowledge of Traditional symbols, as expressed in the Biblical history of the Ten Plagues of Egypt, can help them grasp the meaning of 'signs and wonders' that prefigure the impending culmination of the Crisis of the Modern West. The first chapter has already sketched the outlines of this final crisis of the West, termed the 'Harrowing of Hell', and the chapter following this one will further investigate its social and psychological aspects. But before studying these aspects in more detail, it should be said that it is important that not only the material and physical symptoms of the Crisis of the Modern West, but also its spiritual and psychological causes are understood correctly. Traditional systems of symbolism can offer old, but well-proven ways to interpret 'signs and wonders'. In the final analysis, however, it is up to Modern Western people to truly fathom the meaning of contemporary 'signs and wonders' — and to relate them to the Hamartiology of Modernity. Materialism, scientism and utilitarianism have corroded the mind of Modern Western men, impeding them from recognizing the various historical events of their own lifetimes for what they really are. But the incidents of Late and Postmodern history are not mere random accidents: they point to the 'metaphysical' indictment of Modern Western mankind and prefigure its 'eschatological' trial. With regard to the peoples of the West a correct assessment of contemporary 'signs and wonders', and a correct approach to the 'metaphysical' reality that they reflect, are absolute preconditions for their resurrection. The self-surpassing purification that lies at the heart of an authentically re-lived Christianity offers a viable alternative to the malicious self-annihilation of Postmodern Cultural Nihilism. Whereas Cultural Nihilism is characterized by a downward direction (a negative spiral of self-loathing and self-mutilation), Christianity is characterized by an upward direction (a positive spiral of self-examination and self-renewal). From a Christian perspective, acknowledgement of sins and remorse are even preconditions for spiritual growth and metaphysical hope. In this regard, the Christian thesis of the Resurrection is closely related to the Traditionalist thesis of Palingenesia: in the same way that Christianity teaches that sinful individuals and communities can be purified by confession and re-dedication, so Traditionalism teaches that forgotten forms of civilization and vocation can be recovered and relived by researching their sources and re-experiencing their origins. In this sense, the 'strait gate' of Christianity still offers the Western peoples an emergency exit from the impending 'hellstorm' of industrial ecocide, technological transhumanism, ethnic replacement and social implosion.

Biblical plagues	Physical aspects	Late and Postmodern 'signs'
1. blood	water plague	Amoco Cadiz Oil Spill (1978)
2. frogs	amphibian plague	Bird Flu (2015)
3. lice	earth plague	Southeast Asian Haze (1997)
4. infestation	aerial plague	Bee Colony Collapse Disorder (2006)
5. livestock disease	animal sickness	Mad Cow Disease (1992)
6. sores	human sickness	AIDS (1981)
7. hail	weather disaster	Hurricane Katrina (2005)
8. locusts	famine	Great Ethiopian Famine (1983)
9. darkness	occultation	Paris Solar Eclipse (1999)
death of first-born	human sacrifice	Eastern Christian Genocide (2014)

Chapter Six

The Living Dead

The Theme of Social Implosion in Alexander Wolfheze, The Sunset of Tradition and the Origin of the Great War (Newcastle upon Tyne: Cambridge Scholars Publishing, 2018)

> What was the monstrous evil that brought on God's judgment [in the Deluge]? The Bible does not specify beyond calling it chamas, lawlessness. But lawlessness (or violence as some render it) is the manifestation of a social disease and not its cause. [Bible interpreters] speculate that it was unbounded affluence that caused men to become depraved, that wealth afforded them the leisure to discover new thrills and to commit sexual aberrations. Hand in hand with material prosperity went an overbearing attitude toward God, whom people judged to be incapable of hearing prayers and of enforcing moral standards.
>
> — WILLIAM HALLO

Social Implosion

*Le fil est maintenant cassé. Il n'y a plus d'hommes sur ce continent aban-
donné des dieux: il n'y a qu'une minorité surhumaine... et... une immense
majorité de singes.*

*[The thread has now snapped. There no longer exist humans in this conti-
nent, forsaken by the gods: there is only a super-human minority... and...
an immense majority of apes.]*

— Savitri Devi Mukherdji

The 'Crisis of the Modern World' is a cen-
tral theme of the Traditional School, founded by René Guénon,
Ananda Coomaraswamy and Frithjof Schuon. During the
present Postmodern *époque*, this crisis — which can be more specifically
characterized as the Crisis of the Modern *West* — can be subdivided into
four concrete policy issues that can only be understood and resolved in
terms of mutual interdependence. Chapter 1 described them as the 'Four
Political Realities' of the Postmodern West: global climate change (industrial ecocide), technological trans-humanism (technocatastrophe), ethnic
replacement (demographic inundation) and social chaos (civil disintegra-
tion). The imminent convergence of these Four Political Realities points
to a catastrophic end scenario: a true *hellstorm* that has the power to permanently eliminate the remains of Western civilization. Within this complex scenario, the issue of social chaos takes centre stage: *social implosion*
is the core mechanism driving all of the existential threats that confront
the Modern West. In his recent book *The Sunset of Tradition and the Origin of the Great War*, the writer traced the cultural-historical dynamics of
the Crisis of the Modern World up to the outbreak of the First World War:
Sunset explains the mechanism of social implosion as an inevitable result
of the 'progress' of Modernity. The present chapter seeks to elucidate this
thesis, which is one of the ten theses of *Sunset*.

The accumulating loss of social-psychological cohesion and social-cultural continuity in the Postmodern West results in a collective state of self-induced psychopathy, characterized by institutionalized cognitive dissonance and sub-rational hedonist-materialist conditioning. The silent acceptance of 'politically correct' totalitarianism in the public sphere and of antisocial hyper-individualism in the private sphere are clear symptoms of this development. Only the 'normalization' of collective cognitive dissonance and individual sub-rational conditioning can explain how life-threatening developments such as global climate change, technological transhumanism and ethnic replacement can continue without meeting serious resistance. The fundamental lack of an elementary sense of responsibility — and even of an elementary survival instinct — is only possible in a society that lives in a cultural-historical void. The vacuum lifeworld of the baby boom generation — now permanently structured as a *hostile elite* that regenerates itself by feeding off vindictive 'minorities' — no longer leaves space for authentic identity or a historical sense of responsibility. The ideological counterpart to this cultural-historical vacuum is Cultural Nihilism, i.e. the baby boomer doctrine of militant secularism, social-Darwinist neo-liberalism, narcissist hyper-individualism and totalitarian culture relativism.

Armed with Cultural Nihilism, the baby boomers have eradicated the lifework of generations of ancestors and the civilizational heritage of centuries within one single generation. More than that, they have permanently mortgaged the future of their children by doing irreparable damage to the natural and cultural biotope of the Western peoples. The consistently ruthless manner in which the baby boomers and their *Social Justice Warrior* successors are pursuing this process to its extreme consequences — the utterly unscrupulous manner in which ecological disaster, transhumanist technology and ethnic replacement are poured out over Western humanity — bears the unmistakable stamp of quintessential *inhumanity*. But it is precisely the inhumanity of the *deeds* of the baby boomer hostile elite that provides the key to a correct understanding of its *ideas*. It allows the totalitarian Cultural Nihilist worldview to be understood as subhuman: it is sub-rational, sub-intellectual, psychologically regressive and emotionally atavistic in nature. Thus, it forms a system that is closed in all regards: politically, economically, socially and culturally. It is not primarily a *view* of the world, but rather an *experience* of the world: Cultural Nihilism is not primarily a rationally tangible and logically reversible *ideology*, but rather a pathological psychosocial *condition*.

From a Modern scientific perspective it is easy to explain this condition in terms of rational categories: at an individual level, it can be explained by the psychoanalytic method and at a collective level it can be explained by the psychohistorical method. But such scientific descriptions of the Cultural Nihilist condition offer no more than rational understanding: they fail to address the meta-historical *meaning* of the phenomenon. Rational explanations of Cultural Nihilism can reconstruct objective historical realities — Chapter 1 pointed to relevant bio-evolutionary feedback loops and psychohistorical adaptation mechanisms — but they cannot remedy its present consequences. The Cultural Nihilist 'key values' of militant secularism, shock doctrine neo-liberalism, hyper-democratic consumerism and totalitarian culture relativism have disastrous effects on the natural environment and human society that cannot be remedied through mere scientific analyses. Scientific treatises concerning the realities that are created by these 'key values' — industrial ecocide, economic cannibalism, ethnic replacement, social *anomie*, anti-intellectual 'idiocracy' — are futile as long as they are not framed by meta-historical meaning and metapolitical ethics. A full head is useless with an empty heart.

In this respect, Traditionalist thought can offer a remedy: it offers a meta-historical framework of meaning with an anagogic — holistically pedagogic — functionality. The book *Sunset* is relevant in this respect: it describes the historical background and genealogy of the Postmodern phenomenon of social implosion. The applicable thesis of *Sunset* retraces this phenomenon to a *regressive ontological modality*, i.e. to the reduced 'experiential capacity' of 'modernized' humanity. From a Traditionalist perspective, the cultural-historical background of Postmodern social implosion can be understood as a 'Regression of the Castes' (Julius Evola).

For the reader unfamiliar with the Traditionalist concepts on which *Sunset* is based, a short introduction to this term will be given here.

THE REGRESSION OF THE CASTES

The two main problems of the modern world, demographic expansion and genetic degeneracy, cannot be solved. Liberal principles prevent the solution of the first and egalitarian principles prevent the solution of the second.

— NICOLÁS GÓMEZ DÁVILA

Proceeding from the basic notion of *Sophia Perennis*, 'Perennial Wisdom' in relation to transcendental reality and capital letter Truth, there are various ways by which the concept of 'Tradition' may be approached. Most of these are *esoteric* in nature and therefore irrelevant within the framework of *Alba Rosa*. But there are also three, slightly overlapping *exoteric* definitions: (1) the *scientific* definition (a hermeneutic system that achieves meaning through symbolic structure), (2) the *ideological* definition (a socio-political system founded on charismatic authority, holistic community and anagogic direction) and (3) the *cultural anthropological* definition (a worldview that coincides with an optimal ontological modality).

(1) *Scientific* Tradition is now 'canonized' in the 'Traditional School' that was started, as mentioned earlier, by René Guénon, Ananda Coomaraswamy and Frithjof Schuon. It thus represents a minor but coherent scientific discipline that retains a marginal presence within religious studies, art history and cultural history. It involves a structuralist approach to functionality and symbolism, aimed at epistemological analyses of cosmological, religious, artistic and cultural-historical phenomena. Given its research focus on metaphysical issues and ethical philosophy, scientific Tradition may be considered the last remaining link between pre-modern and Modern knowledge.

(2) *Ideological* Tradition maintains a *concrete presence* in the contemporary world only in the geopolitical margin: the downfall of all Traditional

Imperia during the World Wars of the 20th century has virtually eliminated Tradition as a formally articulated political presence. All that remains are a few symbolic forms (the nominal Japanese Imperium, the sovereign Holy See) and a handful of historical miniature curiosities (Swaziland, Brunei). Formally, there still exists a single larger 'absolute monarchy': Saudi Arabia. But that state is a highly *artificial* creation, historically constructed around Anglo-Saxon oil interests and presently maintained by an American military protectorate. Considering the fact that even hybrid Modern-Traditional experiments such as the Third Reich are merely degenerate reflections of authentically Traditional Imperia such as the Assyrian Empire, such Traditional Imperia constitute socio-political constructs that must now be considered entirely incompatible — because unbearable — for 'Modern men'. On the other hand, ideological Tradition as an *abstract concept* has recently been making an unexpected comeback: the recent phenomenal rise of Archaeofuturism (Guillaume Faye, Jason Jorjani) is largely due to a revolutionary reincorporation of Traditionalist thought in Western metapolitical discourse.

(3) *Cultural anthropological* Tradition has also been reduced to a marginal phenomenon in the human lifeworld: it only continues to exist in the farthest (physical-geographic and psychological-sociological) recesses of the Modern world. On the one hand, authentic Tradition continues to be represented by a handful of 'primitive nature peoples' hidden in isolated locations (e.g. the tropical jungles of Amazonia, the mountain valleys of New Guinea, some of the Andaman Islands). On the other hand, it also continues to be represented by a handful of societal 'drop outs': marginalized thinkers, seers, artists, hermits and other *Aussteiger*. In terms of functionality and symbolism, these include — as hidden and unrecognizable 'antipodes' to Modernity — the 'guardians of the hidden flame' and the 'watchers of the world': the *Tsadikim Nistarim* of Judaism, the 'Latter Day Saints' of Christianity and the *Qalandars* of Islam. It is this *cultural anthropological marginalization* of Tradition that renders the Traditionalist thesis of the Regression of the Castes tangible, scientifically quantifiable, a reality in Modern anthropology and sociology. The book *Sunset* sketches the cultural-historical development of the Regression of the Castes in more detail. Here it suffices to say that early industrial Modern

mankind was already living according to a suboptimal ontological modality, viz. the qualitatively reduced, materialized, damaged and devalued world of repressed nature, metastasizing industry, monetary slavery and lost faith. Late industrial Modern mankind is now living in an ontological modality that is located much *farther below* even this early industrial level: it is living in a hallucinatory world of demonic possession in which the anagogic ideals of Tradition — goodness, wisdom, power and beauty — are systematically reversed into the direction of their perverse antipodes.

The marginal position of Tradition according to all three preceding definitions can be logically explained through the near-total historical defeat of Tradition by triumphant Modernity. *Sunset* specifies the point of no return: it dates the 'sunset' of Tradition in the year 1914 and thus confirms a newly emergent historiographical consensus. The outbreak of the conflict that contemporary observers simply called the 'Great War' is now increasingly taking centre stage in the historical conscience of present-day Western thinkers. Long before the outbreak of the First World War the Bible Students — the predecessors of the present-day Jehovah's Witnesses — had published a count-down system that assumed the year 1914 to be an important milestone in the Biblical plan of salvation. On August 3rd, 1914, on the eve of the British declaration of war against Germany, Foreign Secretary Sir Edward Grey — who was slowly losing his own eyesight — expressed his forebodings in these famous words: *The lamps are going out all over Europe; we shall not see them lit again in our lifetime.* It is only now, over a century later, that Western thinkers are starting to recognize the true significance of 'turning point 1914' (a recent Dutch publication relevant in this regard is Tom Zwitzer's book *Permafrost*).

The Experiential Reality of Modernity

What made it special, made it dangerous. So I bury it, and forget.

— Kate Bush

Modernity, defined as the phased inversion and ultimate negation of Tradition, has meanwhile advanced to the point that all forms of authentic
identity — religion, ethnicity, caste, gender, vocation — are now in an advanced stage of decay. This critical development, which is logically first
reaching its extreme stage in the Western heartland of Modernity, is now
affecting the material and institutional foundations (the bio-evolutionary
incarnations and socio-political structures) of Tradition to such an extent
that there is ever less space for its immaterial and cultural Traditional forms
of civilization (religion and art). In this regard, the present critical state of
all remaining forms of authentic identity is of decisive importance: in the
final analysis, the failure of Tradition is an *anthropological* phenomenon;
it re-defines *what it means to be human.* In the world of Tradition, humanity's experiential reality was of a fundamentally different nature than it is
in the Modern world. The fundamentally *different* capabilities of perception and cognition of Traditional mankind may be considered as functions of a fundamentally *different* experiential reality. The natural world
illustrates the principle of necessary adaption in perception and cognition
to varying experiential modalities: the echolocation of the bat and the
whiskers of the mole are examples of radically different, but functionally
effective systems of orientation adapted to wholly different living environments. It is in this sense that the radically different experiential modalities
of Traditional and Modern mankind can be most easily understood. On
the one hand, Modern mankind is endowed with highly developed capacities for rational calculation and emotional immunity: these capacities are
adjustments to the experiential realities of urban artificiality, scientistic
abstraction, materialist competition and hedonist escapism. Compared to

Traditional mankind, Modern mankind is a true *Übermensch* in terms of abstract and social individualism (monetary profit, sexual experiment). On the other hand, Traditional mankind was endowed with highly developed capacities for mystical insight and applied magic: these capacities are adjustments to the experiential realities of cosmic equilibrium, sublimated naturalism and holistic community. Compared to Modern man, Traditional man was a near-divine being in terms of spiritual perception and instinctive effectiveness. It is this archaic ontological quality that is referred to in ancient lore (e.g. the deuterocanonical 'Books of Adam'). Given the historical primacy of Traditional existential modes and given the increasing distance from the old 'paradisiacal' qualities of humanity, it is inevitable that the tension between the Traditional *nature* of humanity and its Modern *self-image* is building to a breaking point. The inevitable results are intellectual disorientation, cognitive dissonance and emotional instability. These symptoms are the psychohistorical price that must be paid for the *forced devolution* of the human condition, which is most dramatically illustrated by humanity's enforced separation from the Transcendental sphere (through radical secularism) and from the natural environment (through ecocidal urbanization).

Under the aegis of Postmodernism, this denaturalizing devolution is taking on increasingly perverse and totalizing forms. Even the human body itself is now subject to purposeful transformative manipulation ('bio-hacking'): the current epidemic of 'cosmetic surgery', the widespread 'behavioural medication' of children and the public promotion of invasive 'transgenderism' are reliable indicators of a collective loss of Traditional human identity and an accelerated tendency towards enforced physical and psychological 'transformation'. Confronted with the undisputed historical primacy of Traditional human nature — the Traditional identities of religion, ethnicity, caste, gender and vocation — Modern humanity has embarked upon a self-destructive *Flucht nach vorne*, characterized by ideological dogmatism and ethical nihilism. Within the heartland of Modernity, the so-called 'Western world', this direction is now dictated to the masses by a radically anti-Traditional hostile elite — a true 'anti-elite' that may be characterized as truly 'Luciferian' in the Traditional sense of the word.

The prime target of the Postmodern final offensive against all forms of authentic Traditional identity that is being waged by this 'anti-elite' is *ethnicity*, which is the strongest remaining form of collective identity and the historical vehicle of Traditional civilization. Economic 'globalization', political 'hyper-democracy', social 'emancipation' and cultural 'deconstruction' are the 'conventional weapons' of this 'reverse crusade' against Western civilization. Where necessary, these are now supplemented by 'weapons of mass destruction' such as demographic sui-genocide (subsidized 'single-parent households', 'abortion' facilities, liberalized 'euthanasia'), ethnic replacement ('labour migration', 'refugee settlement', 'family unification') and ethnic cleansing (*albanizacija* in Kosovo, *plaasmoorde* in South Africa, *white flight* in the United States). Outside the Western world, in the so-called 'Third World', the destruction of Traditional identities is hastened by a fatal combination of habitat destruction (deforestation, desertification, sea-level rise), industrialization (destruction of Traditional economies), urbanization (destruction of Traditional communities) and acculturation (destruction of Traditional cultures through invasive monocultures, as in Americanization, Islamization and Sinification). The resulting combination of habitat collapse, demographic explosion, ethnic strife and political radicalism in the Third World are encouraging mass migrations that are directed towards the Western world by the hostile elite in a desperate bid to hasten its global vision of an anti-identitarian 'melting pot'. This transforms the Western heartland into the global 'ground zero' of the Cultural Nihilist Maelstrom.

THE CULTURAL NIHILIST MAELSTROM

The earth is full of anger, the seas are dark with wrath;
the nations in their harness go up against our path...

— RUDYARD KIPLING

In the global melting pot, all forms of authentic Traditional identity are subjected to the ultimate test of Modernity. The present form and efficiency of this crucible are determined by the baby boomer ideology of Cultural Nihilism: under the aegis of Cultural Nihilism, the melting pot vision has reached its apotheosis in a moral-free 'American Dream 2.0'. This is a hallucinatory state of urban-hedonist stasis within a total ethical vacuum: Hollywood versions of this vision can be found in Ang Lee's *The Ice Storm* (1997) and Sam Mendes' *American Beauty* (1999). But the actual practice of this 'ideal form' remains the exclusive preserve of the Western baby boomers: as a plague of locusts they have devastated the outer as well as inner worlds of Modernity and in their trail nothing is left but a desert. For the globalized masses of rootless prospective consumers the practical implementation of the global melting pot project is an entirely different reality: their experiential reality is not that of the shaded suburb and the gilded shopping mall, the Brazilian *favela*, the South African *shanty town*, the American *inner city* ghetto and the French *HLM banlieue*, where the teeming billions of *damnés de la terre*, the masses of professional have-nots, are condemned to live under permanent conditions of 'bio-industrial' deprivation and moral degradation. This global reservoir of human misery is the ultimate driving force from which the global process of social implosion derives its impetus. Within the Western world this reservoir functions as a 'labour reserve' to decrease wages, a 'consumer mass' to increase profits and a 'democratic electorate' to vote for the Cultural Nihilist regime. Outside the Western world, it functions as a major psychological catalyst for global subversion through religiously and ethnically inspired violence. Globally escalating demographic pressure, failing ecosystems, denaturalized living conditions, competitive consumer fetishism and structural social-economic marginalization are building up a global 'anger capital', i.e. a sum total of despair, resentment and anger that is deposited in a 'world anger reservoir' (Peter Sloterdijk 2006). This 'global anger bank' constitutes a permanent mortgage on all Traditional forms of authentic identity and social structure. From this perspective, the ultimate foreclosure of Western civilization is inevitable and must result in the final dispossession and permanent debt slavery of the Western peoples. What is truly arising is nothing less than an anti-Western exercise in cosmic revenge: a final overflowing of this 'world anger reservoir' will finally sweep away Western civilization in an incoherent and all-consuming Last Wave of apocalyptic violence.

Until the collapse of the Soviet 'Evil Empire' in 1991 and the declaration of the American 'New World Order' in 1992, the 'world anger reservoir' was still largely contained within the Third World. The phenomena of social implosion and societal atavism were limited to the post-colonial world of Latin America, Africa and Asia and their exponentially breeding populations of impoverished *métèques*. During the subsequent Postmodern Age the Third World still remains the most important stakeholder in the 'global anger bank', obtaining ever higher returns on the Western 'investments' of 'intervention' (Somalia 1992, Iraq 2003), 'sexploitation' (UN Mozambique 1992, Oxfam Haïti 2018) and 'low cost outsourcing' (Nike 'sweatshops' 2005, H&M/Zara child labour 2009). The difference is that the Postmodern Age is characterized by a purposeful 'globalization' of the 'world anger reservoir', which is deliberately being imported into the West itself. After the fall of the Berlin Wall and the Soviet Union, the former Eastern Bloc countries were the first to be subjected to the neo-liberal 'shock doctrine' (Naomi Klein, 2007), with the entirely predictable results of de-industrialization, endemic poverty, brain drain and demographic implosion. With the introduction of the Euro and the start of the 'credit crisis', the Southern European countries were next in line. In the ex-Protestant economic heartland of the West — North-Western Europe and the overseas Anglosphere — the process is more gradual. To maintain political stability in the heartland of

Western consumer society, which is still a vital part of the world economy, the demolition of labour laws and social services proceeds at a slower pace: the process of *Verelendung* is replicated in 'slow motion'. It is reasonable to assume that the final abolition of the last borders of the 'world anger reservoir' will coincide with the biological end of the Western baby boom generation (somewhat arbitrarily defined as the cohorts of 1940–65).

But finally, it will be in the Western heartland that the strongest Cultural Nihilist 'therapy' will have to be prescribed to achieve the abolition of the last borders of the global melting pot. In the face of the highly educated and politically emancipated indigenous populations of the Western heartland, the hostile elite will have to resort to its ultimate weapon: *ethnic replacement*. To the extent that the indigenous peoples of the Western heartland are proving themselves unfit for the melting pot — demographically infertile under totalitarian dictatorship, economically unproductive in urban-hedonist stasis and politically unreliable in debt slavery — they are simply replaced by less intellectual, less demanding and less self-conscious slave peoples that are more easily manipulated. In this regard, the dominant Cultural Nihilist discourse of anti-identity is essential, because it allows for a refined exploitation of the historical traumas and demoralization of the Western peoples. The psychohistorical burden of two world wars, four decades of decolonization and total post-ideological disenchantment makes them ripe for sadomasochistic self-annihilation. The Cultural Nihilist programme of ethnic replacement is based on a subtle combination of demographic 'shrinkage' (deconstruction of the family through 'female emancipation', self-sterilization through 'contraception', child sacrifices through 'abortion', senicide through 'euthanasia'), genetic 'outcrossing' (exogamic role pattern with indigenous people as 'wife-givers' and immigrants as 'wife-takers') and evolutionary 'cropping' (genocidal role pattern with 'decadent' indigenous peoples and 'vital' migrants). The indigenous peoples of the West, starting with the progeny of the baby boomers, are sacrificed in a ritualistic 'holocaust': they are the necessary offering on the altar of the cult of Cultural Nihilism. Once they are in the grip of the Cultural Nihilistic Maelstrom they are doomed to disappear into the bottomless pit of the global melting pot, which is the final destination of all forms of authentic Traditional identity. Thus, in the early 21ˢᵗ century the Western peoples are facing an ultimate choice: either they submit to sadomasochistic self-destruction, or they will struggle free from the Cultural Nihilist anti-identitarian agenda in a self-surpassing act of supreme willpower.

THE ANTI-IDENTITARIAN AGENDA

And now, open your eyes and see... What we have made is real:
we are in Xanadu
— OLIVIA NEWTON-JOHN

The greatest inner power of Modernity resides in its powers of suggestion. The greatest fraud it has perpetrated on Modern mankind is arguably the historical materialist illusion of the infinite malleability of human nature: this illusion causes man to believe that identity is a 'choice'. This illusion, as seductive as it is absurd, is a central tenet of the Enlightenment, inducing Modern mankind to indulge in a self-defeating and self-destructive battle against all forms of authentic identity. In Cultural Nihilism, this tenet becomes doctrine and in the Postmodern melting pot, it becomes reality. This Cultural Nihilist doctrine is implemented by means of an *anti-identarian agenda*. The crucial mechanism by which this agenda is realized is the *mutual cancellation* of all forms of authentic identity, according to the old maxim *divide et impera*. Thus, authentic Christianity (supersession of fate, salvation through grace) is twisted, opposed and cancelled out against authentic Islam (acceptance of fate, salvation through submission). Thus, authentic Indo-European ethnicity (Bringer of *Evangelion*, Creator of *Nomos*, Master of *Techne*) is cancelled out against authentic Semitic ethnicity (Prophet of the Word, People of the Covenant, Servant of the Law). Thus, authentic femininity (private dedication, self-surpassing sacrifice) is cancelled out against authentic masculinity (public authority, self-surpassing responsibility).

This process of mutual cancellation is operational at all levels. At the lowest individual level, all authentic personal vocations are supplanted by competing 'lifestyle' options. Women are made to believe that matrimony and motherhood are somehow 'incomplete' vocations and that they are somehow compatible with relationship and labour-market experiments: this has reduced entire generations of women to eternally immature and eternally unhappy creatures. Men are made to believe that labour and family are merely random and temporary life choices and that public responsibility is an obsolete idea: this has reduced entire generations of men to money-grabbing weasels, striving to imitate the role model of *The Wolf of Wallstreet*. At the highest collective level, all authentic forms of religion, ethnicity and culture are buried in a globalist 'zero-sum' fantasy of 'international competition'. The inevitable geopolitical implication of the Cultural Nihilist anti-identitarian agenda, aimed at realizing the 'New World Order' (George Bush 1990) and the 'End of History' (Francis Fukuyama, 1992), is an apocalyptic 'Clash of Civilizations' (Samuel Huntington, 1997). The anti-identitarian agenda dictates that to the extent that the authentic forms of religion, ethnicity and culture do not disappear of their own accord during the great fire sale of the contemporary Postmodernity, they will be removed by force in the near future.

From this perspective, it is easy to understand why the globalist hostile elite is deliberately creating artificial conflicts: domestically against 'Islam' (the abstract representation of authentic religious life) and internationally against 'Russia' (the abstract representation of authentic national sovereignty). Such conflicts are created on purpose: these artificially created domestic and international 'enemies' function as lightning conductors on the Cultural Nihilist new Tower of Babel. These psy-op machinations, which effectively continue the successful psychological warfare strategies of the Cold War, represent intentional programmes by which the globalist hostile elite means to win the domestic and international Clash of Civilizations. It realizes its anti-identitarian agenda through a combination of ruthless suppression, perverse propaganda and refined psychological manipulation: Third World barbarity is systematically imported under the guise of 'human rights' ('asylum rights', 'refugee status'), fundamentalist terror is systematically sponsored under the guise of 'freedom fighters' (*Jabhat al-Nusra, Da'esh*) and authentic state authority is systematically undermined under the guise of 'colour revolutions' (Georgia 2003, Ukraine 2004). The increasing brinkmanship of the globalist hostile elite — which may lead to civil war in the Western heartland or nuclear war with Russia — indicates its increasing impatience. Knowing that its days are numbered, the old baby boomer elite is seduced by the Cultural Nihilist mirage of the global melting pot and is losing its grip on geopolitical reality. This means that the risk of fatal miscalculation and *va banque* hubris is rising exponentially: the demonically possessed leaders of the West have nothing to lose: their souls are dead already.

'Dead Souls'

> *Dämonen seyd ihr, keine Genien!*
> *Der Hölle, die Verzweiflung haucht, entstiegen.*
> *[You are devils — not genii!*
> *rising up from the hell, breathing despair]*
>
> — Johann Wolfgang von Goethe,
> *Des Epimenides Erwachen*

The global hostile elite represents a power complex that is ruled by a handful of literally *dehumanized* 'dead souls'. These are the 'Davos Men' — the top business tycoons, top politicians, top economists and top ideologues that regularly meet in institutionalized settings such as the World Economic Forum (Samuel Huntington). Occasionally, one of the *éminences grises* of this hostile elite is recognized by opponents of the globalization project, illustrating the 'dead soul' principle. They are a mere handful of new 'rulers of the earth', exploiting the triumph of Modernity — technically defined as the end of the *Nomos* and the occultation of the *Katechon* — to unleash their megalomania on innocent nature and naive mankind. In their case 'humanism' is not a mere ideological slogan but a literally *totaler Krieg* against God; and the *Novus Ordo Seculorum* is not a mere fantasy between lodge 'brethren', but a literal *Griff nach der Weltmacht*. Compared to these dead souls' chief vampires, the political 'cartel creatures' of Western 'democracy' (Thierry Baudet, 2017), the Social Justice Warriors of the 'Leftwing Subsidy Network' (Martin Bosma, 2010), the *Gekaufte Journalisten* of the Western 'free press' (Udo Ulfkotte, 2014) and the 'affirmative action' appointees of the Western academia (Jordan Peterson 2017) are merely insignificant and disposable extras. The anti-identitarian agenda, including its 'open borders', its 'open societies' and its 'open relations', is officially portrayed as a 'democratic' bottom-up project, but it is actually realized in an entirely top-down fashion.

The real strength of the anti-identitarian 'New World Project' resides in the intangible informality and judicial immunity of its largely anonymous leadership. The handful of new Godfathers and new Untouchables that is ultimately responsible for the monstrous network of 'global governance', 'high finance' and 'multinational business' always manages to stay out of public sight — and out of the reach of justice. The ontological 'quality' and the basic 'motivation' of these dead souls are determined by a (micro-cosmic) inner void, and by the (macro-cosmic) 'Outer Void' that is its inevitable downward extension. Their quality and motivation can only be understood as quint-essentially *subhuman* phenomena: only the ancient archetypes of Absolute Evil can shed light on them. It cannot be a coincidence that contemporary art forms are characterized by a massive resurfacing of the archetypes of 'demons' and 'vampires', often in the typically modern incarnations of 'aliens' and 'zombies'. *The Lord of the Rings* offers a poetic stereotype of such an archetype in 'Shelob': a monster living in underground hiding, ruthlessly fixed on the maximal sadistic *inversion* of all authentic Light — all strength, beauty, goodness, innocence — that still exists in a darkening world. Like the dead souls that lead the global hostile elite, Shelob 'lives' without any fixed allegiance and without any fixed affinities, patiently feeding off her eternal resentment and waiting for new victims. The only thing she truly fears is the Light: like the dead souls that lead the global hostile elite, she is only at ease hiding in the shadows of her webs of deceit. It is only in the dark that the global hostile elite prospers and they can only maintain their power by clouding the judgment and intellect of the Western peoples, hoping to catch them in their webs and to devour them in darkness.

> *Woe until them that call evil good and good evil;*
> *that put darkness for light and light for darkness;*
> *that put bitter for sweet and sweet for bitter!*
> — ISAIAH 5:20

THE POISONED CUP OF ANTI-IDENTITY

> *Hence to fight and conquer in all your battles is not supreme excellence;*
> *supreme excellence consists in breaking the enemy's resistance without fighting.*
> — SUN TZU

A Traditionalist analysis clarifies the Cultural Nihilist agenda of the globalist hostile elite. A central theme in Traditionalist thought is how all temporal power, beauty, goodness and innocence in the microcosm of the earthly sphere reflect eternal archetypes in the macrocosm of the heavenly sphere. For Traditional mankind, with its Traditional experiential capacities, these heavenly (transcendental) archetypes are therefore earthly (immanent) *realities*. For Modern mankind, they can only be rationally reconstructed as *archetypal identities*, i.e. 'model identities' of which the *earthly identities* of Traditional mankind were merely temporal and imperfect reflections. Modernity causes a fading and loss of these reflections: the downward — negative, inverse — movement of Modernity is gradually distancing mankind from all forms of authentic identity. From a Traditionalist perspective, it is the 'cosmic task' of the Cultural Nihilist hostile elite to maximize this distance, and to finally abolish all authentic forms of identity. The highest priority of its anti-identitarian agenda is the eradication of the most powerful remnants of authentic identity that still exist in the world: if these remaining identities can be 'tamed', then the other remnants will fall into line soon enough. Thus, the highest priority target of the anti-identitarian agenda is Western *ethnic identity*, as structured around a sublimely transcendental *Evangelion*, a superlatively interiorized *Nomos* and a masterly command of *Techne*. Given the insurmountable material power of Western civilization, the success of the anti-identitarian assault depends on immaterial factors. Western civilization has proven its remarkable material resilience: even after the unprecedented sacrifices of two world wars, the total loss of four centuries of imperialist expansion during four decades of 'decolonization' and the radical anti-Traditional tyrannies of Communism and Fascism, the West is still at the pinnacle of material development. Therefore, the only way in which Western civilization can be destroyed is through the psychological manipulation and intellectual disorientation of the Western peoples. In other words: the Western peoples have to be tricked into destroying *themselves* — this is the strategy behind the anti-identitarian agenda.

The globalist hostile elites have diagnosed the Western people as 'terminally ill' and they have prescribed a recipe in accordance with this diagnosis: the fatal cup of Cultural Nihilist poison. Thus, the globalist hostile elite means to end Western civilization by self-medicated euthanasia, after a short respite of palliative care for the baby boomers, to whom it owes its power. Here applies the maxim that the greatest lie is most readily believed. The first politico-philosophical draught that the Western peoples took from the poisoned cup of anti-identity included the greatest lie of human history since the Seduction of Eve, viz. the fundamental *denial* of Traditional identity embodied in the basic premise of 'The Communist Manifesto': *The history of all hitherto existing society is the history of class struggles.* This lie is so patently absurd that even the authors of the Manifesto felt obliged to backtrack somewhat by immediately adding the most dramatic footnote of all times: *That is, all written history.* But even after discarding the 99% of human presence on Earth that is *unwritten*, this lie remains breathtakingly audacious. Decades of politically correct academic historiography has yet to unearth a single trace of 'classes' — let alone 'class struggle' — in Ancient Mesopotamia, Ancient Egypt, Classical Greece or Medieval Europe. There have been forbidding hierarchies, hermetically closed castes, privileged estates and marginalized slave populations, but in the world of Tradition, all social groups were always holistically positioned in self-regulating communities and integrated within coherent ethnic structures. 'Classes' did not exist until they were programmatically 'invented' by the resentful nihilist ideologues of Historical Materialism: in Western public discourse, 'classes' did not exist before the so-called 'Enlightenment' and 'class struggles' did not exist before 'The Communist Manifesto'. That is something entirely different than the 'history of all hitherto existing society'.

Nevertheless, the grotesquely absurd lie of the history of 'class struggle' still remains effective in the Postmodern West: the Cultural Nihilist hostile is inventing ever new 'classes' on whose behalf it 'struggles'. After the *social-economic* 'class struggle' between 'labour' and 'bourgeoisie' was shipwrecked on the cold rocks of capitalist reality at the end of the Cold War, 'Cultural Marxism' shifted its agenda to the *cultural-identitarian* 'class struggle' (Paul Cliteur, 2018). The collective defeat of the European peoples in two world wars, multiple decolonization wars and the Cold War — and the historical settling of accounts with Imperialism, Communism and Fascism — created an appropriate mental climate for the new anti-identitarian agenda. Deep historical trauma, a twisted self-image and extreme cultural discontinuity resulted in a nihilistic 'slave discourse' of hedonistic escapism, sublimated self-hatred and pathological sadomasochism: an ideal climate for an anti-identitarian 'class struggle' aimed at the *mutual cancellation* of 'repressive' Traditional identities. New 'classes' with repressive 'privileges' and 'reactionary' worldviews were quickly identified in the last outer symbols of power and identity: ethnicity, gender and vocation. The top priorities listed on the Cultural Marxist agenda are obviously the white race and the male gender — especially in their fatal combination of the 'white male', on whom the Cultural Marxists consistently *project* their anger complexes. This is the new spectre of the cultural-identitarian 'class struggle' that is now haunting the Western world: it is the spectre of *anti-identitarian resentment*.

This new spectre is much more effective than the old spectre of 'The Communist Manifesto': it works on a subtly sub-rational level and it exploits *immaterial* (psychohistorical) instead of *material* (social-economic) realities. The anti-identitarian spectre literally *possesses* Postmodern mankind and changes it *from the inside out*: it accurately reflects the outer Postmodern existential reality of *Entfremdung, anomie* and disenchantment in an inner experiential modality of soulless possession. The poisoned cup of anti-identity works in stages: the pleasurable sensation of hedonist exhilaration extends across the entire baby boom generation and only changes into spasmodic convulsions in their children; only their grandchildren will have to swallow the last bitter draught. Through hyper-individualism and hyper-democracy, the poison of anti-identity is gradually spreading through the whole of Western society and civilization. Individuals can arm themselves and bravely resist the resulting wave of collective hallucination, regression and atavism, but in the long term, every form of mere individual resistance is doomed. There is no individual psychoanalytic cure that can match the collective psychohistorical condition of anti-identity: even the elegant 'antidotes' of Jordan Peterson (*12 Rules for Life: An Antidote to Chaos*, 2018) are doomed to fail. From a psychohistorical perspective, such 'antidotes' can be no more than individual 'palliatives': they can lessen the social-psychological suffering of an individual, but they cannot combat the structural causes of that suffering.

Only a collective *volte-face* can still prevent *der Untergang des Abendlandes*. In the hour of their need, the Western peoples can still resort to the oldest and strongest weapon in the cultural-historical arsenal of the West: Traditionalist thought. The Western peoples will have to dislodge the Traditionalist Sword of Knowledge from the silent stone of history before they can hack a way through the deceptive webs of Cultural Nihilist anti-identity. At an intellectual level, this requires in-depth epistemological archaeology to uncover the psychohistorical roots of the 'anti-identitarian movement'. This epistemological-archaeological project will require nothing less than a macro-historical diagnosis of the archetypal powers that direct Modernity itself. Here Traditionalist thought can offer solutions, but only if the Western mind is still strong enough to accept its last consequences and to reject some very comfortable Modernist illusions — the illusion of 'equality' above all. The first illusion of 'equality' that needs to be relegated to the museum of historical curiosities is at the same time the most comfortable of all: the 'equality' between man and woman.

KALI YUGA

A basic characteristic of the last [of the four Hindu Ages of the World], the so-called Dark Age, [or the] Kali Yuga, is that during this era Kâli is fully awake... [A]nd thus that entire era is under her power... in her basic role as goddess of destruction, lust and sexuality.

— JULIUS EVOLA

A central tenet of Traditionalist thought is the cyclical concept of world history. Traditionalist consensus teaches that the Modern Age represents the last era of the present time cycle (*Sunset* places its commencement somewhat arbitrarily in the year 1488). In cosmological terms, the Modern Age is the 'Dark Age', i.e. the age during which the world is farthest removed from the Divine Light. Different Traditions have different expressions to deal with this concept: in Norse mythology, it is the *Ragnarök* (the Wagnerian *Götterdämmerung*); in Christian eschatology, it is the 'Endtime'; and in Spenglerian historiography, it is the 'Winter Time'. In the oldest historically preserved Indo-European Tradition, the Vedic Tradition, this era is termed the *Kali Yuga*, i.e. the reign of the demon Kali, the 'Torturer', incestuously born from the demons Anger and Violence, in their turn born from the demons Impropriety and Falsehood. In Traditional symbolic systems, the Dark Age is consistently characterized by the blind creative force of the *female archetype*: it is characterized as the gradual eclipse of the 'heavenly', ordering and legislating male principle by the 'earthly', irrepressibly fertile female principle. In the world of Tradition the universal binary opposition male-female is consistently projected on cosmology: from an anthropologically structuralist perspective, the fundamental symbolic-mythological opposition between Tradition/Male and Modernity/Female is a fixed feature of all Traditional cultures.

From a Traditionalist perspective, the final total eclipse of the heavenly male principle, symbolically associated with authority as representative of law and order, is an inevitable feature of the Dark Age. Its logical counterpart is the final supremacy of the earthly female principle, symbolically associated with irrepressible fecundity and unrestrained promiscuity. Under the aegis of Dark Age Matriarchy, the collapse of Traditional male authority will inevitably end with the removal of all restraints on materialism and hedonism, resulting in apocalyptic atavistic regression. Conforming to this principle the contemporary world is simultaneously witnessing an unprecedented combination of collective Narcissism, demographic catastrophe and unrestrained Ecocide. Matriarchy, which represents the hypertrophy of the female gift of protecting all life with unreasoning devotion, will inevitably destroy all higher forms of life — everything that is strong, intelligent and beautiful — by fostering all lower forms of life — everything that is weak, stupid and ugly.

— *Sunset*

There is a number of ancient literary texts that specify this terrifying prospect. The Mesopotamian Tradition preserves the threat spoken by the great goddess Ishtar, who is less the goddess of 'love' and 'procreation' than the goddess of elementary sex and war. In case she is hindered in fulfilling her ritual obligations, she pronounces the following warning: (Babylonian) *Shumma la tapatta babu, la erruba anaku, amahhats daltum, sikkuru ashabbir, amahhats sippuma, ushabalakat dalati, ushella mituti, ikallu baltuti, eli baltuti ima'idu mituti.* 'If you do not open the gate [and] I cannot enter, [then] I will force in the door, break the bolts, tear down the doorposts, throw down the doors, raise the dead [and] they will eat the living — the dead will outnumber the living!' (*Inanna's Descent into the Underworld* — K[uyuncuk-Nineveh] 162 Obv. 16-20). Here the 'doorposts' refer to the border between the world of men and the underworld: in the world of Tradition, this border was ritually and institutionally guarded by the *Katechon* provisions of Royalty, Nobility, Temple and Scholarship. The existential threat that emanates from the creative primordial chaos that underpins the archetypal female principle — permanently lurking as 'primordial nature' under and beyond the 'doorposts' of high culture — marks the entire ancient world of Tradition.

A reflection of this profound insight may also be found in a well-known Ancient Near Eastern trope that has been incorporated in the Old Testament: (Hebrew) *Mi-zot, hannishqafah kmo shachar, yafah chalwanah, barah kachamah, ajummah kanniedgalot?* 'Who is she that looketh forth as the morning, fair as the moon, clear as the sun, and terrible as an army with banners?' (Solomon's Song 6:10). In this context, 'she' refers to the archetypal female principle, both abstractly and concretely. Abstractly, it can refer to the terrifying 'Great Goddess', as it does in Robert Graves' *The White Goddess* (1948). Concretely, it can also refer to a dangerously seductive peasant girl, as it does in Umberto Eco's *Il nome della rosa* (1980). At both levels, it unites the female blessing of stainless purity (the virgin theme of the *hortus conclusus*) and the female curse of the black death of the soul (the theme of Durga and Kāli as a destructive force of nature). This elementary duality is still explicitly expressed in contemporary cults such as the Roma cult of *Sara-la-Kali*, 'Black Sarah', in Saintes-Maries-de-la-Mer. It is this negative (blind earthly and sub-rational downward) potential within the female principle which increasingly dominates Modernity as the balancing and the mitigating forces of the male principle fail. In this sense, Modernity can be understood as a combination of the deflation of the male principle to a state of ultimate degeneracy and the inflation of the female principle to a state of ultimate perversity. The extreme consequence of this double development is the perverse reign of the Great Whore: in the Bible, this reign is identified in the context of the Seven Plagues of the Endtime.

> And there came one of the seven angels which had the seven vials, and talked with me, saying unto me, Come hither; I will shew thee the judgment of the great whore that sitteth upon many waters: With whom the kings of the earth have committed fornication, and the inhabitants of the earth have been made drunk with the wine of her fornication. So he carried me away in the spirit into the wilderness: and I saw a woman sit upon a scarlet coloured beast, full of names of blasphemy, having seven heads and ten horns. And the woman was arrayed in purple and scarlet colour, and decked with gold and precious stones and pearls, having a golden cup in her hand full of abomination and filthiness of her fornication: And upon her forehead was a name written, MYSTERY, BABYLON THE GREAT, THE MOTHER OF HARLOTS AND

ABOMINATIONS OF THE EARTH. And I saw the woman drunken with
the blood of the saints, and with the blood of the martyrs of Jesus: and when
I saw her, I wondered with great admiration.

— REVELATION 17:1–6.

In xiv and lxxxviii good hope is (g)rounded,
The Torturer's Time (con)founded,
In The Sunset it is expounded.

Hortus Conclusus

Arcite and Pacamon admire Emilia (unknown master, ca. 1470), illustration from the
oldest French translation of Boccaccio's La teseida delle nozze d'Emilia, MS 2617 Folio
53, Vienna National Library. Hortus conclusus, 'enclosed garden', is one of the titles of
the Virgin Mary (Solomon's Song 4:12, 'A garden enclosed is my sister, my spouse; a
spring shut up, a fountain sealed.'): it is the archetypal representations of the sublime
female principle in the Western Tradition. It is often depicted in conjunction with a
plantatio rosae, in reference to the rose as another attribute of the Virgin (Solomon's
Song 2:1, 'I am the rose of Sharon, and the lily of the valleys.'). In terms of cultural
anthropological analysis, it is important to note that the decline of the Christian devotion
to the Virgin Mary throughout the West is structurally juxtaposed with the rise of an
inverted — entirely degraded — vision of the female principle.

MATRIARCHY

When the patriarchy that was founded by the warriors is finally eliminated, the individualist and martial society of the last millennia returns to its prenatal state of collectivist atavism.

— NICOLÁS GÓMEZ DÁVILA

The Biblical vision of the Great Whore is psychohistorically realized in the *Matriarchy* of the Modern West. This Matriarchy is not the literal exclusive exercise of power by hyper-emancipated women — although this fashionable aspect is increasingly visible — but rather the effective *feminization* of Western civilization. Who exactly exercises power is of secondary importance: 'neutered' males, preferably explicitly identifiable as gays, transgenders and docile affirmative action creatures, can direct a Matriarchy as effectively as 'denatured' women. The only thing that counts is the final destination of the journey towards total feminization: anti-identity.

Sunset dates the matriarchal *Machtübernahme* to the aftermath of the First World War: the male population of the West has been decimated by four years of trench warfare and the female population of the West is forced to take over male societal functions. The remaining males of the West are — mostly subconsciously — suffering from collectively humiliating *survivor guilt* and find themselves bereft of the Traditional structures that used to explicitly represent the male principle of *auctoritas*. The Monarchy, the Nobility and the Church have lost their remaining world power after the total victory of Modernity and the total defeat of Tradition, as illustrated by the fall of the supranational Imperia of the Hohenzollerns, the Hapsburgs, the Ottomans and the Romanovs. Instead, the Western peoples are taking their final steps towards Matriarchy. The female electoral franchise combined with female economic emancipation results in totalitarian 'social security': the government takes on the function of *abstract* 'super husband and father' and forces the remaining *concrete* husbands and fathers into tributary payments in the form of 'taxes' and 'alimonies'.

Thus, the collectivist totalitarian super-state of 20th century Matriarchy is born. 'Social security' combined with 'judicial equality' inevitably results in the breakdown of the traditional family as a societal norm: once they are economically and judicially covered, 'emancipated' women can indulge in relationship and labour experiments with impunity. In the course of a few decennia all traditional values and rules are dissolved in the historical acid of the *Realmatriarchat*, characterized by totalitarian doctrines such as 'emotional experience' (sub-rational communication), 'equal opportunities' (potency reduction) and 'self-development' (narcissist role-playing): this is the start of *The Century of the Self* (Tony Curtis, 2002). It is important to note that, from a Traditionalist perspective, there can be no question of assigning 'blame': from a Traditionalist perspective, Matriarchy is simply the logical societal projection of a cosmic process of feminization that is characterized by the dislocation and hypertrophy of the archetypal feminine principle and that finally ends in anti-identity.

This process accelerates after the Second World War and reaches full speed in the baby boomer *counterculture* of the '60s: it intensifies in a vicious cycle of mutually reinforcing social 'deconstructions': political hyper-democracy, social collectivism, hedonist materialism and culture relativism. From a meta-historical perspective, the semi-reactionary counter movements of the 20th century (Fascism, Corporatism, National Socialism) are nothing more than hopelessly doomed rearguard actions. The inevitable defeat of these movements merely served to strengthen and accelerate the historical development of the Modern Western Matriarchy. The end of the Second World War marks the final psychohistorical 'castration' of Western manhood: biological reproduction and cultural transmission soon start to falter. The ebbing of the last demographic boom — the *baby boomers* are the children of the last authentically 'Western' generation, the *great generation* — is followed by demographic sui-genocide. During the Postmodern Era (*Sunset* places its commencement in the year 1992) the Modern Western Matriarchy achieves a position of social-political and cultural-historical monopoly. But total Matriarchy is doomed to be short-lived: the imminent failure of biological reproduction and cultural

transmission in the Western heartland are creating a fatal psychohistorical void: the stage of individual psychological implosion and collective
malignant narcissism is at hand (Christopher Lasch, 1979). Inevitably,
every Matriarchy eventually abolishes itself by the absence of (viable)
offspring. To the extent that indigenous Western biological procreation
continues — a few non-matriarchal sects such as the Mormons and Amish
aside — the remaining offspring is collectively and fatally marked by the
social and psychological havoc of 'single parent families' and 'liberal educational practices'. Many of these *schrecklichen Kinder der Neuzeit* (Peter
Sloterdijk, 2014) are illegitimate children, stepchildren, foster children,
adopted children etc. In their case, matriarchal jurisprudence of the baby
boomers always prevails: baby boomer 'privacy' prevails over the right
to know who one's parents are, baby boomer 'self-determination' prevails
over the right not to be maltreated, abused and neglected and baby boomer 'property rights' prevail over the right to a just inheritance. Thus, the
'impulsive' wish of 'liberated' women to become pregnant, where necessary facilitated by anonymous 'donors', always prevails over the existential
need of every child: to have a (biological, real) father. Thus, the 'second
youth' of 'speed divorcing' baby boomers, where necessary facilitated by
'mail order brides', always prevails over the inheritance rights of the 'step-
child'. Thus, the numerically inferior post-baby boomer generations are
legally, economically and psychologically doomed to societal marginalization. This marginalization — a de facto state of enforced *Verelendung*
and *anomie* — is continuously affirmed and reinforced by the aggressive
Cultural Nihilist agenda of neo-liberalism (demolition of social security),
globalism (demolition of economic opportunity) and *Umvolkung* (demolition of ethnic cohesion).

Matriarchy degrades Western civilization to the status of the Great
Whore of the world: the matriarchal 'open society' is a calculated invitation of boundless exploitation by unscrupulous bankers, political mercenaries, opportunistic criminals, ruthless colonists and resentful barbarians. Matriarchy cannot and *does not want* to defend itself: it represents
unconditional *surrender* and blind *submission*. From a psychohistorical

perspective, Matriarchy is a sadomasochistic mechanism that condemns the Western peoples to a perverse sacrificial death. Matriarchy is more than a mere emotional incapacity for self-defence: it is the blind impulse to *self-annihilation*. The matriarchal ideology of Cultural Nihilism is nothing but a self-administered anaesthetic to allow this impulse to persist as long as possible. Meanwhile, the instruments of physical self-annihilation are put in place: the torture instruments of neo-liberal economic exploitation, globalist political repression and ethnic replacement are ready to grind the remnant post-baby boomer population of the West into the dust of history.

Undoubtedly, ethnic replacement is the most stereotypically cruel instrument within the matriarchal torture machinery: it explicitly expresses the new 'disposable' status of the Western peoples and it simultaneously represents the ultimate sadomasochistic 'punishment' of Matriarchy. The culturally most highly advanced, the intellectually most refined and the physically most vulnerable peoples of the world are confronted, in their own homelands, with an invasion of the culturally least receptive, mentally least responsible and physically most hardened peoples of the world. The innocent children of the West, the exquisitely sensitive and vulnerable heirs to the most refined civilization of human history, are forced to fight a perversely unequal social-Darwinist struggle for survival against ruthless barbarians from the darkest corners of the Third World. The hostile elite of the Western Matriarchy has opened the gates of the sheep-fold so that the sheep can engage in 'dialogue' with the wolves for the sake of 'diversity'.

Matriarchy is symbolized by an unspoken perversion which is realized in ever increasing numbers of 'broken families': self-hating 'single moms' are indulging in a sick impulse to open the doors of their children's room to her 'guests'. The cult of Matriarchy always depends on child sacrifice — in the Bible the punishment for this cult of ultimate sin is nothing less than the eternal damnation of the People of the Covenant:

> *And they have built the high places of Tophet, which is in the valley of the son of*
> *Hinnom, to burn their sons and their daughters in the fire; which I commanded*
> *them not, neither came it into my heart. Therefore, behold, the days come, saith*

the Lord, that it shall no more be called Tophet, nor the valley of the son of Hinnom, but the valley of slaughter: for they shall bury in Tophet, till there be no place. And the carcases of this people shall be meat for the fowls of the heaven, and for the beasts of the earth; and none shall fray them away. Then will I cause to cease from the cities of Judah, and from the streets of Jerusalem, the voice of mirth, and the voice of gladness, the voice of the bridegroom, and the voice of the bride: for the land shall be desolate.

— JEREMIAH 7:31–34

Ethnic replacement by means of mass immigration is a typical 'feel good' project of the matriarchal baby boomer *Gutmensch*: it reflects the typical matriarchal combination of run-away 'maternal instinct' (ruthless colonists as pitiful 'refugees') and sadomasochistic instinctual complexes (gynophobic polygamists as masculine heroes). It expresses the essentially *oikophobic* emotionality of Matriarchy: the essentially anti-identitarian orientation of Matriarchy finds its explicit expression in deliberate deterritorialization ('open borders') and xenophilia ('multiculturalism'). But it will not be the baby boomers that have to empty the poisoned cup of ethnic replacement to its final bitter dregs: this fate is reserved for the post-baby boomers. It is the privilege of disinherited grandchildren of the baby boomers to be fully submerged in the poisoned pool of 'cultural diversity', including its intimate experiences of *rapefugees, loverboys, grooming gangs, Sylvester-Übergriffe* and *tournantes*. The terrifying combination of matriarchal social implosion and ethnic replacement, still largely hidden behind the (self-)censorship of the media cartel, are so unspeakably disgusting that they are effectively indescribable. At most, a few hallucinatory details occasionally emerge whenever social implosion claims some non-Western victims (Samira Bellil 2002, Ilan Halimi 2006, Mireille Knoll 2018). But the collective price paid by the Western post-baby boomers is becoming increasingly visible in official statistics and the public sphere. Their 'White Death' has many faces: disturbing suicide rates, epidemic drug addiction, escalating psychopathology, massive youth unemployment, collective impoverishment and permanent social degradation.

To prolong the pink intoxication of Matriarchy for as long as possible, the reality of matriarchal social implosion remains a public and political taboo. (Self-)censorship, partially subconscious, is an intricate part of the totalitarian 'political correctness' that *must* characterize every Matriarchy. The dogma of social-cultural 'progress' — and its derivate, feminisation — is the last public idol of Modernity. Institutional cognitive dissonance is an absolute psychohistorical precondition for a prosperous Matriarchy. In the same way that Matriarchy is privately characterized by sub-rational (perverse, sadomasochistic) sexuality and nihilistic (anti-intellectual, morally-deconstructive) education, so it is publicly characterized by political indifference and judicial inefficiency. During the 'ethical holiday' of Postmodern Matriarchy, the male principles of *Nomos* and *Katechon* are eliminated from the public sphere. The elimination of Traditional male values such as honesty, courage and fairness means that the gatekeepers of civilization are banished. Thus, the dangers of feminization remain taboo until they are realized in their last consequences. The taboo on Matriarchy will only end when the power of the Matriarchy ends. Until that time, Western civilization is doomed to a true 'harrowing of hell'.

THE ZOMBIE APOCALYPSE

Surely we have perished sleeping, and walk hell; but who these hellish?
— WILFRED OWEN

The final scenes of Western civilization under the aegis of Matriarchy can be easily deducted from the eschatological visions of the world of Tradition. The ancient prophecy of *Inanna's Descent into the Underworld* uses terminology that is enigmatically reminiscent of the 'modern art' theme of the 'Zombie Apocalypse'. Even after it has lost its Transcendental experiential capacity, modern mankind is still haunted by strange nightmares and visions: presentiments and premonitions are plaguing modern artists and visionaries. The dark midnight of the modern world is occasionally lit up by lightning flashes of hierophany and cryptomnesia, showing the warning signs of the horrors that are awaiting mankind. Contemporary books, music, movies and games are increasingly occupied with enigmatic references to an impending catastrophe of ultimate horror: the take-over of the human world by the 'living dead'. As the immense downward power of Matriarchy is pressing Western humanity ever farther into radical secular nihilism and extreme malignant narcissism, it is inevitable that it is falling back on an archetypal subhuman substrate. It is in this prehistoric 'hell' that it finds demonic archetypes to animate its new *anti-identities*. The alternative to authentic Traditional identity is *not* the hyper-democratic and hyper-individualist *dolce far niente* promised by the false prophets of Modernity, but rather a return to what lies hidden *under* authentic Traditional identity. There is the hell of subhuman *anti-identity*: the identity of the 'hardened sinner', the 'lost soul', the 'erring spirit', the 'hungry ghost' and the 'undead vampire'.

The hedonist-materialist nirvana of Modernity, lived by the baby boomers, is a transient fever dream which will shortly end in a horrendous Postmodern nightmare. The baby boom motto of *après nous le déluge* does not take account of the force that truly directs the impending 'hellstorm'. That force is the bodiless spirit of evil that is the counterpart of the Holy Spirit, Biblically personified as the 'Prince of the Power of the Air' (Ephesians 2:1–2). The emptying of all authentic forms of human identity — and the resultant vacuum in the human soul — at long last offers this evil spirit an opportunity to take shape in humanity itself. It is this force that will ultimately take possession of the 'dead soul' of Western man:

> It is the end of the world, hardly the end we imagined. Not so long ago, it was feared fire would rain from the sky, the earth would tremble and crack and the sea would swell over the land. But it is the unseen, the bodiless that holds humankind's end, the end of all things: it ends with the wind. It came quietly, a breath, a breeze, a storm, a lie, a betrayal, a murder. Then it grew relentless and with its never-ending flow came its fever of friend against friend, brother against brother, child against parent and, finally, man against himself. Since then, time, death and chance have hurried by, drifting towards complete decay.

> — *The Wind* (Michael Mongillo, 2001)

The cultural-historical prelude to the Zombie Apocalypse is slow-paced: the first subtle hints at the rise of the 'living dead' date back to the late-19th century artistic genres of the *revenant* and the vampire, fully developed in literature by Joseph Sheridan Le Fanu (*Carmilla* 1872) and Guy de Maupassant (*Le Horla* 1887) and in painting by John Collier (*Lilith* 1892) and Edvard Munch (*Vampire* 1895). The scientific discovery of the phenomenon of the 'living dead' follows in the psychoanalytic description of narcissism by Sigmund Freud (*Einführung des Narzissmus* 1914). But it is only in the late-20th century cultural-historical analyses of Tom Wolfe (*The 'Me' Decade* 1976) and Christopher Lasch (*The Culture of Narcissism* 1979) that a direct psychohistorical link is first made between the old archetype of the classical vampire and the new stereotype of the modern narcissist. During the late 70s cultural historians began to describe the first stages of a 'narcissism epidemic' in the Western heartland. In these same years, the Zombie Apocalypse became a standard element of the Western cinematic repertoire: George Romero's *Dawn of the Dead* (1978) defines the new genre.

The subconscious fears that are projected on the 'Zombie Apocalypse' are fed by the dissolution of all forms of social cohesion caused by the 'narcissism epidemic' that struck Western society during the rise of the baby boomer generation. During the last part of the reign of the baby boomers, this epidemic of atomised extreme hyper-individualism is further strengthened by digital technologies: the effective replacement of personal communication by 'social media' and of social activities by 'virtual reality' amplifies the narcissistic tendency of self-objectification and de-personification. The technological abstraction of social interaction (*Facebook* instead of face time) and the technological manipulation of social identity ('profile' instead of personality) also strengthen the societal tendency towards feminization: external presentation and social consensus are strengthened at the expense of substantive content and abstract ethics. The masculine public sphere is increasingly replaced by the feminine private sphere: the obsessive fixation on 'image' in the 'social media' and on 'smartphone' ego-communication is literally changing the cityscape, the workplace and the political arena. Masses of self-absorbed 'sleep walkers', staring down with glassy eyes, can be seen shuffling around in amorphous crowds in all Western cities. Thus, the first phase of the Zombie Apocalypse is an invasion of the masculine public sphere by the feminine private sphere and a replacement of public affairs by private priorities: egoism and narcissism become the new standards of behaviour and interaction. In this regard, the rise of neo-liberal nihilism in the Reagan/Thatcher years constitutes a watershed moment. The second phase of the Zombie Apocalypse is the loss of rudimentary public norms of behaviour and presentation: the abolition of the public sphere results in the abolition of all sense of shame. The narcissist motto 'be yourself' is increasingly dominating dress, speech and attitude. The massive presence of unwashed 'zombies', dressed in rags and making random growling noises, can be observed in any major Western city. The third phase of the Zombie Apocalypse is unprovoked aggression (random violence, 'school shootings'): the unrestrained dominance of egoism and narcissism in the former public sphere emboldens extremist elements and triggers a chain reaction of verbal and physical violence.

In the final analysis, the dynamics of the Zombie Apocalypse are determined by real existential fears: the cinematographic scenarios in which family members, neighbours and colleagues suddenly attack each other without provocation and without warning reveal much about the society that dreams them up. In these scenarios, the zombies, self-obsessed monsters with which sensible communication is no longer possible, live off the flesh and blood of ever fewer numbers of survivors — like narcissists, they feed off the energy and vitality of their victims. The few healthy individuals that remain 'uninfected' are forced to survive in a deadly landscape lacking any form of law, order and protection (cf. *The Walking Dead*, Frank Darabont 2010), in the same manner that the remaining non-narcissists are marginalized when their world is overtaken by the 'narcissism epidemic'. These non-narcissists know that the real 'zombies' are more than slowly moving dumb brutes: narcissists are sophisticated, smooth and highly adapted to the Modern world; they feel good and do well in the

Modern world. The non-narcissists are at a distinct disadvantage: they are 'handicapped' by obsolete characteristics such as a sense of responsibility, work ethics and professional talent and they are increasingly pushed into the margins of society. The (in)famous 'Frankfurt School' social psychologist Erich Fromm already explicitly recognized the possibility of a systematic 'reversal' of the societal standard of sanity:

> *The sick individual finds himself at home with all other similarly sick individuals. The whole culture is geared to this kind of pathology. The result is that the average individual does not experience the separateness and isolation the fully schizophrenic person feels. He feels at ease among those who suffer from the same deformation; in fact, it is the fully sane person who feels isolated in the insane society — and he may suffer so much from the incapacity to communicate that it is he who may become psychotic (The Anatomy of Human Destructiveness, 1973).*

In other words: *It is no measure of health to be well adjusted to a profoundly sick society* (Jiddu Krishnamurti).

Inevitably, during the narcissism epidemic masculine behaviour will be 'diagnosed' as *Attention Deficit Hyperactivity Disorder*, scientific talent as *Asperger Syndrome*, artistic talent as *Bipolar Disorder* and spiritual inspiration as *Paranoid Schizophrenia*. Thus, the most talented members of Western society become the first victims of the narcissist Zombie Apocalypse: the first to disappear in the 'great levelling' of collective narcissism are the brave soldier, the top scientist, the genius artist and the spiritual guide. Their disappearance hastens the downward spiral of the Regression of the Castes — and the advance of the Zombie Apocalypse. What remains is a 'fake elite' of narcissist frauds (Martin Bosma, 2011) that paves the way for even more extreme forms of narcissism, facilitated by ever lower standards of societal values and ever more dramatic forms of social atavism.

The all-consuming 'World War Z', the ultimate *bellum omnium contra omnes* which is contained in the 'narcissism epidemic', has already started: the artistic Zombie Apocalypse merely projects this new reality in more extreme forms onto the near future. Often these artistic projections are marked by a sinister undertone of irresistibly returning eschatological mythology: thus, the remake of *Dawn of the Dead* (2004) is introduced by Johnny Cash' artistic Bible exegesis *The Man Comes Around*. In this manner, the 'successors' of Western humanity are making their first appearance on the 'event horizon' of Western history. The 'living dead' can be sensed beyond the newly opened gates of hell:

> *Every species can smell its own extinction. The last ones left won't have a pretty time of it. And in ten years, maybe less, the human race will be just a bedtime story for their children — a myth, nothing more. — In the Mouth of Madness.*
> (John Carpenter, 1994)

Perhaps some old-fashioned Westerners still have to get used to the idea that Hollywood's New World 'Zombie Apocalypse' has anything to teach them: for them this chapter concludes with 'Raskolnikov's Dream', the astounding literary prophecy of one of the greatest writers of the Old World:

> *He dreamt that the whole world was condemned to a terrible new strange plague that had come to Europe from the depths of Asia. All were to be destroyed except a very few chosen. Some new sorts of microbes were attacking the bodies of men, but these microbes were endowed with intelligence and will. Men attacked by them became at once mad and furious. But never had men considered themselves so intellectual and so completely in possession of the truth as these sufferers, never had they considered their decisions, their scientific conclusions, their moral convictions so infallible. Whole villages, whole towns and peoples went mad from the infection. All were excited and did not understand one another. Each thought that he alone had the truth and was wretched looking at the others, beat himself on the breast, wept, and wrung his hands. They did not know how to judge and could not agree what to consider evil and what good; they did not know whom to blame, whom to justify. Men killed each other in a sort of senseless spite. They gathered together in armies against one another, but even on the march the armies would begin attacking each other, the ranks would be broken and the soldiers would fall on each other, stabbing and cutting, biting and devouring each other. The alarm bell was ringing all day long in the towns; men rushed together, but why they were summoned and who was summoning them no one knew. The most ordinary trades were abandoned because everyone proposed his own ideas, his own*

improvements, and they could not agree. The land too was abandoned. Men met in groups, agreed on something, swore to keep together, but at once began on something quite different from what they had proposed. They accused one another, fought and killed each other. There were conflagrations and famine. All men and all things were involved in destruction. The plague spread and moved further and further. Only a few men could be saved in the whole world. They were a pure chosen people, destined to found a new race and a new life, to renew and purify the earth, but no one had seen these men, no one had heard their words and their voices.

— FYODOR DOSTOEVSKY,
CRIME AND PUNISHMENT, 1866

POSTSCRIPT: 'THE REMAINS OF THE DAY'

Modernity is not a final destiny: there still exist hidden antidotes.
— NICOLÁS GÓMEZ DÁVILA

The preceding analysis of the Zombie Apocalypse phenomenon will inevitably raise the question what may be the *use* of foreknowledge of such a terrible 'end of the world'. From a Traditionalist perspective, the answer to this question is simple: the catastrophic Crisis of the Modern World that will conclude the historical cycle of Western civilization is also the necessary precondition of the rebirth of Tradition.

Similar to its historical background, Matriarchy, the Zombie Apocalypse can only be short-lived. Similar to how Matriarchy dies out with failing demographic reproduction, the zombie population dies out with its food source. There are indications that Matriarchy may, in fact, end before the physical extinction of the Western peoples. First, the ethnic replacement of the Western peoples means that Matriarchy has doomed itself to a premature demise: the primitive colonists that are settling in the Western heartland are reintroducing patriarchy in various forms; perhaps these will include an Islamic Caliphate. Second, there is a clear reaction — and mobilization — against Matriarchy among Western men of the post-baby boom generations: they are increasingly resorting to Traditional forms of family life and to Traditional worldviews. In this respect, it is significant to note high rates of marriage with feminine non-Western women and of 'conversion' to stable Traditional religious forms. Third, there is an increasing likelihood that a new *inner* immunity against Matriarchy will achieve critical mass in an *outer* revolution: the *théâtre de l'absurde* of Matriarchy and totalitarian repression of Western masculinity may very well become practically unbearable, triggering a sudden and dramatic reversal. It can be hoped that, before it is too late, these factors will converge in a scenario that is still compatible with the survival of Western civilization, including its relatively advantageous position of women, its relatively well-developed sense of social justice and its relatively large degree of personal freedom. But whether these refined achievements can survive the imminent Crisis of Western Modernity is far from certain: the extreme injustices of Matriarchy are bound to trigger equally extreme forms of neo-patriarchal correction, a correction that may leave preciously little space for such sophisticated niceties. Western women would, therefore, be well advised to leave the sinking *Titanic* of Matriarchy discretely — and in time.

It is entirely conceivable that Western civilization will fall together with Matriarchy during its Zombie Apocalypse end phase and that little more will be left than what was left of the drowned world of Atlantis: a handful of survivors — and a myth. From a Traditionalist perspective, the only thing that will count is that handful of survivors — and what survives *in them*. Even the destruction of 99% of Western mankind may be a necessary price to pay for the survival of a small remnant of 'chosen people'. In this sense, Traditionalist thought also has a 'prophetic' functionality: it points to the possibility of 'election' and warns the 'elect' to distance them from the Great Whore of Matriarchy in a timely fashion. From a Traditionalist perspective, Matriarchy is nothing less than the ultimate personification of Modernity; in Traditionalist terms it is nothing less than the doomed city of the Great Whore:

> *Babylon the great is fallen, is fallen.... Come out of her, my people, that ye be*
> *not partakers of her sins, and that ye receive not her plagues. For her sins have*

reached unto heaven, and God hath remembered her iniquities.... Therefore
shall her plagues come in one day, death, and mourning, and famine; and she
shall be utterly burned with fire: for strong is the Lord God who judgeth her.

— REVELATION 18:2, 4–8

Such a 'prophecy' is not directed at all: it is only directed at those who still
have ears to hear — at those who remember their authentic identity and
vocation. In practical terms, these are the people who are 'bio-evolution-
arily' immune to the anti-identitarian 'zombie virus' of Modernity — those
people who still preserve (some part of) the authentic identities of ethnicity, caste, gender and vocation within themselves. The essential function
of Traditionalist thought is the preservation of knowledge of such identities and such vocations: it is the Guardian of Tradition. Traditionalism
stands guard over very precious knowledge — knowledge that has been
bought with the blood, sweat and tears of countless generations of ancestors. This 'Night Watch' carries Tradition across the exile of Modernity.
In this regard, the Western peoples have much to learn from the Jewish
Tradition, which is the oldest surviving historical Tradition in the world.
The Jewish Tradition puts its lesson thus:

> (Yiddish) *Ir vet, kinder, elter vern, vet ir aleyn farshteyn, vifl in di oysyes lign*
> *trern, un vi fil geveyn. Az ir vet, kinder, dem goles shlepn, oysgemutshet zayn,*
> *zolt ir fun di oysyes koyekh shepn, kukt in zey arayn!* 'When you grow older,
> children, you will understand by yourselves, how many tears lie in these let-
> ters, and how much lament. When you, children, will bear the Exile, and will
> be exhausted, may you derive strength from these letters — [so] look to them!'
>
> — *OYFN PRIPETSHIK.*

Only a new generation of 'faithful' — the handful of young people who
have built up immunity from the 'zombie virus' of Cultural Nihilist Matriarchy — can realize a self-surpassing rebirth of Western civilization. The
promises of the Traditionalist Palingenesia, the Archaeofuturist Renaissance and the Identitarian Revolution are directed exclusively at them.

They are standing before the ultimate test of Western civilization. But what does not kill them, will make them stronger.

The early 21st century will be the desperate midnight of the world.

But it always is darkest before dawn.

Let us raise our youth, even if they are only a tiny minority, to be the New Nobility.

— GUILLAUME FAYE

CHAPTER SEVEN

Shutdown

FIVE MINUTES TO MIDNIGHT

Do not go gentle into that good night,
Rage, rage against the dying of the light.

— DYLAN THOMAS

HAPTER 5 DESCRIBED HOW TRADITIONALISM views the Western world as the epicentre of the Crisis of the Modern World and Chapter 6 described the meta-historical interpretation that Traditionalism gives to the historical trajectory of this escalating crisis. This chapter will offer a Traditionalist analysis of the psycho-historical 'options' available to the Western peoples in view of the approaching culmination point of the Crisis of the Modern West. Its emphasis will be on the issue of *ethnic replacement*. In Chapter 5, the Crisis of the Modern West was viewed as a combination of four converging core issues: global climate change (industrial ecocide), technological catastrophe (transhumanism), societal chaos (social implosion) and ethnic replacement (demographic inundation). It is self-evident that the issue of ethnic replacement demands priority treatment: it is the most *urgent* problem within the Crisis of the Modern West. From a Western cultural-historical perspective, solutions to the other problems are useless when the Western peoples are unable to

survive the first 'challenge' of ethnic replacement: the historical event horizon of Western civilization matches the physical expiry date of the Western
peoples. Thus, the crucial question is whether — and, if yes, how — the indigenous peoples of the West can still avert their sui-genocide, which the Cultural
Nihilist global hostile elite has been preparing with mathematical precision.
The answer to this question depends upon their ability to break free from
their Cultural Nihilist psycho-historical conditioning, i.e. upon their ability to
re-cover, re-live and re-activate their authentic identities *in time*.

These words are written during a time in history characterized by the
oppressive atmosphere of the 'lull before the storm': the hellstorm of the
Crisis of the Modern West is near at hand and the event horizon of Western civilization is fading in the increasing chaos of converging crisis phenomena. The precarious prosperity and awareness 'bubbles' into which the
privileged classes of the Western heartland have retreated are still glittering
in this dying rays of the setting sun of Western civilization. Still, the baby
boomer consumer crowds are stampeding through the classical inner cities,
the ancient art temples and the archaic half-nature landscapes of the West,
but this artificially ritualized life is lived on borrowed time and high-per-
centage credit. Western society, Western culture and Western nature have
entered their terminal stage: their historical 'shutdown' is imminent. Western nature is rapidly disappearing through accelerating climate change:
the Alpine glaciers have already shrunken to a historical minimum, wine
production has already moved north into Sweden and the Arctic sea ice is
about to melt entirely. Western culture is rapidly being abolished through
Cultural Nihilist 'deconstruction': 'privatization', 'commercialization', 'internationalization' and 'diversity' have brought down academic and artistic life
to the level of a ridiculous scam. Western society is fast collapsing through
economic cannibalism and social implosion: the drastic transformation
of Western social geography reflects the collapse of all authentic forms of
Western identity. Except for a few small 'reservations' for mindless tourists,
hasty businessmen and spoilt students, the great cities of the West have now
largely been abandoned to the exponentially multiplying immigrant masses. The remains of the indigenous 'common people' are being assimilated

into this rapidly proliferating mass of alien invaders which is living off a poisonous cocktail of improvised entrepreneurship, marginal day labour, social security fraud and street crime. The result is an entirely denaturalized, demoralized and deracinated *métèque* population defined by urban-hedonist stasis, endemic vice and psychosocial instability—a growing reservoir of social resentment and political extremism. On the other side of the social divide there is the shrinking indigenous elite of baby boomer *rentiers*, nihilist *intelligentsia* and privileged *jeunesse dorée*, temporarily shielded from reality in the socio-economic bubbles of well-guarded gated communities and gentrified city enclaves. This combined ethnic-demographic and socio-economic time bomb has been ticking away for quite some time all throughout the heartland of Western civilization, here defined as Western Europe plus the overseas Anglosphere. It is now five minutes to midnight. The Western peoples are about to face their last choice: to silently go into the night of history—or to break free from their fate through a final, self-surpassing assertion of willpower.

'THE FIGHTING TEMERAIRE'

> It was not part of their blood,
> It came to them very late
> With long arrears to make good,
> When the English began to hate.
>
> — RUDYARD KIPLING
> 'THE BEGINNINGS'

In tracing the Postmodern trajectory of Cultural Nihilism an important test case is provided by the 'scouting nation' of Western Modernity and Atlanticist thallasocracy: Great Britain. The case of Great Britain can provide insight into the psycho-historical 'options' available to the Western peoples in the face of Postmodern Cultural Nihilism. On the one hand, Britain's *splendid isolation* has created an ideal insular greenhouse for relatively peaceful experiments in Modernity (the religious Anglican Reformation, the political Glorious Reformation, the economic Industrial Revolution). On the other hand, it provides 'Classical Modernity' a fallback position for heroic stands against the extreme violence of experimental 'Hyper-Modernity'. British history is characterized by continuous resistance to Hyper-Modernist experiments in totalitarian tyranny and collectivist dictatorship. The English victory over the Spanish Armada in 1588 represented a victory over the prospective dictatorship of counter-reformatory centralist absolutism. The British victory over Napoleon's fleet in 1805 represented a victory over the prospective dictatorship of the revolutionary-secularist bourgeoisie. The British victory over the German *Luftwaffe* during the Battle of Britain in 1940 represented a victory over the prospective dictatorship of a genocidal and hyper-nationalist *proletariat*. Despite the historical vanguard role of Great Britain as the scouting nation of Western Modernity and Atlanticist thallasocracy these victories resulted in important modifications — dilutions, diversions — within Modernity. Against this background, it is useful to investigate the present British reaction to the increasingly totalitarian globalism of the Cultural Nihilist hostile elite. This reaction suggests that the British people do not wish to disappear silently into the night of Cultural Nihilism.

Room 34 of the British National Gallery exhibits a painting that provides an unsurpassed symbolic expression of the soul of the British people. William Turner, most known for his marine paintings, gave this modest oil canvas, painted in the years 1838–39 and bequeathed to the British nation upon his death in 1851, the name *The Fighting Temeraire tugged to her last berth to be broken up, 1838*. It shows a steam tugboat on the Thames dragging along an old warship to the place where it is to be demolished so that her materials can be sold off. The old warship of wood and sail, a ship of the line second class built in 1798, is *His Majesty's Ship Temeraire*, famous for its heroic role in the Battle of Trafalgar. It was this sea battle, fought near the Spanish naval base at Cádiz on 19 October 1805 and resulting in the utter destruction of the allied French and Spanish fleets, which effectively scuttled Napoleon's hopes of challenging Britain's global naval hegemony. In fact, the beginning of the Anglo-Saxon thalassocracy — the combined

Anglo-American 'Atlanticist' world power, which up to today remains the greatest geopolitical pillar of Modernity—can be dated to this battle. The mythological meaning of this battle for the British people, which rose to become the world's most powerful people at the imperialist height of Western civilization during the following century, is reflected in the name of the most important public square of the British capital: Trafalgar Square. In the middle of the square stands Nelson's Column, crowned with a statue of the great victor of the Battle of Trafalgar, Vice-Admiral Horatio Lord Nelson. The square pedestal is decorated with four bronze panels, cast from captured French guns, depicting Nelson's four greatest feats: the Battle of Cape St Vincent (1797), the Battle of the Nile (1798), the Battle of Copenhagen (1801) and the Battle of Trafalgar (1805). His heroic death during his last and greatest victory ensured in his immortal glory and his status as the greatest naval hero of the British people—an ultimate example of *mors triumphalis*. Opposite Nelson's Column stands the National Gallery, containing the other iconic reference to the Battle of Trafalgar: Turner's *The Fighting Temeraire*. The *Temeraire* played a crucial role in the Battle of Trafalgar: it came to the aid of Nelson's flagship *Victory* at a crucial moment and subsequently fought off superior Franco-Spanish forces for many hours, with great loss of human life and substantial damage. Her brave action and exemplary conduct brought the *Temeraire* the admiration of British public: after she reached Portsmouth on 1 December the *Temeraire*, together with the *Victory*, became a great attraction for masses of curious visitors. Among these many visitors was the thirty-year-old William Turner.

After four decades of service as a prison, guard and training ship, the *Temeraire* was finally taken out of service in the summer of 1838: she fired her last salute on 28 June, for the occasion of the coronation of Queen Victoria. In the new Victorian Age, an age of steam and steel under the aegis of the Second Industrial Revolution and world-encompassing Modern Imperialism, there was no longer any place for old wood-and-sail warhorses like the *Temeraire*: she was auctioned off to be broken up and on 5 August she commenced her last journey to the mudflats of the Thames off the London suburb of Rotherhithe. It was witnessing this last journey that

inspired Turner to paint his masterwork and the special manner in which
it has continued to touch a chord in the British soul is illustrated by the fact
that in 2005 it was voted as the favourite painting of the British people. The
theme of the painting is appropriately dramatic: the grey-and-white ghost
of the mythical 'White Ship' passes under an eerie moon, the still water of
the windless river that renders sails helpless but is resolutely ploughed by
the blackened steam tug, the white flag that signifies not only a commercial
voyage but also capitulation. In the background, vaguely visible in a ghostly
haze, appear the monstrous factory chimneys and city skylines of Modernity — all under a red sunset. The setting sun indicates the end of the epoch,
symbolized by *The Fighting Temeraire*, the 'saucy dare-devil'. It is the end
of the heroic age of 'steel men in wooden ships', followed by the cowardly
age of 'wooden men in steel ships'. On the mudflats of Rotherhithe the *Temeraire* was finally broken up: pieces of her woodwork found their way all
throughout the British cultural landscape, embedded in artefacts such as a
royal chair, a church altar and a painting frame.

Obviously, Turner's masterpiece first and foremost represents *British*
heritage: it encapsulates the schizophrenic but consistent relation that Great
Britain has with Modernity: as dramatically illustrated in her status as the
world's *First Industrial Nation*, Great Britain is the scouting nation of Western Modernity. This relation is typified by a Faustian application of Modern
Techne that goes hand in hand with a deep awareness of the loss of archetypal Traditional ideal forms. In the British psyche, crude capitalist calculation
and the ruthless sacrifice of nature and culture to the laws of Modernity are
always juxtaposed with subtle nostalgia and sublime melancholy. Archetypal expressions of the double-faced life of the First Industrial Nation, fea-
turing (public, exterior) institutionalized harshness alongside (private, interior) idyllic tenderness, are characteristic of all great British art, including
Dickens' *David Copperfield*, Holst's *The Planets* — and Turner's *The Fighting
Temeraire*.

In a certain sense, the British relation with Modernity, exquisitely expressed in Turner's *The Fighting Temeraire*, can be regarded as a quintessential summary of Modernity in Western civilization *as a whole*: Great

Britain is in the vanguard of that Modernity, it explores it and advances it. Even in the contemporary Postmodern West, long after the British leadership in Anglosaxon thalassocratic world power passed to America, Great Britain still retains its quintessential role as pioneer and test case. Significant developments in this regard are: its early economic de-industrialization (neo-Victorian neo-liberalism: 'Thatcherism', 'de-regulation', 'privatisation') and its early social de-construction (Cultural Nihilism multiculturalism: 'open borders', 'inverse colonization', 'islamization'). Its cultural-historical *anticipatory* role means that Great Britain is an interesting subject in any Traditionalist analysis of the Postmodern West.

An example of contemporary relevance is the Cultural Nihilist programme of *ethnic replacement*: in Great Britain, this programme has advanced much further than in the rest of Western Europe. The resulting symptoms indicated the future direction of development in the rest of Western Europe: endemic and massive Islamist terror ('7/7', 'Manchester Arena'), industrial-scale ethnic 'grooming gangs' ('Rochdale', 'Rotherham'), uncontrollable street criminality and systematic inter-ethnic wealth redistribution. The reaction of the nominally 'British' authorities and the British indigenous people are equally interesting as indicators of the future development in the rest of Western Europe. On the one hand, there is the total abdication of political authority, the official policy of cover-up, the self-censorship in the media and the 'white flight' from the great cities. On the other hand, there is the unexpectedly radical re-emergence of anti-globalist nationalism: with 'Brexit' Great Britain is the first European nation to formally denounce globalist transnational tyranny. Combined, these symptoms and reactions indicate an imminent saturation point in the historical trajectory of Western Cultural Nihilism; in Great Britain, this is due earlier than in the rest of the West. When the Cultural Nihilist programme of ethnic replacement finally reaches a certain (demographic, economic, social) 'critical mass', the global hostile elite will face a potentially lethal 'democratic deficit'. 'Brexit' indicates the potential weakness of the global hostile elite in the present form of 'democratic' governance: for the sake of political survival the British ruling class has decided to bow to the overt manifestation of the will of the indigenous people. This reaction is theoretically possible in other Western countries as well.

The only reliable ways by which the hostile elite can avoid defeats such as 'Brexit' — and 'Trump' — is to either structurally misrepresent the will of the indigenous people, or to simply ignore it. The former strategy forms the basis of parliamentarianism, the second forms the basis of Eurocracy. In the case of Great Britain, both strategies failed: 'Brexit' offers a ray of hope for Western civilization — or at least a delay in its downfall. As long as the ethnic-demographic balance still permits it, authentic (direct, non-parliamentarian) democracy — referenda, direct representation — remains a grave danger to the hostile elite. This explains the hastiness of the hostile elite with regards to the implementation of ethnic replacement: it needs to permanently disable the power of the indigenous population by 'democratically' marginalizing them in terms of ethnic demography. This hastiness, however, implies a rising risk of social unrest, societal chaos, ethnic conflict and even civil war. Until now, the hostile elite has managed to control the process of ethnic replacement by careful socio-economic calibration, but it could be easily derailed by an unexpected incident, followed by an uncontrollable chain-reaction and complete societal breakdown. Thus, the Cultural Nihilist hostile elite is playing with fire: the publicly suppressed but tangible rise in inter-ethnic tensions increases the potential for a fatal catastrophe from year to year.

Its geopolitical insulation and its cultural-historical anticipatory role determine the particular historical development of Great Britain, which greatly differs from that of Continental Europe. It has been spared many of the violent and cruel excesses of Modernity: the victories of 1588, 1805 and 1940 meant that Great Britain escaped the experience of land warfare, foreign occupation and totalitarian experimentation. Great Britain managed to absorb Modernity and to control its development without a total loss of state sovereignty, socio-economic balance and historical identity. 'Brexit' indicates that Great Britain will also live up to its role as scouting nation of Western Modernity with regard to the issues of Cultural Nihilist totalitarianism and ethnic replacement — and find relatively 'restrained', 'reasonable' and 'moderate' answers. In view of the equivalent historical patterns in Continental Europe, it is probable that the development there will lack such self-restraint, reasonability and moderation. At the same time, however, it should be noted that, from a psycho-historical perspective, an *overdose* of self-restraint, reasonability and moderation is fatal for the survival of any civilization: a civilization that is *too* patient, *too* reasonable and *too* moderate vis-à-vis its enemies is doomed to extinction. Thus, the question remains whether or not the British people can find the right balance in view of the imminent final Crisis of Western Modernity. If 'Brexit' turns out to be nothing else but an exterior denial of an inner self-annihilation, then the pioneering role of Great Britain as the scouting nation of Western Modernity implies a worst-case scenario for the future of Western civilization. If 'Brexit' turns out to be nothing else but a propagandistic façade of counterfeit sovereignty to hide the last phase of ethnic replacement and social implosion, then it can only be concluded that the British people have at long last forgotten its *Fighting Temeraire*.

'THE CAMP OF THE SAINTS'

And when a thousand years are expired, Satan shall be loosed out of his prison, and shall go out to deceive the nations which are in the four quarters of the earth, Gog and Magog, to gather them together to battle: the number of whom is as the sand of the sea. And they went up the breadth of the earth, and compassed the camp of the saints, and the beloved city...

— REVELATION 20:7–9

Every serious inquiry into the survival chances of the Western peoples must start with the question of their present psycho-historical conditioning: to what extent are they still able to overcome this conditioning and re-cover, re-live and re-activate their authentic identities? In short: do they still *want* to survive and, if so, are they *able* to? From a psycho-historical perspective *intentional self-annihilation* may be a fully legitimate strategy: in the same way that an existentially saturated person, overwhelmed by sickness, old age or exterior pressures, may have a legitimate reason for intentional self-annihilation at the individual level, so a community may have a similar reason at the collective level. From a Traditionalist perspective, the degree of psycho-historical legitimacy of every form of self-annihilation coincides with the question of authentic destiny. In other words: from a Traditionalist perspective, suicide is fully justified when a specific destiny is experienced as truly 'accomplished'. In this regard, the issue of the 'natural life cycle' is of secondary importance: individuals and peoples may be historically 'young', but meta-historically 'old' at the same time. The degree of 'age' and 'accomplishment' is primarily a 'subjective' *experience*: in the final analysis, authentic destiny — as well as authentic identity and authentic vocation — is determined by an inner experience of transcendental reality. Thus, awareness of destiny is a super-rational experience — rationally, it can only be retroactively 'reconstructed' as a meta-historical 'thesis'.

Thus, the Western peoples have — at least in theory — the psycho-historical 'option' to chose a *Nirvana* end scenario, i.e. the intentional annihilation of themselves and their civilization. An esoteric interpretation of such an end scenario falls outside the cultural-historical scope of *Alba Rosa*, but the archaic archetypes of Western civilization do provide some meaningful avenues of research: the otherworldly ideal of Christianity (the celibate *Sacerdotus*), the monastic life of the Church (the abstemious *Monachus*) and the spiritual tendency to asceticism (the purified *Perfectus*). These spiritual archetypes are institutionally reflected in Traditional Western rites such as the priestly ordination, the monastic vow and the lent fast. Even after the rise of Historical Materialism and the downfall of Christianity, these archetypes retain a residual effectiveness in Modern Western culture: they explain the strongly internalized ethics and strongly self-regulating discipline of the Western peoples. Till today, these highly stylized Western ethics — respect for other life forms, altruism towards socially disadvantaged groups, self-correcting severity regarding ego-impulses — have long been at work in Western civilization. At certain points, this ethical development is still continuing: a growing ecological consciousness contributes to a 'new nature', a growing sensitivity to animal welfare contributes to new bio-ethics and a growing interest in the cosmological plight of women contributes to new social freedoms. At these points, it is possible to speak of objective 'progress' in ethical terms: there is less physical and psychological suffering and there is more space for the pursuit of destiny and vocation at the individual level. A similar positive interpretation can be given to another specific point at which Western ethics are still developing according to their original Christian trajectory: the voluntary anti-natalistic aspect of the negative demographic development throughout the West. To the degree that this development is *not* enforced by the Cultural Nihilist hostile elite as 'sui-genocide' through socio-economic manipulation and ethnic replacement, it may be interpreted as actual *progress* in a spiritual and esoteric sense. But an ecological and social equivalent to this spiritual and esoteric improvement demands a population decline that is not merely *relative*, but *absolute*. In fact, a drastic decline in population is an absolute precondition for any substantial improvement of the natural biotope and the social structure of the West. Simply replacing the indigenous peoples of the West by a mixed population with a large alien ethnic component can only result in a decline in the natural biotope and the social structure, even when absolute numbers remain stable: the replacement population will inevitably regress in terms of economic productivity, technological innovation and ethic development. Thus, the voluntary anti-natalism of the indigenous peoples of the West is negated by the process of ethnic replacement.

On balance, the psycho-historical resonance of Christian archetypes in contemporary Western civilization is negative, rather than positive. Traditional Christian ethical values are effectively negated through the Modern post-Christian *inversion* of these values. The three great Historical-Materialist ideologies of Modernity (Liberalism, Socialism, Fascism: Aleksandr Dugin, 2009) operate on the basis of a systematic inversion of Christian ethics: respect for other life forms is perverted into self-destructive culture relativism, social altruism is perverted into 'oikophobic' sado-masochism and impulse-control is perverted into politically correct self-humiliation. This equally absurd and tragic *Umwertung aller Werte* is the cultural-his-

torical background for the proliferation of Cultural Nihilism in Western
ethics and for the rise of the *Gutmensch* reflexes of politically correct pseu-
do-idealism and totalitarian pseudo-morality. In this sense, Cultural Nihilism can be understood as a 'secularized' and absurdly inverted version of
Christianity: without their transcendental referent, the Christian virtues
of self-denial and asceticism are transformed into morbid self-hatred and
malicious self-abasement. This perverted development is clearly illustrated
in the Postmodern phenomenon of the 'Social Justice Warrior': the ego-
centric, prejudiced, unreasonable and hypocritical personification of 'political correctness', engaged in the systematic suppression of everything that
is still strong, healthy, intelligent, beautiful and good in the world. To the
Social Justice Warrior, ethnic replacement is nothing less than a personal
quest — a theme that is pursued to its logical extreme in the prophetic novel
Le Camp des Saints (Raspail, 1973). In this phenomenological context, Cultural Nihilism achieves its aim of an anti-Christian *Umwertung aller Werte*:
the old *superhuman* ethics of Christianity are negatively projected through
the lens of a narcissist world-view and are transformed into the new *subhuman* ethics of Postmodernity. At the metaphysical level, in contrast, the
self-annihilation aimed at by Cultural Nihilism and personified by the Social Justice Warrior represents a *structural inversion* of Christianity.

THE NIRVANA OPTION

Im Westen wirft die Sonne von sich die Purpurtracht
und träumt im Flutenbette des nächsten Tages Pracht.
[In the west the sun casts off her crimson dress
and dreams in her bed of waves of next day's splendour.]

— ROBERT ARNOLD

From a Traditionalist perspective, there are two reasons why the Cultural
Nihilist self-annihilation scenario does not represent an authentically le-
gitimate 'Nirvana option' — why it lacks the status of legitimate choice for
Western civilization.

(1) First, the legitimacy of the 'Nirvana option' depends on a voluntary choice: *all* individuals within Western civilization would have to collectively agree with this choice without any compulsion. It is highly unlikely that all individuals would simultaneously recognize this destiny as privately applicable to themselves. Especially problematic in this regard is the 'choice' of vulnerable groups such as children, sick people and older people. Only a group that is exclusively made up of adult and healthy people, and which has freely agreed to abstain from procreation, can fully avoid this ethical problem. There are very few historical precedents for a legitimate 'Nirvana option', and then only in the very specific circumstances of an existential external threat (the Jewish Sicarii at Masada in 73 AD, the Cathar refugees at Montségur in 1244, the Balinese *puputan* of 1906). At an individual level, the 'Nirvana option' is an entirely legitimate response for contemporary Western men in the face of Western Modernity: to halt biological procreation, to take leave of worldly affairs and to welcome ritual self-annihilation are deeply embedded within the timeless ideals of Christianity and therefore retain their value as steps to transcendental 'redemption' at an individual level. A Western man looking at the downfall of his civilization from this perspective is still able to fulfil the self-surpassing destiny of that civilization in an entirely unexpected and liberating fashion. From this perspective, all the symptoms of ethnic replacement are transformed into insignificant incidents—at most, the ridiculous hedonism and atavistic cruelty of the immigrant masses will cause a moment of serene pity. To most indigenous Westerners, their ferocious appetite for procreation (polygamy, r-strategy reproduction), their infantile greediness (obsessive car ownership, *free rider* immorality) and their primitive rituals (genital mutilation of children, animal sacrifice) represent long-abandoned stations on their journey to an incomparably more sublime end. But a *voluntary*, individual 'Nirvana' experience never justifies an *enforced*, collective 'Nirvana' strategy. As long as there are Western people who still have worldly wishes and earthly ambitions, the Cultural Nihilist self-annihilation programme of ethnic replacement remains a grotesque perversion.

(2) Second, the legitimacy of the 'Nirvana option' depends upon a

conscious choice: the choice for self-annihilation can only be valid if it is made in a state of mental competence. From a Traditionalist perspective, however, the Postmodern dominance of Cultural Nihilism among the Western peoples renders them mentally incompetent. At a collective level, the Cultural Nihilist programme of self-annihilation does not represent a well-considered journey towards a consciously willed destiny, but rather an unconscious movement in an undetermined direction. The purposeless fatalism and denaturalized instinct that propel this unconscious movement can be understood against their historical background: two world wars, four decennia of imperial collapse and a century of fatal experiments with Historical Materialist ideologies. Regressive genetic selection, totalitarian cultural matriarchy and collective narcissist pathology make it impossible to speak in terms of a conscious and legitimate choice for self-annihilation: the Western peoples are not abolishing themselves, but are losing themselves (Peter Sloterdijk's 'fall into the future'). This is shown by the fact that they *are* abstaining from cultural transmission, but *not* from biological reproduction. In other words: they are distancing themselves from continuity in civilization (culture), but not from continuity in biology (nature): they are regressing from civilization-creating patriarchy into atavistic matriarchy. Thus, the baby boomers are still having children, but they no longer take *responsibility* for them. Thus, the baby boomers still want to continue to live as long as possible, but they no longer have a *destiny* to live towards. Thus, the Cultural Nihilist self-annihilation project for Western civilization, initiated by the baby boomers, is nothing more than narcissist pathology, megalomaniacally played out on the stage of world history: it represents a psycho-historical revenge on Western culture and a sadistic sacrificial offering of the children of that culture.

But a Traditionalist analysis of the Crisis of the Modern West cannot end with a simple statement of the historical facts. Neither the cultural-historical explanation of the Cultural Nihilist annihilation of Western civilization nor the psycho-historical refutation of the Cultural Nihilist 'Nirvana option' suffices as an effective metapolitical discourse when the future of the Western Tradition is at stake. Traditionalism's *raison d'être* resides in its function as Guardian of Tradition — in this case, the Guardian of the Western Tradition — and it is obliged to fulfil its duties in an effective manner. The night watch manning the walls of Western civilization is not only obliged to keep a look-out, but also to raise the alarm when necessary. Traditionalism has recognized the Cultural Nihilist hostile elite as the enemy and it must now call to arms the defenders of Western civilization. The fact that this enemy is a traitor from within and that it has already opened the gates of the West to barbarous invaders is no reason for dereliction of duty. The Guardian of the West has done his first duty by raising alarm and is now bound to take up arms alongside the Katechon of the West. The old Katechon institutions of the West — Monarchy, Nobility, Church, Academy — have a duty to the Western peoples: they must make a supreme effort to fight and defeat Cultural Nihilism — or die in the attempt. Here the probable outcome of the fight is of secondary importance: in every authentic Tradition, duty and honour take precedence over calculus and life.

'GÖTTERDÄMMERUNG'

In certain times suicide is no longer a gesture of pride,
but a last remedy to avoid capitulation to Satan.

— NICOLÁS GÓMEZ DÁVILA

For peoples that have lost their *Wehr- und Waffeninstinkt* through unearned freedom, unappreciated peace and undeserved wealth — peoples that have forgotten the great sacrifices of their ancestors and the costly lessons of their history — it is difficult to achieve a realistic view of the world. This problem is most acute in those who are most privileged: they feel so secure and so comfortable that they easily lapse into classic hubris. If for a long time they have had the illusion that they no longer need their own identity and their own people, and if they long get away with behaving accordingly, they finally become a *hostile elite*. Thus, during the eternal baby boomer generation and under the aegis of Cultural Nihilism, a 'globalist' hostile elite has formed in the West, rejecting all forms of authentic identity — and all forms of authentic debate. Between this hostile elite — a power cartel of shareholder billionaires, usurious bankers, professional politicians, media pundits and politically correct academics — and the 'common people' of the West, there is a rather thick intermediate layer: a well-to-do conglomerate of baby boom *pensionados*, entrepreneurial *nouveaux riches* and *wannabe* social climbers. The large majority of the hostile elite can no longer be saved except by psychiatric intervention — they are lost to their people. But in demographic terms this elite is insignificant — it accounts for no more than ten percent of the population at most. It is the intermediate group that is demographically crucial: it represents up to a quarter of the population and it is permanently vulnerable in terms of wealth and status due to its immediate position. Its self-interest dictates its adherence to the ideology of the hostile elite, but this adherence is superficial and pragmatic. Its acceptance of the obligatory politically correct hallucinations of the Cultural Nihilist elite represents a *survival strategy*, not a *worldview*. Members of the intermediate layer permanently fear social demotion — a relapse into the 'common people' from which they rose with so much difficulty — and they are existentially sensitive to 'real life' developments such as economic cycles, social threats and ethnic transitions. They suffer, at least unconsciously and instinctively, from the existential *Angst* that is caused by the daily reality of the Postmodern West: hyper-capitalist bubble economics, social deconstruction and ethnic replacement.

Thus, it is a good strategy to explain to them that their worst fears are about to be realized and that there is only one way to face them: to move outside the daily 'bubble' of self-absorbed consumerism and outside the *comfort zone* of ideological political correctness. A realistic conversation with members of the intermediate section of the Western population means this: to point out all that they stand to *lose*. In concrete terms: the inheritance of their ancestors, their own gains in the present and the future of their children. To a certain extent, the socio-economic loss — loss of security, loss of wealth, loss of opportunities — can be rationally calculated. The cultural-historical loss may be less tangible, but it is exactly this intangibility that makes it more fearsome. Thus, a successful policy of patriotic and identitarian resistance to the Cultural Nihilist abolition of Western civilization will depend on formulating a coherent and effective answer to the deep-seated — unconscious, instinctive — fears of the Western peoples, fears that are most acute in the intermediate layer of the population.

The effectiveness of the patriotic-identitarian response to the problem of ethnic replacement depends on a correct psycho-historical approach of the elementary fears of the Western peoples. This approach must allow them to master these fears by recognizing their own strength and potential. In other words: the Western peoples must be brought to re-cover their authentic identities and to re-live the archaic power that once created these identities. In this regard, Traditionalism has an important task: its knowledge of authentic identity and authentic heritage allows it to accurately predict the real price tag attached to the Cultural Nihilist self-annihilation programme of ethnic replacement. Traditionalism can point out the direct link between the ancient eschatological visions of Western culture and the contemporary self-annihilation programmes cherished by the hostile elite. Traditionalism permits insight into the psycho-historical background to the programme of ethnic replacement by 'naming and shaming' its sub-rational, counter-instinctive and sadomasochistic motives — and by exorcizing them. The most important exorcism spell is the counter-motif, i.e. the contemporary re-activation of archaic eschatological motifs. In concrete terms: to pronounce the actual implications of the impending *Götterdämmerung* of Western civilization. The future of Western civilization is at stake and the time has come to ask questions about the concrete prospects of its highest creations when the programme of ethnic replacement reaches its conclusion. These questions even concern the hostile elite: the hostile elite has appropriated these creations, identifies with them and derives its status from their ownership. Thus, in the final analysis, it must all fall when it loses these 'trophies'.

How will Da Vinci's *La Gioconda* end when the advance guard of *Da'esh* finally reaches the Louvre? The bullet-proof glass that already covers it is meant to protect it from lone-wolf crazies, not from armies of psychiatric patients. Will it end in a Chinese *Wunderkammer* dedicated to the extinct tribes of the West, bought up by a business tycoon during a last execution sale? Or will the last curator happen to be an 'angry white man' who will choose to sink it into the Seine, rather than let it fall in the hands of jihadist vandals?

How will Bach's *Hohe Messe* be heard for the last time after the last Christians have been smoked out of their end-time catacombs? The sum total of technique, skill and tradition that is necessary to reproduce this masterwork is incompatible with the intellectual atavism and cultural-bolshevik barbarity that will inevitably result from *Umvolkung*. Will the last note sound just before the first *'aḏān* sounds from the mosque into which the Dresden Frauenkirche has been converted, three hundred years after the composer played it on the organ there? Or will it resound in the ear of the last commander of rocket forces when he chooses the *schreckliche Ende* of nuclear euthanasia over the *Schrecken ohne Ende* of eternal barbarity?

And how will the last performance of Tchaikovsky's *Spyashchaya krasavitsa* take place before the final introduction of Shariah Law? The precarious performing arts—a girl's foot *pointe en relevé*, an ethereal angel in a transparant *tutu*—are no match for *hudūd* executioners. Will the last performance take place in some obscure provincial town in the last native-held enclave, just before the *Endsieg* of the Eurocaliphate? Or will it be held in a last outburst of spectacular splendour as a last gesture, in the manner of the performance of Wagner's *Götterdämmerung* by the Berliner Philharmoniker on 16 April 1945 during the final act of Hitler's *Götterdämmerung*?

The Samson Option

Earth! render back from out thy breast
A remnant of our Spartan dead!
Of the three hundred grant but three,
To make a new Thermopylae!

— Lord Byron

Still, the Western peoples have been given a short respite during which to reconsider their options: a short moment to recognize the counterfeit 'Nirvana option' of the Cultural Nihilist hostile elite as a historical Fata Morgana — and to choose another road before it is too late. But it is entirely conceivable that, after half a century of Cultural Nihilist delusions, they are no longer capable of rational observation and authentic autonomy, and that the fate of the Western peoples has been sealed. In the latter case, from a metaphysical perspective, it is entirely justified that the Western peoples submit to the 'judgment' and 'punishment' befitting the 'unrepentant sinner': the Bible expresses this metaphysical dimension as the 'Final Judgment' and the 'Lake of Fire'. But for 'Modern men' this fate is perhaps more easily understood in its immanent dimension, i.e. as the natural law of cause and effect. In terms of natural law, the earthly home of humanity constitutes a single 'living' organism that is ruled by cosmic time cycles and bio-evolutionary feedback loops of immense duration and width in time and space. Within this network of interrelated, overlapping and simultaneous cycles and loops it is inevitable that every *action* is followed by *reaction* — and every *mistake* by *correction*. Within this imminent reality, it is therefore inevitable that the actions of the Western peoples throughout the Modern Age are eventually followed by reactions. In terms of Traditional metaphysics, this cycle of 'action and reaction' may be interpreted as 'crime and punishment'. From that perspective, it is simply inconceivable that the enormities committed by the Western peoples during the Dark Age of Modernity — global ecocide through anthropogenic climate change, billion-fold animal cruelty through

bio-industrial commerce, hellish idiocracy through institutionalized matriarchy—will remain without consequences.

In a certain sense, these enormities punish themselves in Western Cultural Nihilism and its self-annihilation programmes of climate catastrophe
(abolition of the Western biotope), social implosion (abolition of Western
communal life) and ethnic replacement (abolition of Western ethnicity).
From a Traditional metaphysical perspective, Cultural Nihilism can, therefore, be interpreted as the just 'punishment' of the Western peoples, con-
demning them to a slow death in blindness, slavery and humiliation. In the
Bible this was the fate of the mighty judge Samson, the Christian anti-type
of the miracle-working and miraculously resurrected Messiah: he ended
'Eyeless in Gaza at the Mill with Slaves' (John Milton, *Samson Agonistes*).
But the Bible also recounts how Samson decided not to accept his fate: before his death, he reconciled with God and took revenge on his enemies.
In pre-Christian Indo-European paganism such a heroic death, the *mors
triumphalis*, was considered the highest possible destiny: it guaranteed an
honourable reception in Valhalla. Thus, the double Christian and pagan
heritage of the Western peoples provide them with a double vision to escape
from the dark fate of blind slavery. They do not have to go silently into the
night of history: even if their downfall proves inevitable, they can still reach
eternity through a last effort of supreme willpower. It is the will to self-surpassing heroism that has etched the name of Judge Samson and the name of
his people, Israel, into history for all eternity.

And Samson called unto the Lord, and said, O Lord God,
remember me, I pray thee, and strengthen me, I pray thee, only this once, O God,
that I may be at once avenged of the Philistines for my two eyes.
...And Samson said, Let me die with the Philistines.
And he bowed himself with all his might; and the house fell upon the lords,
and upon all the people that were therein.
So the dead which he slew at his death were more than they which he slew in his life.

— JUDGES 16:28, 30

The Fighting Temeraire

The Fighting Temeraire Tugged to Her Last Berth to be Broken Up, 1838 (Joseph Mallord William Turner, 1839), The National Gallery.

A danger -

I want to be a danger -

I want to be a danger to the world.

So that after my destruction not a single blade of grass will remain upon the Earth,

upon the Earth where, since I was born, I am a danger.

Because it is my right when I have to die,

to annihilate my annihilators.

When in the setting sun I read the newspapers, full of treason,

when in an old atlas I see the old fatherlands,

now annihilated by and for barbarians,

then I know that we still have this right:

to be annihilated -

but to take with us into oblivion the whole old world,

with all its books of wisdom, all its arts of beauty and all its melodies of magic.

So that, after we descend into the grave, the Earth will also swallow our annihilators-

this is our right after two thousand years.

So that, when the West descends into its final night, we can say:

'If you force us to descend from the face of the Earth,

then also let the Earth itself roll descending into Nothingness.'

— 'The Right to Exist',

FREELY INSPIRED BY Itamar Yaoz-Kest

CHAPTER EIGHT

The Archaeofuturist Revolution

Traditionalist and Identitarian Notes on
Jason Reza Jorjani's Prometheus and Atlas *(London: Arktos, 2016)*

audax Iapeti genus

NIBIRU RETURNING

Nēberu nēberet shamê u ertseti lū tamehma
[Let Nibiru hold the crossing of heaven and earth]

— ENUMA ELISH

O OLDER EUROPEANS RAISED IN THE CONTI-
nental intellectual tradition, it may seem implausible, but it is
the contention of this chapter that America has at long last pro-
duced a philosopher worthy of the name. Obviously, the snobbery and
condescendence of older European intellectuals are more substantially
inspired by their postwar geopolitical inferiority complexes than by their
actual postwar intellectual achievements. But the fact remains that the
term 'American philosopher' is still widely considered a *contradictio in
terminis* — though perhaps, given the obvious dementia and decadence of

Old Europe, many Americans might actually consider this 'Old Europe' qualification to be a badge of honour. At any rate, the actual rise of an authentic philosopher in America is *news* — whether it is good or bad news will depend on political colour and intellectual orientation. To ethno-nationalist 'critics', his name — Jason Reza Jorjani — may sound 'un-American', but for Traditionalist thinkers it will immediately resolve the riddle: apparently the Old World genius of *Persian* philosophy has in some mysterious way resurfaced in the New World. In some unfathomable manner, a little branch of philosophical life has grown up in the shallow soil of the anti-intellectual American 'melting pot' and it has managed to survive the blistering heat of the hedonist 'American dream'. In an unexpected way, this proves that not all of the hundreds of thousands of Iranian immigrants that have flooded into the West since the Islamic Revolution are 'asylum' frauds, 'business' opportunists and 'pop culture clones'. One Jorjani may outweigh the burden of the entire millions-strong Iranian immigration to the West (at any rate bearable because Iranians tend to be among the most-assimilated immigrants) — if his role as *avant garde* philosopher, identitarian idealist and geopolitical critic is properly understood. He may yet have to write his defining work and he may not yet have done all he can do (supposing his jealous enemies leave his talent time and space to prosper), but his first work *Prometheus and Atlas* already firmly establishes his credentials as a pioneering philosopher. Its stature was first recognized by John Morgan of Arktos Publishing, Jorjani's predecessor as Arktos' Editor-in-Chief. Jorjani's oeuvre, which now also includes *World State of Emergency* and *Lovers of Sophia*, is at the cutting edge of contemporary Western thought.

Jorjani's appearance on the Western philosophical scene comes at a critical juncture in Western history: the remnant peoples of the West, now facing the quadruple challenge of ecological disaster, demographic inundation, social implosion and trans-humanist supersession, are approaching the 'event horizon' of Western history. From a Traditionalist perspective, the approaching 'world state of emergency' means that, as the Western peoples face the ultimate test of history, the ancient forces that once created them and the submerged archetypes that once shaped them are bound to resurface — even if only at the *moment suprême* of their *mors triumphalis*. Jorjani not only views these forces and archetypes through the prism of the oldest strata of Indo-European mythology, but also points to their epistemological relevance in relation to cutting edge transhumanist and 'supernatural' technologies. Jorjani's uniquely specialized knowledge in abstract and applied parapsychology allows him to historically contextualize the rising hybrid technologies of cybernetics, bioinformatics, artificial intelligence and psychotronics. Much of the content of Jorjani's *Prometheus and Atlas* is devoted to these subjects — and reads better than most literary science fiction. In the final analysis, this pioneering exploration of transhumanist-futurist technology may very well turn out to be *Prometheus and Atlas'* primary philosophical achievement. A substantial secondary achievement may be found in the way in which it reintroduces Western thinkers to the historic relevance of the archaic Iranian Tradition for the Western Tradition as a whole: *Prometheus and Atlas* re-appropriates their long-suppressed common heritage. Jorjani rightly considers the re-appropriation of this common Indo-European heritage — 'Aryan' in its original etymological sense of 'noble' — as a vital precondition for achieving a new and sustainable Western metapolitical and geopolitical worldview. This stance — which must overcome the historical association of the 'Aryan' archetype with the failed political experiments of 20th century — is directly relevant to the emerging Western identitarian movement. It is the contention of this chapter that *Prometheus and Atlas* provides a valuable contribution to the metapolitical discourse of this movement.

Given Jorjani's stated opposition to Perennial Philosophy, a Traditionalist approach to *Prometheus and Atlas*, as chosen for this chapter, may seem somewhat incongruous, but it should be remembered that Jorjani himself recommends the *dialectic* approach as an essential tool of Western philosophy. If Western civilization is to shift into its final culminating and defining phase — provided it is to survive at all — a *synthesis* of Tradition and Modernity must be assumed to be imminent. The historical *va banque* course of Western Modernity, now openly evident in the wholesale ethnic displacement of the native Western peoples and the extremist neo-liberal globalism implemented by the Cultural Nihilist hostile elite, clearly points in the direction of an approaching crisis. The author of this article — tracing the development of Western Modernity from a Traditionalist perspective and effectively complementing Jorjani's Archaeofuturist perspective on the impending 'World State of Emergency' — has pointed out this possible historic synthesis in his own work, *The Sunset of Tradition*. It is this tantalizing possibility of a superlative self-renewal of Western civilization — against historical probability, even against civilizational fate itself — that requires the few authentic thinkers who still survive in the Dark Age of Western civilization to study the signs of a possible new Golden Dawn. From a Traditionalist perspective, Jorjani's work represents one of the first attempts in Western philosophy to cross the approaching 'event horizon' of Western history. In Traditionalist symbolism this crossing is also expressed as the return of a 'death star' at the turning of the cycle of Sacred Time: this return indicates a macro-cosmic Nemesis that cleanses the human microcosm. Thus, the concept of 'Nibiru returning' — a fringe 'conspiracy theory' with esoteric overtones — contains an unlikely element of truth.

The Postmodern Prometheus

> *Sail forth — steer for the deep waters only...*
> *For we are bound where mariner has not yet dared to go,*
> *And we will risk the ship, ourselves and all.*
>
> — Walt Whitman

It is important that a discussion of the metapolitical relevance of *Prometheus and Atlas* for the identitarian movement be preceded by a brief sketch of its philosophical background. If the identitarian movement wants to be more than a political mayfly, then it needs a solid metapolitical basis. If the identitarian movement proves unable to outgrow short-sighted political pragmatism and superficial ethno-nationalist rhetoric, then it is doomed to be consigned to the rubbish heap of history. That fate would deprive the Western peoples of their best — and probably last — chance to survive the imminent crisis of Western Modernity. It is with this reality in mind that this and the following sections will briefly sketch the wider philosophical background to Jorjani's work. This section will give its Traditionalist context; the following section will give its Archaeofuturist context.

From a Traditionalist perspective, Jorjani's trailblazing work contains many 'risky' ideas. Some of these are directly relevant to the foundational tenets of Traditionalist thought. Apart from the fact that daring exploration is entirely legitimate in any substantive philosophical *début*, however, it is necessary to state that Jorjani's ideas must be understood as *useful* and *necessary*. The Traditionalist School, founded by Guénon and reaching its apogee in Evola, has arrived at its end station in the work of Seyyed Hossein Nasr: it is now history. Beyond its hermeneutical functionality Traditionalism is now reduced to an esoteric discourse and an apolitical worldview. Its ideas and ideals can only survive and thrive when they are incorporated in — and transformed by — future forms of philosophy and historiography. They can only be incorporated into new thought architectures, such as Archaeofuturism and those grander philosophies and arts that lie beyond Archaeofuturism, in as far as they stand the test of time. But until these grander philosophies and arts have fully materialized, Traditionalist thought will remain the highest standard against which new ideas and ideals can be measured. Thus, it is particularly important to apply this standard to two of Jorjani's core ideas, viz. his analyses of (1) the emergent civilization of a 'New Atlantis' and (2) the meta-historical position of the remnant Abrahamic religions.

(1) Jorjani's sketch of a future Atlantean world order — mirroring the titanic nature, the cosmopolitan trajectory and the daemonic powers of ancient Atlantis — philosophically contextualizes the dangers of heaven-storming cultural universalism and technological ecocide: these are the exact features of the cultural and natural destruction caused by the

'New World Order' as it has spread outward from the Anglophone shores of the Atlantic since the fall of the Soviet Union. The transformation of the proto-Atlantean New World Order into something not merely destructive is the greatest geopolitical challenge of the contemporary Western world. Jorjani's subtle stance on an alternative Atlantean project reminds all critics of the New World Order and the Cultural Nihilist hostile elite that there can be no retreat into primitive pre-Modernity. If Western civilization is to survive in a cultural-historically recognizable form, it will be necessary to incorporate, harness and master the technological sciences of Modernity: these sciences will have to be tamed and overcome. Russian Eurasianists, as well as Western identitarians, would be well advised to study the archetypal dynamics of 'Atlantean Modernity' uncovered by Jorjani. In this respect, Jorjani's analysis of the 'Atlantean' metamorphosis of Japan in the wake of the atomic bombings of 1945, resulting in the materially hybridized and psychologically deracinated culture of contemporary Japan, contains an important warning. It reminds identitarian critics of the globalist New World Order — now faltering under internal dissent in its Western heartland — of the awesome physical power of their enemy. The ultimate resort of the Cultural Nihilist hostile elite to sheer brute violence must be taken for granted — and it is the wounded snake that bites deepest. The Western hostile elite, inhabiting a mental bubble that is ethically as well as cogitatively divorced from reality, can be expected to resort to increasingly irrational means to hold on to its crumbling power. As its projected 'end of history' fails to materialize and as it faces resurgent geopolitical opposition, it may resort to all-out 'decapitation' strategies against its international and domestic enemies. As its 'ethnic replacement' projects run into determined identitarian resistance in the Western homelands, it may resort to violently totalitarian strategies against its domestic opposition — perhaps even adopting an artificial 'civil war' strategy aimed at the annihilation of the native Western population as a whole. A dispassionate reading of Modern history teaches that Modernity did not defeat Tradition through superior philosophy, 'soft power' persuasion or materialist-hedonist consensus. In the final analysis, it has only succeeded through 'black magic' military technology applied with ruthless inhumanity: this is the most obvious lesson of Jorjani's 'Promethium Sky over Hiroshima'. Thus, a 'Jorjanian' — deep archaeological and mythological— reading of Modern history is particularly relevant to the emerging outer and inner resistance to the New World Order. The rising 'anti-thalassocratic' Eurasian movement, which is gathering pace in Russia and Eastern Europe, already gives evidence of commensurate awareness, as visible in Dugin's concept of the 'Last War of the World Island'. The rising Western identitarian movements would similarly be well advised to give serious thought to Jorjani's reading of Modern history: the looming spectres of totalitarian repression, enforced colonization, native societal dissolution and civil war call not only for strong nerves and steely determination, but also for cool-headed calculus and rational anticipatory strategies.

(2) Jorjani's sketch of the old Abrahamic religions as outdated megalomaniacal schemes for human enslavement and subjugation, based on the supernatural interventions by inhuman — ultimately malevolent — spirit forces, may be considered an 'activist' Archaeofuturist restatement of the Traditionalist thesis that nearly all the remaining institutional 'religions' of the contemporary world are effectively equivalent to Modernist inversions — and perversions — of the authentic religions of the long-lost world of Tradition. The difference is that Jorjani assumes that these religions have always been negative spirit forces, while Traditionalism assumes their origins to have been positively powered and anagogically directed. But from a Traditionalist perspective, it is equally true that, while on a private and esoteric level, traces of these authentic religions may have retained a degree of existential spiritual relevance, on a collective and exoteric level, they are almost all subject to the Dark Age degeneracy and subversion. Abstractly, the remnants of these religions may have retained a certain 'commemorative value', but concretely the historical closure of the Transcendental realm during the Modern Age has caused these 'inverted religions' to become 'possessed' by *subhuman* forces, operating in a psychological void of collective narcissism and feeding off cross-cultural

resentments. Thus, without questioning private religious convictions and without doubting sincere religious adherence, it is important to recognize the generally downward direction of organized and institutional religion under the contemporary aegis of 'latter-day' Modernity. Jorjani recognizes that, by and large, the 'false religions' of the contemporary world effectively constitute 'demonically possessed' counterfeits: programmes for socio-political manipulation and bio-evolutionary group strategies for primitive peoples. As a committed Iranian nationalist, Jorjani's belligerent stance against the contemporary Abrahamic religions is obviously inspired by Iran's highly traumatic historic experience with militant forms of political Islam. His vision of a Promethean rebellion against the false 'one true god', the 'god' propagated by pseudo-religions such as atavistic pseudo-Islam, may be understood against this background: any Iranian who is truly aware of the great past of Imperial Iran can be forgiven for resenting the socio-political primitivism imposed by its current pseudo-Islamic usurpers. Nevertheless, Jorjani's core argument remains valid: the opposition between the mentally 'closed' atavism of 'inverted religions' (as dominant among the primitive nations of Asia and Africa) and the Faustian 'openness' of Western Modernity (as dominant among the developed nations of Europe and America) is undoubtedly the core dialectic driving contemporary global metapolitics and geopolitics. By explicitly recognizing the 'demonic' quality of this contest, Jorjani's Archaeofuturist 'dialectic' analysis validates the Traditionalist thesis that Dark Age Modernity, although operating through human agents, human ideas and human institutions, is of an ultimately *non-human* origin (Jorjani uses the term *Luciferian*), geared to *in-human*, diabolical interests.

Thus, by Traditionalist standards, Jorjani's work is epistemologically valid. The next step is to determine its position within the framework of contemporary philosophy and its relevance for identitarian metapolitics.

ARCHAEOFUTURISM RISING

The higher the cause, the less important is the number of its supporters.
An army is needed to defend a nation,
but only one man is needed to defend an idea.

— NICOLÁS GÓMEZ DÁVILA

In metapolitical terms, Jorjani's work represents yet another—very substantial—breach in the dominant Postmodern ideological discourse of Cultural Nihilism, which is characterized by secular nihilism, globalist neo-liberalism, narcissist hyper-individualism and extreme culture relativism. Metapolitically, Jorjani's work can be located in the—admittedly rather vague—spectrum of 'Archaeofuturism', a philosophical school historically related to what is ironically termed the 'Dark Enlightenment'. Both terms are essentially misnomers, most frequently applied in a disparaging way by ideological critics of the supposedly 'anti-democratic' and 'reactionary' thinkers and movements that they are meant to cover; but these terms are nonetheless useful as provisional markers. From a Traditionalist perspective, both movements are—inevitably, given their Postmodern subsoil—ideological hybrids. They tend to engage with particular aspects of Modernity (technological achievement, scientific exploration, futurist aesthetics) while rejecting its nihilistic, materialistic and relativistic ideologies and attitudes. It would be more accurate to say that these movements tend to be interested in 'timeless', rather than 'archaic' alternatives to these ideologies and attitudes. They tend to reject the Enlightenment premises of Modernity precisely because they associate these premises with spiritual and intellectual *darkness* rather with *light*. In this regard, Archaeofuturism and the Dark Enlightenment share considerable ground with Traditionalist thought, which views the Modern Age as the equivalent of a cosmic Dark Age (the Christian 'End Times', the Hindu 'Kali Yuga', the Spenglerian 'Winter Time'). They differ from Traditionalism, however, insofar as their metapolitical discourse tends to be operational: it provides a basis not only for activist consensus-breaking, but also for revolutionary identitarian politics. In other words, Archaeofuturism and the Dark Enlightenment have the potential to expand into fully operational socio-political ideologies and into effective political programmes. This potential is visible in the manifold crossovers from Archaeofuturist and Dark Enlightenment thought into the Western identitarian movement.

Throughout the last decades, the institutional and academic disciplines of the humanities and social sciences have lost virtually all credibility and respect among the young generation throughout the West — and rightly so. The anti-rational hallucinations and 'Social Justice Warrior' activisms triggered by Cultural Nihilist ideology have caused scientific standards and intellectual integrity to give way to politically correct dogmas. The deliberate 'dumbing down' imposed by hyper-democratic mass education has eliminated basic quality standards. The invasion of 'affirmative action' appointees has resulted in an 'idiocratic' tyranny by an incompetent and resentful cabal of 'gender' and 'minority' activists. The institutional and academic disciplines of the humanities and social sciences are now effectively reduced to tools of ideological censorship and intellectual repression in the service of the Cultural Nihilist *hostile elite*. Their politically 'embedded' and comfortably tenured representatives are now fully incorporated into this hostile elite: they have sold out the prestige and legacy of one of the oldest and most precious Traditional institutions of the Western world: the Academy. The academic elite is now divided into two parts: on the one hand, there are the 'technocrats' representing the exact sciences, still credible within their narrow specializations but lacking public policy commitment and meta-political authority, and on the other hand, there are the pseudo-scientists who have usurped the former humanities and social sciences and who now effectively function as the 'priestly class' within the Cultural Nihilist establishment. As long as they limit themselves to the mundane tasks of technological research and industrial development, the 'technocrats' are tolerated as part of the Postmodern academic elite — they include the last remnants of the former white-race all-male intellectual *avant garde* of Western civilization. The rest of the old Academy, however, is now ruled by resentful political correctness appointees, feeding off the decaying remnants of the humanities and social sciences: these power-hungry *homines novi* — 'second wave feminists', 'gender activists', 'diversity representatives' and other assorted Social Justice Warriors — have now usurped the societal position formerly held by the now-extinct Western Church. These new high priests of Cultural Nihilism are working hand in hand with the journalistic and political cartels to maintain, deepen and expand the Postmodern socio-political status quo across the Western world and they are increasingly doing so in an openly dictatorial fashion. Media censorship and politically correct witch hunts are now reaching epidemic proportions — these are sure signs of the rising desperation of the Cultural Nihilist hostile elite.

With the fading of the Brave New World myopias and utopias of the baby boomer generation and with the rise of a hard-eyed, digitally liberated and politically inoculated new generation, Cultural Nihilism is now about to face its historical Nemesis. Increasingly, the counterfeit 'academics' of the Cultural Nihilist hostile elite are publicly recognized for what they are: cowardly mercenaries, who owe their hollow status and privilege to a collective betrayal of all forms of authentic community, authentic identity and authentic knowledge. Jordan Peterson's ongoing exposure of the Western academic 'anti-elite' is following up on Charlotte Iserbyt's earlier exposure of the Western primary and secondary 'anti-educational' system. Together they expose the larger Cultural Nihilist agenda of ideological indoctrination and deliberate 'dumbing down'. These exponents of the incoming tide of a Post-Postmodernist 'New Realism' are harbingers of the impending demise of Cultural Nihilism. The hostile elite's desperate effort to shore up its tottering Cultural Nihilist ideology of secular nihilism, globalist neo-liberalism, narcissist hyper-individualism and culture relativism is now taking on openly totalitarian forms through violent crackdowns ('Charlottesville'), workplace harassment (Google's 'diversity drive') and digital censorship (Alt-right's 'deplatforming'), but it is ultimately doomed. A determined strategy of media blackout, as in the case of the Cologne 'rape jihad', the British 'grooming gangs', the French 'hell of the *tournantes*' and the South African 'farm killings', may artificially prolong the life of the Cultural Nihilist hostile elite, but cannot save it indefinitely. Politically, Cultural Nihilism will be simply swamped by the rising tide of the Western identitarian movement. Intellectually, it is already dead in the water—the first waves of Archaeofuturism have already drowned it. Jorjani's contribution to the long-overdue euthanasia of Cultural Nihilism is considerable: as co-founder of the Alt-right movement and as Editor-in-Chief of Arktos Publishing—but above all as an Archaeofuturist thinker in his own right. He has thus far done as much as is humanly possible to further the identitarian resistance to Cultural Nihilism. It is now time for all identitarian thinkers and activists to ask whether they can sincerely say the same about themselves—and to measure the progress of the Western identitarian movement as a whole.

Killing by silence

Le silence. Les camps de reconcentration au Transvaal (Jean Veber, 1901), L'assiette de beure (French Anarchist periodical). One of the earliest examples of a government-sponsored media black-out to cover up genocidal practices was the British white-wash of the ethnic cleansing of the Afrikaner civilian population during the Second Boer War (1899–1902), when no less than 26,000 defenceless women and children died in British concentration camps. The Western hostile elite has imposed a *mokusatsu* (Japanese: 'killing by silence') policy with regard to ongoing White Genocide.

Μολὼν λαβέ

And reap his old reward,
The blame of those ye better,
The hate of those ye guard...

— RUDYARD KIPLING

The young intellectuals of the West are now abandoning the sinking ship of the institutional humanities and social sciences *en masse*. Even as the old baby boomer elite and their intended feminist and minority successors are still enjoying the comforts and privileges of the upper decks, the supposedly unsinkable *Titanic* of the Western academic cartel is already foundering. Young seekers, students and scholars are already scrambling for the life rafts, but they face a very dark ocean with little or no guidance. Intellectually and ideologically, they are abandoning the doomed *Titanic* of Cultural Nihilism, but they are finding themselves in the very dark and cold waters of an entirely uncharted 'New Realism'. Only a few living intellectual reference points remain available to the *génération identitaire* after the shipwreck of the Postmodern West — a mere handful of institutionally marginalized and journalistically demonized thinkers. In the overseas Anglosphere, these include Kevin MacDonald (1944), Jared Taylor (1951), Jordan Peterson (1962) and Stefan Molyneux (1966). In Europe, these include Alain de Benoist (1943), Roger Scruton (1944), Guillaume Faye (1949), Robert Steuckers (1956) and Aleksandr Dugin (1962). Much courage is required from young people to break the taboo on their work. Throughout the entire West, there are other, lesser-known and unknown writers and activists — those few individuals among the baby boomer and members of generation x who have broken ranks and have had the courage to stand up, who have joined their quest. But still this anti-establishment *avant garde* is pitifully underdeveloped: it is understaffed, underfunded and often forced to operate semi-underground. Against the monstrously powerful army of mercenary journalists, academics, lawyers and politicians that is still at the disposal of the Western hostile elite this small *avant garde* obviously does not stand a chance — but its brave stance will not be forgotten.

But even as they fight their heroic delaying action, these few older generation outposts are providing a precious breathing space during which the young generation of the West can gather and prepare for an all-out final battle with Cultural Nihilism. Shielded by the prolonged rearguard action of the anti-establishment *avant garde*, the Western *génération identitaire* can gear up to avenge the inevitable defeat and heroic sacrifice of their *avant garde*. The formidable and urgent task of mentally preparing and intellectually arming the entire Western *génération identitaire* now requires courageous young scholars to formulate entirely new metapolitical frames and recipes. Jorjani has fully risen to this challenge — his ferocious persecution by the American academic and journalistic establishment bears witness to the cold terror that his work is striking in the heart of the hostile elite. His intellectual validation of archaic cultural archetypes and futurist technological spectres, his iconoclastic realism in matters of ethnicity and identity and his devastating appraisal of the historical trajectory of Western civilization represent an entirely unexpected and unprecedented challenge from a generation that the baby boomers had supposed to have been entirely 'burnt out', i.e. entirely conditioned and deformed by Postmodern Cultural Nihilism. Ironically, Jorjani has inverted the expectations of the Cultural Nihilist academic establishment. Undoubtedly, his 'minority' (part-Iranian) heritage should presumably have guaranteed his political correctness. Undoubtedly, his 'innovative' (parapsychological) specialization should presumably have guaranteed academic vacuousness. Instead, Jorjani has turned out to be a formidable champion of philosophical tradition, authentic identity and intellectual integrity. Without compromising his own Iranian heritage, he has taken his place in the Western philosophical tradition. His work reminds Western thinkers of the fact that the wars between Greeks and Persians of the Ancient World were wars between closely related peoples — even as the World Wars of the 20th century were in fact largely wars between peoples that were closely related in blood, culture and history. Having taken his place in Western philosophy, and having proven his commitment to Western civilization as a whole, Jorjani should be respected when he calls for a re-evaluation of the common Indo-European heritage — and when he demands a place of honour for the long-suffering (Arab-colonized, theocratically suppressed) Iranian people among the Indo-European peoples. Having taken his stance for a redefined and resurrected Indo-European civilization, Jorjani should be recognized as a courageous fighter against its common enemies.

Whether or not Jorjani can be brought down by his 'Social Justice Warrior' enemies still remains to be seen, but the only honourable thing for his former identitarian friends to do is to stand by him in his hour of need. Subjected to 'academic review' after character assassination in the system press and duped by foreign policy intrigue, Jorjani has been shamefully let down by many people in the very identitarian movement he has helped found. Within the identitarian movement, Jorjani's subtle stances on sensitive topics such as ethno-nationalism and Middle Eastern geopolitics may be controversial, but this does not justify vindictive smears and undignified slurs. Within a successful identitarian movement, there will always be space for a wide range of ideologies and worldviews. Totalitarian dogmas and ideological witch hunts risk bringing it down to the unworthy level of its subrational Social Justice Warrior enemies. Thus, from a European Traditionalist perspective within this larger movement, some of Jorjani's ideas may be risky — if not downright dangerous — and some of his ideals may be overly utopian, but they represent *exploratory challenges* rather than *sources of conflict*. From this perspective, the failure of American identitarian publicists and activists to decisively rally around one of their key intellectuals is therefore regrettable. It demonstrates not only the persisting lack of cohesion within the larger Trans-Atlantic identitarian movement — one of the explicit aims of the Alt-Right organization co-founded by Jorjani — but also the intellectual immaturity of this movement as a whole. Thus, it may be useful to briefly revisit Jorjani's *Prometheus and Atlas,* and re-state the key importance of philosophic inquiry and intellectual boldness for the whole Trans-Atlantic identitarian movement. Eventually, the metapolitical position of the movement will be decisive for its political success: a new identitarian Thermopylae requires not only a brave heart, but also a shrewd choice of terrain. The fate of the identitarian movement is intricately bound up with the Archeofuturism revolution that is proposed by the Persian philosopher from Manhattan.

THE SPECTRAL REVOLUTION

There appears to be an archaic force that projects an inexhaustible variety of mythic symbols onto nature, irresistibly framing the world in terms of meaningful relationships. This projection is most commonly expressed in pre-modern cosmologies in terms of 'firmament of Heaven', the boundless ocean of space conceived as a cosmic ordering principle that begins with astronomical certainties and that reiterates these patterns in the nomos, or worldly order, that governs more mundane levels.

— JASON REZA JORJANI,
PROMETHEUS AND ATLAS

The above-given opening statement of Jorjani's first chapter basically conforms to the Traditionalist perception of (macro-micro) cosmic order: it confirms the validity of Jorjani's epistemological premise, realistically recognizing the limits of human perception and conception. Jorjani's concern, however, is with the historic plasticity of human perception — and with the resultant historic alterations in human social and cultural structures. As he sees it, all great revolutions in human history, whether long-term technological, social, cultural or political in nature, depend on such shifts — and the greatest revolution of all of human history is about to take place.

Jorjani describes the threats that impending shifts pose to present socio-political structures in terms of a Spectral Revolution, approaching them from his specialization in paranormal research. Thus, he re-creates the link between the micro-cosmic (natural and human) order and the macro-cosmic (supernatural and superhuman) sphere that has always

been recognized in Traditionalist thought, but which has been systematically ignored in Modernist (what Jorjani terms Cartesian) thought. Jorjani correctly points out that, unlike Modern Western 'culture', Traditional
cultures have always accepted the 'supernatural' phenomena as part and
parcel of the human condition. In fact, the potential dangers and benefits
of direct 'trans-dimensional' disturbances and procedures — including the
intrusion of the past and the future (respectively, *legacies* and *possibilities*
shaping present thoughts and intentions) — into present reality signifi-
cantly shaped the behaviour and mindset of all of pre-Modern humanity.
This accounts for the intangible 'magic' quality that suffuses all Traditional social structures, artworks and belief-systems. In all of recorded history,
it is only Modern humanity that has attempted to break away from this
respectful *modus vivendi* by suppressing the spectral world. Jorjani rightly
emphasizes the relation between epistemological shifts and cognitive marginalization mechanisms, and the relevance of 'spectral' phenomena and
'supernatural' realities to the shifting definition of science and technology.
Thus, most modern technology would count as 'magic' in any Traditional
culture; indeed, much of it would count as 'black magic'. In Traditionalist
hermeneutics (pre-Modern 'natural science', e.g. alchemy) the relation between the natural-human world and the supernatural-superhuman world
was always recognized for what it was: precarious and dangerous. The
lack of an equivalent recognition in Modernist hermeneutics effectively
reduces contemporary scientists to presumptuous 'sorcerer's apprentices'
who are incapable of mastering the forces they are tampering with. From
a Traditionalist perspective, Modernity is simply a *reduced* existential and
perceptual modality, inevitably resulting in spiritual and intellectual implosion — its effects are now most acutely felt in the academic humanities
and social sciences. Jorjani re-states this fact in a highly original Archaeofuturist manner by indicating the inextricable link between Modernist
(historical-materialist) epistemological frames and Modernist (technological) discursive practices. He shows that Modernist historical-materialist 'theories' cannot be tested against Modernist scientific 'facts', because
such 'facts' lack autonomous existence and objective reality outside the

Modernist scientist frame. The inextricable link between Modernist epistemological frames and Modernist discursive practices predetermines the
uncontrolled trajectory of Modern science and technology. It also invali-
dates the 'objectivist' and 'positivist' pretences of the Modern humanities
and social sciences, reducing them to ridiculous post-Wittgensteinian
Sprachspiele.

Jorjani correctly predicts that the impending *Post*-Postmodern
re-definition of the Western knowledge system will require an entirely
new language — and a resort to pre-logical categories. The dynamics of
the transitional phase are vitally important in shaping the future boundaries of a new knowledge system.

> To break new ground in thought, to express ideas for which there is as yet no ap-
> propriate discourse, already existing language must be distorted, misused, beat-
> en into new patterns appropriate to unforeseen situations... A new worldview
> is built only out of fundamental conceptual changes, after which it takes time
> for a new language to be clearly defined in its internal structure. Thus, in tran-
> sitional phases between worldviews, we have to be open to more free-flowing
> discussing with a view to creating 'a language of the future' (Jason Reza Jorjani,
> *Prometheus and Atlas*, 12–13).

From a Traditionalist perspective, this insight refers to the *creative act*
that underpins all authentic forms of cultural palingenesia, a creative act
which is per definition *transcendentally* defined. *In the beginning was the
Word, and the Word was with God, and the Word was God* (John 1:1).
In other words, supernatural and superhuman forces will eventually have
to re-enter the natural and human world in order to break the anachronistic dominance of Western civilization by the Modernist historical
materialism discourse. This increasingly unbearable dominance is predicated on the increasingly unsustainable epistemology of Modernity, as
expressed in exclusively mechanical-scientist and materialistically functional tenets of Copernican cosmology, Darwinian biology and Freudian
psychology. From a meta-historical perspective, these historical materialist 'revolutions' actually represent intellectual 'devolutions' because they
have eliminated the only possible referent point for authentic anagogic

direction: Jorjani's 'supernature', better known to the world of Tradition as 'transcendence'. Jorjani points to the desperate manner in which various Modernist thinkers have attempted to maintain this highly artificial status quo in Western thought: in his view, Descartes' rationalist exclusion of the occult, Kant's philosophical rejection of Swedenborg and Robespierre's political suppression of the *Culte de la raison* are conscious attempts at deliberate (self-)censorship.

Jorjani instinctively grasps the impending climax of what the Traditional School terms the 'Crisis of the Modern World' and he manages to couch this awareness in terms of a radical transformation of the human condition (transhumanism) and an ultimate epistemological abyss (parapsychology). With incisive insight, he states that *terror* in the face of this looming Spectral Revolution is the occulted foundation of the entire Modernist (Cartesian) *épistème*. From this perspective, at a certain level, the phenomenon of globalist Postmodernism (the infrastructure of the New World Order and the superstructure of Cultural Nihilism) appears as simple hedonist escapism. Postmodern 'philosophy' — a *contradictio in terminis* if ever there was one — appears as nothing more than a superficially *deconstructive* but ultimately *desperate* feeding off the receding world of Tradition: it is fundamentally unable to cope with epistemic frameworks that are *not* immanently (psycho-socially) pre-structured. Only a ruthlessly iconoclastic Archaeofuturist Revolution can hope to keep up with Jorjani's Spectral Revolution, i.e. the return of macro-cosmic and archetypal (supernatural and superhuman) forces into the natural and human world. Jorjani expresses this impending revolution as the return of Prometheus and Atlas as the titanic spectres of a future *Art* of Science and Technology. This new *Techne* will require a superlative level of human consciousness and spiritual development: it therefore requires the *readmission* of macro-cosmic and archetypal spirit-powers into micro-cosmic human reality.

THE IDENTITARIAN REVOLUTION

Our sensations are mediated by our education as members of a group with the same experience, language, and culture. ... [I]t is only parochialism that makes us suspect that members of very different groups sense the world in the same way. ... [But b]ecause they have systematically different (and internally consistent) sensations in response to the same stimuli, members of different groups do in some sense live in different worlds.

— JASON REZA JORJANI,
PROMETHEUS AND ATLAS

Jorjani approaches the challenge of readmitting 'supernature' into Western civilization through 20th century continental philosophy, which allows him to exploit Bergson's and Heidegger's critical analyses of the experiential limitations of Modernity. In this regard, Jorjani's approach again shows an implicit parallel to the Traditionalist approach of the same problem. Bergson's re-appropriation of intuition and *élan vital* in reaction to the Modernist atrophy of intellectual instinct not only validates Jorjani's Archaeofuturist reintroduction of 'supernature', it also validates the Traditionalist view of Modernity as a perceptual and conceptual 'handicap'. Heidegger's fundamental critique of mechanist scientism as a cause of the artificially reduced spatial-temporal experience of Modern humanity not only validates Jorjani's Archaeofuturist reassertion of primordial 'supernatural' abilities, it also validates the Traditionalist insistence of the essential reality of humanity's 'magic' abilities. The Modern atrophy of these ancient perceptual and conceptual abilities also explains Modern humanity's inability to cope with its own existential identities, which Traditionalist thought holds to be doubly communally and individually specialized according to race, ethnicity, gender, caste and vocation. Only a degree of reappropriation of these abilities will allow a rediscovery, reappropriation and reactivation of these identities.

Having appropriated Heidegger's concepts of specialized time (the bounded time-horizon of *Kulturkreisen*) and specialized space (the sheltering spatial horizon of *Blut und Boden*) as vital preconditions for every authentic form of world-historical human existence, Jorjani discusses the danger of world-encompassing, run-away technological science by pointing out its exceptional archetypal power to subdue the whole of the natural world and all human cultures. This power allows it to dissolve specialized time and specialized space through anticipatory projection and predictive models: it tends to alienate humans from nature, from culture and from community. At this point, Jorjani's Archaeofuturist analysis matches the classic Traditionalist thesis that the Modern scientist worldview represents a grave danger to all forms of authentic identity. It is precisely at this point that Jorjani's *Prometheus and Atlas* offers its most powerful metapolitical contribution to the identitarian movement: it offers a devastating philosophical 'counter-deconstruction' of the Cultural Nihilist myth of culture relativism — and it restates the incalculable value of the authentic Western identity. Jorjani explicitly stresses the importance of reappropriating what lies at the core of Western identity: the Indo-European cultural substratum historically known as 'Aryan'. Proceeding from his unencumbered Iranian heritage, he courageously reclaims the term 'Aryan' for the archetypal essence of Western identity, as represented in its original etymological meaning: 'noble'. In doing so, he is able to re-explore the spiritual root identity and cultural-historical heritage of the Indo-European peoples (cf. Chapter 4). From the Archaeofuturist as well as the Traditionalist perspective this identity and this heritage are primarily spiritual in nature: they must be *earned* and *conquered*. It is up to the Indo-European *génération identitaire* to claim its rightful inheritance so that the Indo-European people may again *inhabit* the *specialized* worlds that are their rightful heritage. Outside authentic identity there can be no authentic knowledge; only if the *génération identitaire* re-experiences authentic identity can they hope to gain empowering knowledge. Power starts where taboo ends: the breaking of the Cultural Nihilist stranglehold on authentic identity is the first Rubicon that the Identitarian Revolution will have to cross. It is now up to the Western *génération identitaire* to boldly follow in the footsteps of its philosophical pioneers — and to stake an existential claim in the future that lies beyond the imminent event horizon of Western history.

De l'audace, encore de l'audace, toujours de l'audace et la Patrie sera sauvée!

CHAPTER NINE

Twelve Rules for the Archaeofuturist Revolution

accipe quam primum; brevis est occasio lucri

— MARTIAL

DIAGNOSIS

adhuc coelum volvitur

— ERASMUS

RULE ONE. *RECOGNIZE THE PATHOLOGY:* UNDER-
stand the *Four Political Realities* that confront the Western peoples at the imminent height of the Crisis of the Modern World
(cf. Chapter 1). These Four Political Realities are: global climate change
(industrial ecocide), technological transhumanism (socio-economic de-
humanization), ethnic replacement (demographic inundation) and social
implosion — realities that are increasingly likely to converge into the single catastrophe of a final 'hellstorm' scenario. The most urgent of these realities is ethnic replacement, but the most fundamental is social implosion
(cf. Chapter 6).

(2) Rule Two. *Recognize the disease*: understand *Cultural Nihilism* (cf. Preface) as a historical-materialist and secular-humanist worldview that has its origin in the Early Modern complex of Renaissance, Reformation and Enlightenment. The Four Political Realities derive their contemporary power from the ideological monopoly of Cultural Nihilism within the public discourse of the Postmodern West. The sub-intellectual charge of Cultural Nihilism has caused the Western peoples to lapse into a state of psycho-historical trance and urban-hedonist stasis, resulting in cultural-historical self-annihilation.

(3) Rule Three. *Recognize the pathogen*: understand the *hostile elite* (cf. Chapter 6). The Western hostile elite is the *vector* (the 'carrier') of Cultural Nihilism: it arises by social implosion (class warfare, feminization, xenification), it thrives on cultural oikophobia (globalism, universalism, cosmopolitanism) and it dominates in political idiocracy (hyper-democracy, hyper-liberalism, hyper-humanism). The political power of the hostile elite resides in sub-democratic, trans-national institutions. The Western peoples are in a de facto state of *alieni juris* after the supercession of national borders (Schengen), national sovereignty (EU, UN), national currencies (Euro), national defence (NATO) and national legislation (international laws and treaties). The inevitable results of this transnational 'alien occupation' are: economic 'fracking' (neo-liberal 'privatization'), collective debt-slavery ('sovereign debt'), state-sponsored mass-usury (high finance dictatorship), institutional corruption (elusive political 'cartels'), judicial chaos (bureaucratic abuse of power) and socio-cultural self-annihilation (mass-immigration). The globalist power of the hostile elite is characterized by a sociological dynamic of self-reinforcing and self-radicalizing feedback loops. The 'democratic mandate' of the hostile elite provides it with an irresistible quantitative superiority: it continually mobilizes and absorbs new 'repressed' groups ('women', 'gays', 'minorities', 'refugees'). This hyper-democratic 'race to the bottom' causes a vicious cycle of continuing radicalization within the hostile elite. These nihilist-collectivist dynamics determine the increasingly overt ultimate incarnation of the hostile elite: a transnational totalitarian regime. This totalitarian regime, and the Cultural Nihilist worldview on which it is based, deserves to be eradicated from the face of the earth — even to the point of an irrevocable *damnatio memoriae*.

Only the ruthless pursuit of the Archaeofuturist Revolution can provide the appropriate therapy for this deadly disease.

THERAPY

...for verily I say unto you, If ye have faith as a grain of mustard seed,
ye shall say to this mountain, Remove hence to yonder place;
and it shall remove; and nothing shall be impossible unto you.

— MATTHEW 17:20.

(4) Rule Four. *Recognize the crisis*: accept the consequences of the *Ernstfall* (cf. Chapter 2). The *Machtergreifung* of the Cultural Nihilist hostile elite confronts the Western people with the ultimate *Ernstfall*: this requires an *Ausnahmezustand* to facilitate a *controlled descent*—an 'emergency landing'. An effective fight against the hyper-democratic, hyper-individualist and 'idiocratic' excesses of Cultural Nihilism requires a fundamental reform of nearly all contemporary institutional, judicial, economic and social structures. Externally, the restoration of authentic state sovereignty requires the wholesale abolition of present transnational institutions. Internally, the restoration of authentic national communities requires the (re-)introduction of socio-political hierarchies and holistic-anagogic visions. At the same time, the toxic legacy of over half a century Cultural Nihilism requires pragmatic *Realpolitik*. The residue of mass-immigration (ethnic minorities) and multiculturalism (mixed families) requires carefully calibrated policies, with correctly calculated dosages of mutually reinforcing medication, including (voluntary) resettlement, segregation and assimilation (cf. Chapter 4). The highly poisonous residue of social feminization (informal matriarchy) and social deconstruction (broken families) requires finely attuned 'detox' programmes. The most effective cure for the Crisis of the Modern West is the psychological internalization of the necessity of societal reforms. In this regard, the restoration of the transcendental referent of Western civilization is of vital importance. From a Christian perspective, this means the restoration of metaphysical *faith*—the kind of faith that moves mountains.

(5) Rule Five. *Recognize the treatment*: accept the side-effects of the restoration of the *Nomos*. The only legitimate aim of an *Ausnahmezustand* can be the restoration of the Nomos, viz. of an authentic hierarchical order based on transcendental reference. The restoration of the Nomos is only possible on the basis of individual acceptance of a super-individual *anagogical direction* of society as a whole, i.e. individual acceptance of the *holistic structuring* of society. This requires an individual willingness and ability to tolerate *hierarchy*: the natural hierarchy according to age, gender and talent as well as the cultural hierarchy of caste, ethnicity and vocation. The most effective cure for the grotesque hubris and demonic ideology of *liberté, égalité, fraternité* is the psychological re-activation of the ana-gogical-holistic compensatory mechanisms that are built into all authen-tic Traditions. In this regard, again, the restoration of the transcendental referent of Western civilization is of vital importance. From a Christian perspective, this means the restoration of metaphysical *hope* — hope that what is humanly impossible, may be possible in other ways.

(6) Rule Six. *Recognize the surgeon*: accept the authority of the restored Katechon. The authority of archetypal institutions such as the Monarchy, the Church, the Nobility and the Academy rests on their function as Kate-chon, i.e. their guardianship with respect to the Nomos. To the extent that they have been weakened, they must be strengthened. To the extent that they have been lost, they must be re-invented. The re-definition, re-con-struction and re-activation of the Katechon is the *primary task of the Ar-chaeofuturist Revolution*: this implies the re-introduction of the Primacy of the Political Sphere and the abolition of the Primacy of the Economic Sphere. This requires the recognition of authentic Charisma and authentic Auctoritas because the legitimacy of the Katechon rests on the transcen-dental vocation that is expressed through Charisma and Auctoritas. The regressive 'anti-theocracy' of Cultural Nihilism, with its 'separation of church and state', undermines this legitimacy and therefore fails to pro-vide a viable political dispensation. In this regard, once more, the res-toration of the transcendental referent of Western civilization is of vital importance. From a Christian perspective, this means the restoration of

metaphysical *love* — the super-natural love that inspires dedication, loyalty and honour.

(*) *Note that in Appendix A the interested reader can find Article 7 of the United Nations' Declaration on the Rights of Indigenous Peoples. Thus, even within current international law, there is sufficient legal basis for legitimate resistance to the ongoing ethnic replacement of the Western peoples — and for the judicial persecution of Western regime members that politically facilitate this replacement.*

Dietary Restrictions

And why beholdest thou the mote that is in thy brother's eye, but considerest not the beam that is in thy own eye? Or how wilt thou say to thy brother, Let me pull out the mote out of thine eye; and, behold, a beam if in thine own eye? Thou hypocrite, first cast out the beam out of thine own eye; and then shalt thou see clearly to cast out the mote out of thy brother's eye.

— Matthew 7:3–5

(7) Rule Seven. *Resist the temptation of conspiracy theories*: take responsibility for your own predicament. Even if the Crisis of the Modern West is partially shaped by external 'enemies of the West', its cause resides in its internal dynamics. The fact that *outside* forces — evolutionary group strategies (e.g. 'Inverted Judaism'), occultist elite organizations (e.g. Freemasonry), subversive ideological programmes (e.g. 'Cultural Marxism') — are able to negatively affect the Western peoples essentially reflects a decay *within*. The present predicament of Western civilization — its existential spiritual crisis, its historical-materialist ideological bankruptcy, its deep psycho-social regression — will not be alleviated by scapegoat mechanisms and conspiracy theories. In the final analysis, the efficacy of the *outer* immune system of the West depends on its *inner* state of health.

(8) Rule Eight. *Resist the temptation of facile Islamophobia*: see Islam for what it objectively is. It should be remembered that there is a profound

difference between Islam as an authentic Tradition, which historically prevails among the people of the Middle East and North Africa, and Islam as
Modern evolutionary group strategy. From a Traditionalist perspective, the
recent spread of so-called 'contemporary Islam' — nominally 'Islamic' populations, 'political Islam', 'Islamist' terrorism — into the heartlands of the
West is a purely *socio-biological phenomenon*: it does not disqualify Islam as
an authentic Tradition. The fact that this recent spread leaves the term 'Islam' superficially charged with residual Traditional prestige, is highly mis-
leading because it actually reduces the term to a mere ethnic identity marker for migrating African and Asian populations. Theoretically speaking,
'political Islam' is a contradiction in terms, but in practice it is highly effective because it serves to 'weaponize' ethnic identity. The contemporary use
of the term 'Islamic' among migrant populations provides a heterogeneous
conglomerate of ethnic identities with a common origin myth: it provides
their colonization projects with a false imprint of 'supernatural' sanction.
The common Western association of 'Islam' with an inability to innovate
('fatalism'), a lack of self-discipline ('primitivism') and irredeemable obtuse-
ness ('arrogance') does not reflect the actual authentic Tradition of Islam,
but rather the primitive ethnic substrate that carries this Tradition in the
Modern world. From a Traditionalist perspective, every authentic Tradition — including Islam — is superior to every Modernist social construct.
This is proven by the fact that only peoples that adhere to authentic Tradition survive in human history. The Western peoples have not been brought
to the brink of extinction by Traditional Islam, but by modern secularism.

Rehabilitation

There only exists one true form of vulgarity: not to accept who we are.
— Nicolás Gómez Dávila

(9) Rule Nine. *Restore your identity*: rediscover your authentic essence, as
expressed in your natural identities of phenotype, age and in your cultural

identities of ethnicity, caste and vocation. All authentic forms of identity represent a precious heritage: their rehabilitation — the reversal of their Cultural Nihilist deconstruction — is the *primary aim of the Archaeofuturist Revolution*. Cultural Nihilist deconstruction aims at the founding of an anti-identitarian 'dictatorship of the proletariat' and at the destruction of all that is still strong, healthy, wise, good and beautiful in the world. Its ideology of 'manufacturability' undermines and vulgarizes: it replaces gender identity by 'transgenderism', religious identity by narcissistic 'self-expression', ethnic identity by oikophobic 'universalism' and natural hierarchy by atavist collectivism. The restoration of authentic identity requires an authentic communal vision, i.e. a vision with anagogical direction, holistic perspective and synergic dynamics.

(10) Rule Ten. *Restore your ethics*: recover your ethical superiority. Ethical superiority is the *primary strength of the Archaeofuturist Revolution*. The rubble to which Western civilization has been reduced after half a century of Cultural Nihilism proves the final bankruptcy of the 'humanist', 'universalist' and 'cosmopolitan' discourse of the hostile elite: ethics and morality are now the exclusive domain of its enemies, including the Archaeofuturist movement. This movement can now occupy the moral high ground that was vacated by the hostile elite: it can stand for *real* animal rights (against the bio-industry and ritual slaughter), *real* workers' rights (against neo-Victorian working conditions and social-Darwinist exploitation), *real* women's rights (allowing women to be wives, mothers and grandmothers instead of merely workers, consumers and voters) and *real* human rights (the right to authentic identity and a place in the sun). But ethical superiority obliges: it demands a just and equitable resolution of the toxic legacy of Cultural Nihilism, i.e. a correct treatment of its legacies of multicultural demography (ethnic minorities, mixed families), materialist conditioning (consumerism, criminalization), socio-cultural feminization (emancipated women, broken families) and psycho-social implosion (pandemic addictions, collective narcissism).

(11) Rule Eleven. *Restore your ethnicity*: recognize your ethnic roots. There are various perspectives from which to scientifically describe and

analyze a people — or any ethnic group. From a bio-evolutionary perspective, every ethnic group can be formally described as a 'polygenetically homophenic group' (definition Alfred Vierling, 1985) and functionally as a *stigmergic super-organism*, characterized by self-organizing networks, swarm intelligence and synergic surplus value. Cooperative reproduction strategies, labour diversifications and altruistic defence mechanisms allow ethnic groups to channel energy into self-surpassing creativity. From a sociological perspective, every ethnic group represents a uniquely specialized form of collective transcendence, varying in complexity from primitive totemism to highly stylized messianism. The eusocial implication of these combined perspectives is the obligation to pursue solidarity and unity at a super-individual level — and to the functional acceptance of the sometimes harsh reality of natural and cultural differences within and without the ethnic group. But these scientific perspectives are actually nothing but vague reflections of the supra-scientific reality of ethnicity. In the final analysis, any ethnicity stands or falls with the intuitive intentionality and transcendental experience of its members, without this intentionality and without this experience the people will cease to exist.

(*)Note that in Appendix B the interested reader can find two excerpts from Nietzsche's Untimely Meditations, translated into English by the author, with direct relevance to the issue of scientific and ideological 'modesty' as regards authentic ethnic identity.

Prognosis

Then shall thy light break forth as the morning, and thine health shall spring forth speedily: and thy righteousness shall go before thee, the glory of the Lord shall be thy reward. Then shalt thou call, and the Lord shall answer; thou shalt cry, and he shall say, Here I am. If thou take away from the midst of thee, the yoke, the putting forth of the finger, and speaking vanity; And if thou draw out thy soul to the hungry, and satisfy the afflicted soul; then shall thy light rise in obscurity, and thy darkness be as the noon day...

— Isaiah 58:8–10

(12) Rule Twelve. *Strive for the Golden Dawn*: prepare for the *Katharsis* that precedes the re-introduction of the *Nomos*. The Golden Dawn means this: to fulfil pledges that are archaic as well as futuristic and to realize possibilities that are very old as well as brand new. The Katharsis that it implies is the *realization of the Archaeofuturist Revolution*. Elements of this Katharsis are: *Jubilee* ('collective debt remission' — an end to the usurious dictatorship of the banks), *Amnesty* ('collective pardon' — an end to party politics and social divisions), *Manumissio* ('liberation of slaves' — the repatriation of guest workers and displaced persons), *Gaia Principle* ('bio-ethical revolution' — the end to industrial ecocide and bio-industry) and *Purification* (ritual cleansing — the re-consecration of desecrated places). The resulting *restitutio in integrum* implies the final fulfilment of the destiny of the Western peoples. All that counts is to strive towards this — irrespective of success or failure in the here and now.

Postscript: 'Aṣḥāb al-Kahf (The Seven Sleepers)

When the youths took refuge in the Cave, they said, 'Our Lord!
Grant us a mercy from Yourself, and help us on to rectitude in our affair.'
So We put them to sleep in the Cave for several years.
Then We aroused them that We might know
which of the two groups better reckoned the period they had stayed.

— Quran 18:10–12

Traditionalist thought can provide the Archaeofuturist Revolution with these Ten Rules. It can offer insight into Postmodern Cultural Nihilism: provide a diagnosis, prescribe a therapy, project a rehabilitation trajectory and give a general prognosis. By preparing the ground for the Archaeofuturist Revolution — and pointing it in a general direction — it can contribute to the fall of Cultural Nihilism and to the arrival of the Golden Dawn. What it cannot do, however, is to provide assurances: history cannot be forced and the future cannot be predicted. The question of whether the Archaeofuturism and the Golden Dawn will even take place during the 21st century — and, if so, when, where and how — cannot be answered on the basis of mere human thought. It is very well possible that the long night of the Dark Age has only just begun and that Traditionalist thoughts can only serve as acts of witnessing. It is very well possible that Western civilization is doomed to an undiluted 'descent into hell' — and utter destruction. But in that case, Western Tradition still has a use: its doctrine of *mors triumphalis* still gives the Fall of the West an ultimate meaning. Nietzsche, the Classical Modern prophet of Postmodern Nihilism, incorporated this doctrine in his concept of the *ewige Wiederkunft*. From a philosophical perspective, this *ewige Wiederkunft* represents nothing less than a reference to the Traditionalist principle that all macrocosmic archetypes are bound to cyclically resurface in microcosmic realities.

Thus, the macrocosmic archetypes that are expressed through Western civilization — Bringer of *Evangelion*, Creator of *Nomos*, Master of *Techne* — are bound to somehow survive and return. But whether or not these archetypes — and all other archetypes that have been displaced by Modernity — are still to be found somewhere on Earth during the night of the Dark Age is a mystery. Deep into the Modern Era, great prophets, genius scholars and inspired artists have occupied themselves with this mystery; they have touched upon the theme of the Great Occultation of the Sacred and the Numinous (definition Rudolf Otto, 1917). It is this 'Occultation of Revelation' (definition Alexander Wolfheze, 2018) that has continued to inspire a handful of seers and pilgrims until deep into the 20th century. They have continued the age-old doubly spiritual and physical quest for the hidden earthly hide-outs — often thought of as literally located underground — of the 'Discarded Image' (definition Clive Lewis, 1964). It is against this background that Nicholas Roerich sought 'Agharta' in Central Asia, that Percy Fawcett sought the 'City of Z' in Amazonia and that László Almásy sought 'Zerzura' in the Sahara. The exponential growth of the world's human population, the pandemic spread of the tourist industry and the reckless desecration of nature make it likely that this quest must be finally abandoned because the light of Tradition retreats as the darkness of Modernity blankets the world. Thus, buried deep under the ashes of the Modern world, the world of Tradition has been lost. It remains undiscovered, forgotten and unsuspected, until the Golden Dawn.

Und nun vernehmt! — Wie einst in Grabeshöhlen
Ein frommes Volk geheim sich flüchtete,
Und allen Drang der himmlich reinen Seelen
Nach oben voll Vertrauen richtete,
Nicht unterliess auf höchsten Schutz zu zählen
Und auszudauern sich verplichtete:
So hat die Tugend still ein Reich gegründet
Und sich zu Schutz und Trutz geheim verbündet.
Im tiefsten, hohl, das Erdreich untergraben
Auf welchem jene schreckliche Gewalten
Nun offenbar ihr wildes Wesen haben,
In majestätisch hässlichen Gestalten,
Und mit den holden überreifen Gaben
Der Oberfläche nach Belieben schalten;
Doch wird der Boden gleich zusammenstürzen,
Und jenes Reich des Uebermuths verkürzen.

[And now hear! — How once a pious people
Went into hiding in secret caverns and,
Maintaining the heavenly purity of their souls
And their trusting faith,
Continued to count on the Highest Help
And promised to endure:
Thus, a Hidden Realm was founded by piety,
Pledged to stand guard and keep vigil,
And it dug deeply under the earthly realm,
Now usurped by the wild powers
And horrible terrors of
Those demonic spectres that
Still desecrate its surface at will
With their unholy arts;
But soon the ground will cave in
And shorten that empire of insolence.]

— Johann Wolfgang von Goethe,
Des Epimenides Erwachen

The Seven Sleepers

The Seven Sleepers of Ephesus, illustration from a Fāl-Nāmeh, a Persian 'Book of Omens' (16th Century). Oracle books such as this one were widely used for practicing bibliomancy in the Islamic East (cf. the practice of *sortes sanctorum* common in the Christian West). The *sortes* of the 'Seven Sleepers' for the last chapter of *Alba Rosa* involves the apotropaic theme of animal rights: in the lower right corner is depicted their faithful guard dog, explicitly referred to in the Quran (Quran 18:18, 'And thou wouldst have deemed them waking though they were asleep, and we caused them to turn over to the right and the left, and their dog stretching out his paws on the threshold. If thou hadst observed them closely thou hadst assuredly turned away from them in flight, and hadst been filled with awe of them.').

CHAPTER TEN

The White Rose

dedicated to Alfred Vierling — in lieu of the white tornado

PROLOGUE: THE DUTCH REVOLT

tanto monta cortar como desatar
[it amounts to the same, cutting as untying]

A S STATED IN THE PREFACE, *ALBA ROSA* APPEARS in two alternative editions: a Dutch-language edition, which is meant for the author's native Netherlands and its Flemish brother nation, and this English-language edition, which is meant for an international public. The author has deemed it worthwhile to draw attention to the Postmodern predicament of his native people because in many ways it is exemplary of the predicament of the other native peoples of Western Europe and the overseas Anglosphere. In this sense, the analyses of some contemporary Dutch themes included in the international edition of *Alba Rosa* serve to indicate the overall tendency and general direction of the Crisis of the Modern West. Awareness of the contemporary Dutch predicament under the aegis of Cultural Nihilism can remind other Western peoples facing a similar predicament of the usefulness — even necessity — of cooperation to remedy their shared plight. It can also remind the peoples of Eastern Europe and the ex-Soviet Union of the imperative need to avoid the road taken by their Western European neighbours. Even so, it is important to emphasize the unique historical destiny of each of the European peoples separately — the Dutch included.

It should be remembered that the Netherlands is a 'scouting nation' of Western Modernity, in a manner not dissimilar to Great Britain (cf. Chapter 7): the Dutch people are also a quintessentially 'Modern' people (cf. Chapter 4). The historical genesis of the Dutch nation dramatically illustrates this: the radical-Protestant and radically progressive Dutch Republic was born out of one of the most extreme caesuras in Western history. In a storm of fire and blood, in defiance of the full force of its mighty Hapsburg over-lords, it fought itself free of the Catholic Counter-Reformation and monar-chic Absolutism. The Dutch Reformation came relatively late, but once it came it was driven by the full historical impetus of Modernity: the Dutch Revolt — an improvised rising by disaffected traders, preachers, fishermen and peasants led by a few adventurous nobles and spearheaded by a handful of pirates and desperadoes — miraculously managed to fight off, bankrupt and humble the mighty Spanish world empire. The Dutch Revolt derived its inner compass and moral strength from a carefully calibrated amalgam of archaic values and 'futuristic' visions: it combined a rightful claim to ancient rights (local autonomy, devolved governance, civil freedom) with an au-dacious insistence on 'futuristic' exploration (entrepreneurial experiment, social reform, religious diversification). In this sense, the Dutch Revolt and the resultant rise, in the course of its Eighty Years' Independence War, of the Dutch Republic to great power status was a truly *Archaeofuturist Revo-lution*. As a radical-Protestant sovereign republic, the Dutch state was truly the 'firstborn' of Modernity: it was the 'scouting nation' of Early Modernity in the same way that, two centuries later, the United States would be the 'scouting nation' of Classical Modernity.

It is not entirely inconceivable that, given the right ingredients and cir-cumstances, the Dutch nation will once again play a similar pioneering role in the future. If the Postmodern predicament of the Netherlands is particularly alarming in nature and if the Dutch entanglement in the Gordian Knot of Cultural Nihilism is particularly difficult to solve, it may be that the Dutch solution to Postmodern Cultural Nihilism will be particularly decisive as well. With this in mind, *Alba Rosa* concludes with a 'manifest' that takes its paragraph titles from three documents that were essential in inspiring and guiding the 16th century Dutch Archaeofuturist Revolution. These three key texts of the Dutch Revolt eloquently represent its doubly intellectual and spiritual force. The first, *Vindiciae contra tyrannos*, or 'Defences against Tyrants', provides a staunch theological defence of justified resistance to unjust rule. It was written in 1579, the year in which the northern provinces of the Low Countries laid the foundation for Dutch statehood in the Union of Utrecht. The second, the *Plakkaat van Verlatinghe*, or 'Placard of Abjuration', legally sets the Union of Utrecht free from its allegiance to its nominal overlord King Philip II of Spain, deeming him to have forfeited his sovereign rights due to the systematic violation of his sacred trust and tyrannical abuse of power. It was written in 1581 and constitutes the de facto 'declaration of independence' of the Netherlands as a sovereign state. The third, the *Wilhelmus*, the national anthem of the Netherlands — the oldest known in the world — is a prayer poem dedicated to the leader of the Dutch Revolt, William I, Prince of Orange, Father of the Nation and forefather of the present King Willem-Alexander; it compares William I to King David in his quest to free the People of Israel from the unjust rule of the apostate King Saul. All three of these texts emphasize trust in God, respect for the law and a longing for peace. They reflect the old national character of the Dutch, traditionally known as a particularly God-fearing, law-abiding and peace-loving people. These characteristics explain the Dutch people's highest priorities in combating all forms of tyranny: intellectual resistance, civil disobedience and — above all — non-violence. It is in this spirit that *Alba Rosa* concludes with the following 'manifest', which takes its inspiration from what is perhaps the bravest non-violent resistance movement of the Modern Age: *Die Weisse Rose*, in which a few brave German students took on the all-powerful Nazi regime, perhaps the most formidable totalitarian dictatorship of the Modern Age. May their intellectual, moral and spiritual superiority in the face of a mindless, brutal and inhuman dictatorship inspire the young people of the West in their coming battle with the dark power of the Cultural Nihilist hostile elite.

Hope:

Nun begegn' ich meinen Braven,
Die sich in der Nacht versammlet,
Um zu schweigen, nicht zu schlafen,
Und das schöne Wort der Freiheit
Wird gelispelt und gestammelt,
Bis in ungewohnter Neuheit!

[Now I meet my brave companions
Who have come together in the night
To keep silent, not to sleep,
And the fair word of freedom
Is murmured and stammered
As an unsuspected novelty!]
— JOHANN WOLFGANG VON GOETHE,
DES EPIMENIDES ERWACHEN

'VINDICIAE CONTRA TYRANNOS'

— *freely inspired by the first leaflet of* Die Weisse Rose

Nothing is more unworthy of a people of high culture than a mindless and feeble acceptance of 'governance' by an irresponsible clique that itself is governed by dark instincts. Is it not true that at present every decent Dutchman is ashamed of his 'government' of 'Lying Dutchmen'? And who of us can imagine the shame which will come over us and our children when finally our eyes are fully opened to the whole mendacity and criminality by which this hostile elite is betraying our country and our people? If the Dutch people have so far degenerated in soul and heart that they are willing to give up their free will — the highest good of humanity and the thing that raises man above all other creatures — without a fight, in the frivolous belief in the dubious 'progress of history', then they deserve to disappear. If they are willing to give up their human freedom to decide the course of history and to shape history according to their will, and if they have lost their sense of human individuality in the shapeless 'grey zone' of mindless and cowardly collectivism, then they deserve to be consigned to the dustbin of history. During their Eighty Years' fight for freedom and independence, the ancestors of the modern Dutch saw themselves as a new Chosen People in a new Promised Land, which was liberating itself from a new Egyptian bondage. But now it seems that the Dutch people have become an effeminate and spineless herd of sheep, deprived of any sense of honour and dignity, willing to be meekly led to an ignominious end.

Thus it seems, but it is not so. Rather, each individual Dutchman has been reduced to spiritual bondage by a slow, treacherous and systematic suppression of independent thinking and mature conscience. Only when he was down on the ground in chains did he realize what his fate was. Only a few noticed the approaching disaster; the wages of their warnings were murder (Pim Fortuyn, Theo van Gogh) and persecution (Hans Janmaat, Geert Wilders). The final verdict on these names will have to be spoken by future historians. But if everybody waits until others do something, then the harbingers of merciless Nemesis will inexorably come closer and closer, until the last senseless sacrifice will have vanished into the gaping jaws of the insatiable demon of Cultural Nihilism. For this reason, every individual must be aware of his responsibility towards his Christian culture and his Western civilization and resist, as much as he is able to, the scourge of Western humanity: Cultural Nihilism and its totalitarian grip on state authority. Prepare yourselves for passive and non-violent resistance — *resistance* — wherever you are: prevent the advance of this godless machine of destruction before it is too late, before the last remnants of our civilization disappear in the abyss of history and before our last descendants are sacrificed to the satanic madness of the subhuman and unworthy hostile elite! Pierce the transparent ritual with which it facilitates, tolerates and hides dark evil! Do not forget the crimes that are coming ever closer to your door-step: the South African 'farm killings', the Rotherham 'grooming gangs', the Cologne New Year's Eve — and the daily larger and smaller terror that is creeping into your cities, villages and streets! Do not forget that every nation gets the government that it deserves, that it allows itself to be ruled by!

'PLACARD OF ABJURATION'

— freely inspired by the second leaflet of Die Weisse Rose

It is impossible to combat Historical Materialist movements such as Liberalism and Cultural Nihilism with spiritual weapons because these movements do not possess a spirit. It is incorrect to call Liberalism or Cultural Nihilism 'worldviews'. If this were the case, they should be combated with spiritual weapons, but reality shows us an entirely different picture: from their very beginnings Liberalism and Cultural Nihilism depend on simple deceit; from the very start, they were rotten to their core and could only maintain the appearance of substance by continuous lies. Initially, these cancerous growths were not clearly visible in the body politic, because there were still enough positive powers available to combat them. But when they grew larger and larger, when they obtained a monopoly on power through a last and malignant transformation and when they finally took over our country and people in a Neo-Liberal New World Order, then most of these earlier resistance forces hid themselves from reality: the Dutch intelligentsia took refuge in a dark hole, to slowly decay and die like little poor indoor plants lacking sun and light.

Now we are facing the bankruptcy of Historical Materialism in its final incarnations of Neo-Liberalism and Cultural Nihilism. Now it is essential that we find each other again, that we clear our minds by talking to each other, that we think through our predicament and that we do not allow ourselves to rest until everybody is convinced about the absolute necessity of our personal commitment to fight the hostile elite that is attempting to artificially prolong the life of the Neo-Liberal New World Order. If in that manner, a wave of resistance is generated, if a new idea pervades the air, if many join the cause, then it is still possible to shake off this satanic system in a last, mighty exertion of our collective willpower. A terrible end is better than terror without end.

It is not up to us to pronounce the final verdict on our historical destiny. But if our present Cultural Nihilist predicament can still be of value, then only thus: to be purified by our ordeal, so that we may look up from the darkest night to the new dawn. Thus, we can pull ourselves together and help dislodge the yoke that is pressing down on our country and on the whole of the Western world.

Not only *ethnic replacement* is an issue of vital importance: this issue is merely one of the *symptoms* of Cultural Nihilism. With subtly disguised mass-immigration our country is being colonized in front of our very eyes: our people and culture are being slowly strangulated — this is indeed an immense crime. But even these 'immigrants' are still *people*, whatever one's feeling about 'immigration'; they are mere pawns in the evil game of the Cultural Nihilist hostile elite. Neither the colonized indigenous peoples of the West nor the rootless immigrant populations that are being imported by the hostile elite benefit from mass-immigration: the former lose their home and the latter is eternally homeless. The Cultural Nihilist project of ethnic replacement is a dead-end street that offers no exit except self-destruction: ethnic conflict and civil war. But the other symptoms of Cultural Nihilism are just as fatal: especially industrial ecocide and social implosion. The continuation of *industrial ecocide*, driven by absurd hyper-capitalism and unbridled consumerism means that the mindless cruelty of the horrendous bio-industry is allowed to roll on undisturbed and that unprecedented climate change is allowed to reach catastrophic proportions. The continuation of the *social implosion* that inevitably results from the Postmodern realities of matriarchic feminization and collective narcissism means that the 'deconstruction' of our people, our family and our society is allowed to proceed unchecked. A whole generation of young people has already been scarred for life by the results of this 'deconstruction': 'broken families', 'libertarian childrearing', 'education reform', 'permissiveness', 'pornification' and 'transgenderism'. In the same way that ethnic replacement leads to 'ethnic deconstruction' and that industrial ecocide leads to 'environmental deconstruction', so social implosion leads to 'identitarian deconstruction'. The resulting combination of demographic inundation, climate catastrophe and failing cultural transmission is the death sentence of our people.

Why does all of this have to be said to you in these words, if yourself you already know it—if not in detail, at least in substance? Because the issue of Cultural Nihilism is an issue of life or death: it must be addressed, as our fate as a people depends on it. Why do the people respond with apathy to this terrible, inhuman development? Almost nobody gives it any serious thought. This development is accepted as a fact of 'progress' and set aside. Again the nation falls asleep, stupefied and exhausted, and again it encourages the Cultural Nihilist hostile elite to take another step down into the abyss—and the fall continues. Perhaps this is a sign that the people have been damaged in their most primitive human dignity—that their conscience has atrophied to the point of being silent even in full view of the most disturbing sights, that they have fallen into a lethal urban-hedonist trance and a spiritual coma from which there is no waking up. It appears to be the case. And it *is* true, if the people cannot shake off their stupor, if they do not protest—at every opportunity—against this criminal hostile elite, if they do not feel pity for the countless innocent creatures that are its victims —

For the millions of defenceless animals that are tortured to death in the maniacal bloodbath of the 'bio-industry' every year. For the hundreds of thousands of children who live through the narcissist madness of the 'libertarian' society, children who will never know who their real father is or what a real family feels like—and who have to go through life as broken reeds after being neglected, maltreated and abused. For the hundreds of thousands of youngsters who feel the daily effects of globalist Neo-Liberalism in unbearable 'student loans', permanent work insecurity and unfair competition with inflowing masses of cheap 'migrant labour'. For the hundreds of thousands of young women who have been brainwashed and manipulated into embracing an empty 'emancipation' that robs them of their chances of marriage, motherhood and family life. For the hundreds of thousands of 'redundant' old people who are deprived of natural family life, dignified care environments and well-earned social respect, only to be subtly encouraged to quickly quit their supposedly 'completed lives'. *So I returned, and considered all the oppressions that are done under the sun: and behold the tears of such as were oppressed, and they had no comforter; and on the side of their oppressors there was power; but they had no comforter. Wherefore I praised the dead more than the living which are yet alive,* — Ecclesiastes 4:1–2.

Not only should the people feel pity for these innocent victims, but much more: they should be aware of their guilt as *accomplices*. Because, by their apathy, they make it possible for the hostile elite to do what it does: they tolerate a regime that is guilty of atrocious negligence and criminality. More: they themselves are guilty because they have allowed it to rise to power! Everybody wants to deny this guilt and gloss it over — and this is exactly what everybody does, dozing off into an undisturbed sleep with an unburdened conscience. But the people cannot escape their responsibility: they themselves are *guilty, guilty, guilty.*

But still, it is not yet too late to remove the disgusting dirt that is supposed to be our 'government' and our 'elite' — and to avoid further incrimination. Now that, at long last, our eyes have opened and now that we know who we are dealing with, the time has come to remove the hostile elite of fake leaders and fake authorities. Until recently, most of the people were blind: the Cultural Nihilist hostile elite was able to hide behind the politically correct mask of 'humanism' and 'progressiveness'. It is only recently that the evil conjoined twins of the regressive left and the kleptocratic right have finally discarded this mask. So now, now that we know who they truly are, it is the sacred duty of the people to remove the suicide pilots of the hostile elite from the cockpit of our national government.

'And Tyranny Away'

— *freely inspired by the fourth leaflet of* Die Weisse Rose

A shield and my reliance
O God, Thou ever wert.
I'll trust unto Thy guidance.
O leave me not ungirt.
That I may stay a pious
Servant of Thine for aye,
And drive the plagues that try us
And tyranny away.

— The Dutch national anthem 'Wilhelmus', VI

It is an ancient wisdom, as we repeat to our children, that whoever refuses to hear, must feel. A clever child will only burn his finger on the hot stove once. You have been warned: every word that comes out of the hostile elite is a lie. If it says 'multicultural tolerance', it means mass immigration that you pay for yourself and ethnic replacement that is fatal to your children's future. If it says 'free movement of goods, capital, services and labour', it means offshore accounting, mailbox companies, money laundry, narcostate, industrial dumping, outsourcing and wage-suppressing migrant labour. When it says 'environmental awareness', it means bureaucratic whitewashing of bio-industrial horrors, profitable self-deception of commercial 'greening' and paper-only animal rights. When it says 'progress' and 'enlightenment', it means atavistic regression and demonic darkness. Its media outlets are the stinking mouths of hell and its governmental institutions are inwardly rotting.

Of course, it is laudable to fight the false ideology and dictatorial regime of the hostile elite with rational arguments, but whoever still doubts the existence of the demoniacal power that stands behind this regime has not grasped the metaphysical context of the Crisis of the Modern World. Behind the concrete realities that can be discerned by the senses and behind the logical deliberations that are founded on tangible affairs, there is an irrational dimension. It is in that dimension that the struggle against the demon and the antichrist is fought. Everywhere and at all times the demons have been waiting in the dark, waiting for the hour that humanity becomes weak, the hour that of its own free will it abandons the place that God has granted it in freedom. That is the hour that humanity surrenders to evil temptation, that it turns its back on higher powers and higher aims. After this voluntary first step follows a second and a third — and more steps follow at an ever-accelerating pace. But everywhere and at all times, whenever human distress reaches unbearable levels, people have stood up: prophets, holy men who remembered humanity's original freedom. They remembered the One True God and, with His help, called the people to turn back. Humanity may be free, but it is helpless against evil without the One True God: without Him, it is as a ship without a rudder, an infant without a mother, a cloud that dissolves into nothing. If you believe this, you should ask yourself if, in the present struggle against Cultural Nihilist evil, there is still any legitimate reason to hesitate, to prevaricate or to postpone the outstanding final confrontation. Do you hope that another person will take up arms on your behalf if God has given you the power and the courage to fight? We have to fight evil where it is strongest — and it is strongest in the regime of our Cultural Nihilist hostile elite.

It should be emphatically stated that every authentic Dutch resistance to our hostile elite must reject service to any foreign power. Even if it is clear that our own hostile elite represents a global power and that the Dutch people should join other Western peoples in a common effort to destroy that power, it is of vital importance that the deeply wounded Dutch spirit is cured from *within*. The Dutch Renaissance must be preceded by a clear awareness of the burden of guilt with which the Dutch people have charged themselves through their own tardiness, passiveness, laziness and collaboration. They have to detach themselves from the hostile elite and stop their slavish deference to greedy bankers, looting venture capitalists, political straw men, corrupt journalists and compromised academicians. Next, there should be created a clear delineation between the *real* Dutch people and the treacherous *hostile* elite of 'transnational' hyper-capitalists, 'europhile' political stooges, 'cosmopolitan' media pundits and 'internationalized' pseudo-academicians. For the 'hard core' of the hostile elite, who have not only betrayed their country and their people, but who have also abandoned their humanity and conscience, there is no punishment on this Earth that befits their crimes. But, for the sake of coming generations, they should be made an example of after their downfall — so that never again will anybody feel the slightest temptation to repeat a similar betrayal of their nation and their people, or to repeat a similar disdain for God and God's Law.

Until the Cultural Nihilist hostile elite has fallen, silence is no longer an option: until that time, may the White Rose be your conscience.

⚜

> *Ave, formosissima, gemma pretiosa,*
> *ave, decus virginum, virgo gloriosa,*
> *ave, mundi luminar,*
> *ave, mundi rosa!*
> — CARMINA BURANA

> *Completed at The Hague on 20 June 2018,*
> *half a century after the* Machtergreifung of the soixante-huitards.

* albus in albis *

Ave, mundi rosa

Offrande à la Vierge, 'Offering to the Virgin' (Simon Saint-Jean, 1842),
Museum of Fine Arts Lyon.

APPENDIX A

'Human Rights'

A Traditionalist Reality Check

NOTES ON THE UNIVERSAL DECLARATION OF HUMAN RIGHTS

(RESOLUTION 217 OF THE UNITED NATIONS GENERAL ASSEMBLY, 10 DECEMBER 1948)

chassez le naturel, il revient au galop

Article 1. *All human beings are born free and equal in dignity and rights. They are endowed with reason and conscience and should act towards one another in a spirit of brotherhood.*

All human beings are born subject to God's Law and natural law: they are not free. They are born in different physical bodies: they are not equal. They are born in different social realities: they do not have the same rights. They are not naturally endowed with reason and conscience: these must be culturally instilled and are therefore also culturally determined. They are not naturally capable of solidarity and brotherhood: these must be socially cultivated and are therefore also socially determined.

Article 2. *Everyone is entitled to all the rights and freedoms set forth in this Declaration, without distinction of any kind, such as race, colour, sex, language, religion, political or other opinion, national or social origin, property, birth or other status. Furthermore, no distinction shall be made on the basis of the political, jurisdictional or international status of the country or territory to which a person belongs, whether it be independent, trust, non-self-governing or under any other limitation of sovereignty.*

Nobody is automatically entitled to any rights or freedoms: these must be earned and conquered. Rights and freedoms are always situational and conditional: they are related to ethnicity, nationality, gender, language, religion, social origin, material property, physical birth and other ascribed status. Further differences are imposed by the political, judicial and military authorities that claim to rule over territories and peoples.

Article 3. *Everyone has the right to life, liberty and security of person.*

Everyone is born mortal and is exposed to the common calamities of life in the form of natural and manmade dangers. In the universal struggle for survival and in the universal fight to overcome restrictions and dangers there are no enduring rights to life, liberty and security beyond the temporary rights gained by communities on behalf of individuals and by individuals on behalf of communities.

Article 4. *No one shall be held in slavery or servitude; slavery and the slave trade shall be prohibited in all their forms.*

Everyone is born in a natural state of slavery and servitude: everyone is born subject to God's Law, to natural law, to human law, to social convention and to cultural tradition.

Article 5. *No one shall be subjected to torture or to cruel, inhuman or degrading treatment or punishment.*

No one is exempt from the natural and man-made diseases, frailties, tortures, cruelties, inhumanities and degradations that are inherent in the natural human condition ever since the Fall of Adam and Eve.

Article 6. *Everyone has the right to recognition everywhere as a person before the law.*

Everyone is subject to the vagaries and uncertainties of biased and arbitrary human law ever since it has parted from God's Law, and even more so since the advent of Dark Age Modernity.

Article 7. *All are equal before the law and are entitled without any discrimination to equal protection of the law. All are entitled to equal protection against any discrimination in violation of this Declaration and against any incitement to such discrimination.*

Mere human law can never offer total constancy, total protection and total equality. Since it must take account of natural law it is obliged to discriminate on the basis of biological identity, including age, gender, infirmity, ethnicity and genealogy. Since it has parted from Tradition, modern law is furthermore bound to discriminate on the basis of social status, financial resources and political expediency.

Article 8. *Everyone has the right to an effective remedy by the competent national tribunals for acts violating the fundamental rights granted him by the constitution or by law.*

Everyone is subject to the incompetence and violence of unjust modern law, without effective remedy. A lessening of its injustice depends on the attempt at reincorporating a measure of Divine Law into secular law. Modern law systematically precludes this attempt and is therefore historically bound to be the most unjust.

Article 9. *No one shall be subjected to arbitrary arrest, detention or exile.*

Arbitrary arrest, detention and exile are inevitable under unjust modern law: these serve to aggravate the anguish of the modern human condition.

Article 10. *Everyone is entitled in full equality to a fair and public hearing by an independent and impartial tribunal, in the determination of his rights and obligations and of any criminal charge against him.*

Everyone can be exposed to insidious slander, public character assassination and judicial persecution within the framework of unjust modern law: 'human rights' and 'civil rights' are mere ideological constructs.

Article 12. *No one shall be subjected to arbitrary interference with his privacy, family, home or correspondence, nor to attacks upon his honour and reputation. Everyone has the right to the protection of the law against such interference or attacks.*

No one is sure of his privacy, family, home or correspondence, nor of his honour and reputation within the framework of unjust modern law. Legalized government surveillance and marketing manipulation intrude into privacy and correspondence, legalized educational and media indoctrination threaten the family, unjust taxes and debt slavery threaten the home, matriarchy and feminisation threaten honour and reputation.

Article 13. *(a) Everyone has the right to freedom of movement and residence within the borders of each state. (b) Everyone has the right to leave any country, including his own, and to return to his country.*

(a) The semi-legalized anarchy of globalized free movement and residence is a fundamental threat to national security, civic freedom, private property and rooted identity. (b) The semi-legalized anarchy of globalized free movement and residence institutionalizes abandonment and betrayal of ethnicity and nationality, and imposes anti-identitarian ethno-morphosis.

Article 14. *(a) Everyone has the right to seek and to enjoy in other countries asylum from persecution. (b) This right may not be invoked in the case of prosecutions genuinely arising from non-political crimes or from acts contrary to the purposes and principles of the United Nations.*

(a) To reside abroad is a privilege to be granted by a host nation, not a right to be claimed by a guest. (b) For guest 'migrants' to force themselves on their host nations through legal pressure, administrative fraud and illegal residence is sufficient reason for expulsion and persecution.

Article 15. *(a) Everyone has the right to a nationality. (b) No one shall be arbitrarily deprived of his nationality nor denied the right to change his nationality.*

(a) It is a vocation and privilege to be born into a nation: nationality is a birth pledge privilege that should be constantly redeemed throughout life. (b) Every one is called upon to proof him- or herself be worthy of their nationality: to lose and change nationality is to lose and change identity — it is fraught with trauma, tragedy and moral hazard.

Article 16. *(a) Men and women of full age, without any limitation due to race, nationality or religion, have the right to marry and to found a family. They are entitled to equal rights as to marriage, during marriage and at its dissolution. (b) Marriage shall be entered into only with the free and full consent of the intending spouses. (c) The family is the natural and fundamental group unit of society and is entitled to protection by society and the State.*

(a) Men and women must first earn the right to marry and found a family. This right is conditional upon respect for the institution of marriage, which is existentially shaped by race, nationality and religion. Individual rights are substantially affected by marital and family status. Marriage and parenthood are social functions with duties and restrictions: neither marriage nor family can be dissolved at will. (b) Marriage is not merely a contract between two individuals, but also affects families and nations and therefore demands a minimum degree of societal consent. (c) In Tradition, the family is a sacred and crucial element of communal unity, but in Modernity it is threatened by social chaos and governmental intervention.

Article 17. *(a) Everyone has the right to own property alone as well as in association with others. (b) No one shall be arbitrarily deprived of his property.*

(a) Individual property rights can never be absolute: they must be balanced by communal sanction to avoid social implosion. (b) Individual property obtained by exploitation, extortion and fraud is liable to expropriation.

Article 18. *Everyone has the right to freedom of thought, conscience and religion; this right includes freedom to change his religion or belief, and freedom, either alone or in community with others and in public or private, to manifest his religion or belief in teaching, practice, worship and observance.*

Everyone is bound to honour the contracts and obligations due to his or her religious affiliation and to conform to the public and private rules and observances that regulate his or her religion. Religion regulates not only divine worship, but also social structure: it is neither to be trifled with nor to be discarded at will.

Article 19. *Everyone has the right to freedom of opinion and expression; this right includes freedom to hold opinions without interference and to seek, receive and impart information and ideas through any media and regardless of frontiers.*

No one has the right to opinions and expressions, except to the degree that they conform to strict criteria of competence, relevance and etiquette. Information and ideas should be restricted to those competent to handle them.

Article 20. *(a) Everyone has the right to freedom of peaceful assembly and association. (b) No one may be compelled to belong to an association.*

(a) Everyone is bound to associate with his or her birth community (family, caste, nation) and according to his or her birth vocation (marriage, religion, profession) — an association beyond this must be undertaken only with extreme caution and with proper guidance. (b) No one can freely dissociate from birth community and birth vocation.

Article 21. *(a) Everyone has the right to take part in the government of his country, directly or through freely chosen representatives. (b) Everyone has the right of equal access to public service in his country. (c) The will of the people shall be the basis of the authority of government; this will shall be expressed in periodic and genuine elections which shall be by universal and equal suffrage and shall be held by secret vote or by equivalent free voting procedures.*

(a) No one has the right to busy themselves with government and politics except those called upon by privileged birth, proven vocation or exceptional talent. (b) Access to public services and social amenities depends on a combination of individually earned privilege and voluntary communal goodwill: it is never an absolute right. (c) Governance should be for the good of the people, not by the will of the people: just rulers are bound to treat their people as their children: they must strike a due balance between control and freedom, sternness and kindness.

Article 22. *Everyone, as a member of society, has the right to social security and is entitled to realization, through national effort and international co-operation and in accordance with the organization and resources of each State, of the economic, social and cultural rights indispensable for his dignity and the free development of his personality.*

No one has an absolute right to economic, social and cultural rights: individual rights should be earned and individual irresponsibility should be punished. Social security should be predicated on responsible individual choice and behaviour as much as on communal solidarity.

Article 23. *(a) Everyone has the right to work, to free choice of employment, to just and favourable conditions of work and to protection against unemployment. (b) Everyone, without any discrimination, has the right to equal pay for equal work. (c) Everyone who works has the right to just and favourable remuneration ensuring for himself and his family an existence worthy of human dignity, and supplemented, if necessary, by other means of social protection. (d) Everyone has the right to form and to join trade unions for the protection of his interests.*

(a) Everyone should pursue his personal and professional vocation irrespective of material reward — everyone should choose useful activity over 'productive' work. Dedicated motherhood, religious duty, scientific exploration and artistic expression are no less valuable than industrial production and mercantile endeavour. (b) The reward of activity should be of a primarily personal and social nature — material wealth should be commensurate with biological functionality and societal functionality and should never be an aim in itself. (c) Just wages for labour should allow the labourer to maintain himself and his family in materially adequate circumstances, but no more than that — just wages do not imply luxury and do serve vanity. (d) Owner and worker, employer and employee should corporate for mutual benefit: their interests are intertwined and not opposed.

Article 24. *Everyone has the right to rest and leisure, including reasonable limitation of working hours and periodic holidays with pay.*

Rest and leisure should be commensurate with exertion and labour — they should not be aims in themselves.

Article 25. *(a) Everyone has the right to a standard of living adequate for the health and well-being of himself and of his family, including food, clothing, housing and medical care and necessary social services, and the right to security in the event of unemployment, sickness, disability, widowhood, old age or other lack of livelihood in circumstances beyond his control. (b) Motherhood and childhood are entitled to special care and assistance. All children, whether born in or out of wedlock, shall enjoy the same social protection.*

(a) Communal provisions for social security are a matter of basic civilization, but should not be frivolously extended to criminal, irresponsible and foreign elements. (b) Motherhood demands support by the family and protection by the community, but only to the extent that mothers respect the rules and norms of the family and the community.

Article 26. *(a) Everyone has the right to education. Education shall be free, at least in the elementary and fundamental stages. Elementary education shall be compulsory. Technical and professional education shall be made generally available and higher education shall be equally accessible to all on the basis of merit. (b) Education shall be directed to the full development of the human personality and to the strengthening of respect for human rights and fundamental freedoms. It shall promote understanding, tolerance and friendship among all nations, racial or religious groups, and shall further the activities of the United Nations for the maintenance of peace. (c) Parents have a prior right to choose the kind of education that shall be given to their children.*

(a) Education should be appropriate to situation, vocation and talent: it is not an aim in itself. Education should be provided by idealistic and competent teachers and paid for by responsible and prudent parents. (b) Education should be appropriate to authentic identity: it should foster the reproduction of a specific tradition and a specific culture. The reproduction of authentic national, ethnic, social and religious identity, rather than the pursuit of cosmopolitan ideologies and universalist doctrine, should be the true aim of education. (c) Educational choice should depend on authentic collective (national, ethnic, social, religious) identity, rather than short-sighted 'fashion statements' by individual parents.

Article 27. *(a) Everyone has the right freely to participate in the cultural life of the community, to enjoy the arts and to share in scientific advancement and its benefits. (b) Everyone has the right to the protection of the moral and material interests resulting from any scientific, literary or artistic production of which he is the author.*

(a) Authentic cultural life is inextricably linked to authentic community identity: individuals should experience themselves as active participants, rather than passive 'consumers' of the arts and sciences. (b) Scientific, literary and artistic achievement should benefit the community: the author should be honoured and rewarded, but he is above all a servant of his or her community.

Article 28. *Everyone is entitled to a social and international order in which the rights and freedoms set forth in this Declaration can be fully realized.*

Individual rights and freedoms are determined by communities and nations — there are no universal rights and freedoms.

Article 29. *(a) Everyone has duties to the community in which alone the free and full development of his personality is possible. (b) In the exercise of his rights and freedoms, everyone shall be subject only to such limitations as are determined by law solely for the purpose of securing due recognition and respect for the rights and freedoms of others and of meeting the just requirements of morality, public order and the general welfare in a democratic society. (c) These rights and freedoms may in no case be exercised contrary to the purposes and principles of the United Nations.*

(a) Yes — even a broken watch is right one time per day. (b) Individual rights and freedoms should be balanced by communal obligations and limitations — holistically-defined common good and intergenerational continuity should always prevail over individual rights and freedoms. (c) There are no purposes and principles that are of a higher order than the holistically-defined common good and the intergenerational continuity of the largest authentic human community groups, viz. ethnicity and nation.

Article 30. *Nothing in this Declaration may be interpreted as implying for any State, group or person any right to engage in any activity or to perform any act aimed at the destruction of any of the rights and freedoms set forth herein.*

The Universal Declaration of Human Rights is the product of a secular-nihilist and cultural-relativist ideology that stands opposed to authentic identity and traditional religion. Its semi-binding status in 'international law' reflects the interests of the Cultural-Nihilist 'New World Order': these interests — and all attempts at formulating non-sacred 'international law' — are harmful to the holistically-defined common good and the intergenerational continuity of the largest authentic human community groups, viz. ethnicity and nation.

Encore: From the Declaration on the Rights of Indigenous Peoples

(Resolution 61/295 of the United Nations General Assembly, 13 September 2007)

Article 7. *(1) Indigenous peoples and individuals have the right not to be subjected to forced assimilation or destruction of their culture. (2) States shall provide effective mechanisms for prevention of, and redress for:*

(a) Any action which has the aim or effect of depriving them of their integrity as distinct peoples, or of their cultural values or ethnic identities;

(b) Any action which has the aim or effect of dispossessing them of their lands, territories or resources;

(c) Any form of population transfer which has the aim or effect of violating or undermining any of their rights;

(d) Any form of assimilation or integration by other cultures or ways of life imposed on them by legislative, administrative or other measures;

(e) Any form of propaganda directed against them.

ceci tuera cela

Appendix B

'Stultitiae Laus'

Excerpts from Friedrich Nietzsche, Untimely Meditations — orig. Unzeitgemässe Betrachtungen (translation Alexander Wolfheze)

'The Gay Science'

('Die fröhliche Wissenschaft')

*Gewiss, wir brauchen Historie, aber wir brauchen sie anders, als sie die ver-
wöhnte Müssiggänger im Garten des Wissens braucht, mag derselbe auch
vornehm auf unsere derben und unmuthlosen Bedürfnisse und Nöthe her-
absehen. Das heisst, wir brachen sie zum Leben und zur That, nicht zur
bequemen Abkehr vom Leben und von der That, oder gar zur Beschönigung
des selbstsüchtigen Lebens und der feigen und schlechten That. Nur soweit
die Historie dem Leben dient, wollen wir ihr dienen: aber es gibt einen Grad,
Historie zu treiben, und eine Schätzung derselben, bei der das Leben verküm-
mert und entärtet: ein Phänomenen, welches an merkwürdigen Symptomen
unserer Zeit sich zur Erfahrung zu bringen jetzt eben so nothwendig ist, als
es schmerzlich sein mag. ... Unzeitgemäss ist ... diese Betrachtung, weil ich
etwas, worauf die Zeit ... stolz ist, ihre historische Bildung, hier einmal als
Schaden, Gebreste und Mangel der Zeit zu verstehen versuche, weil ich sogar
glaube, dass wir Alle an einem verzehrenden historischen Fieber leiden und
mindestens erkennen sollten, dass wir daran leiden. ... Jedermann weiss,
[dass] eine hypertrophische Tugend —wie sie mir die historischen Sinn unserer Zeit zu sein scheint— so gut zum Verderben eines Volkes werden kann
wie ein hypertrophyisches Laster...*

Certainly, we need History, but *differently* than spoilt tourists sightsee-ing in the Garden of Knowledge, even if they look down on our uncouth and ill-humoured needs and wants. That is to say: we need History for Life and Action, not as a leisurely vacation from Life and Action or as a justification for an egoistic life or for a cowardly and evil action. We will serve History only to the extent that it serves Life. But there is a de-gree of practising History that actually damages Life — a degree at which the former actually damages and degenerates the latter. To recognize this phenomenon in the strange symptoms of our time may be painful, but it is also necessary. ... This meditation ... is untimely, because here I must re-interpret something of which our time ... is particularly proud: its his-torical consciousness. I have to interpret it as an injury, a defect and a deficiency — I even believe we all suffer from a consuming historical fever and that, at the very least, we should recognize that we are suffering from it. ... Everybody knows that an exaggerated virtue — and I interpret the historical consciousness of our time as such — can be equally damaging to a people as an exaggerated vice...

'The Will of the People'

('Gesundes Geschichtsempfinden')

...*[E]s gibt einen Grad von Schlaflosigkeit, von Wiederkäuen, von historischem Sinne, bei dem das Lebendige zu Schaden kommt und zuletzt zu Grunde geht, sei es nun ein Mensch oder ein Volk oder eine Cultur. Um diesen Grad und durch ihn dann die Grenze zu bestimmen, an der das Vergangne vergessen werden muss, wenn es nicht zu Todten-gräber des Gegenwärtigen werden soll, müsste man genau wissen, wie gross die plastische Kraft eines Menschen, eines Volkes, einer Cultur ist; ich meine jene Kraft, aus sich heraus eigenartig zu wachsen, Vergangnes und Fremdes umzubilden und einzuverleiben, Wun-den auszuheilen, Verlornes zu ersetzen, zerbrochne Formen aus sich nachzuformen. ... Das, was eine solche [Kraft] nicht bezwingt, weiss sie zu vergessen; es ist nicht mehr da, der Horizont ist geschlossen und ganz, und nichts vermag daran zu erinnern, dass es noch jenseits desselben Menschen, Leidenschaften, Lehren, Zwecke giebt. ... [J]edes Lebendige kann nur innerhalb eines Horizontes gesund, stark und fruchtbar werden; ist es unvermögend, einen Horizont um sich zu ziehn, ... so siecht es matt oder über-hastig zu zeitigem Untergange dahin. Die Heiterkeit, das gute Gewissen, die frohe That, das Vertrauen auf das Kommende — alles hängt, bei dem Einzelnen wie bei dem Volke, davon ab, dass es eine Linie giebt, die das Uebersehbare, Helle von dem Unaufhellbaren und Dunklen scheidet; ... davon, dass man mit kräftigen Instinkte herausfühlt, wann es nöthig ist historisch, wann, unhistorisch zu empfinden. ... [D]as Unhistorische und das Historische is gleichermassen für die Gesundheit eines Einzelnen, eines Volkes und einer Cultur nöthig. ... [D]as historische Wissen und Empfinden eines Menschen kann sehr beschränkt, sein Horizont eingeengt wie der eines Alpenthal-Bewohners sein, in jedes Ur-theil mag er eine Ungerechtigkeit, in jede Erfahrung den Irrthum legen, mit ihr die Erste zu sein — und trotz aller Ungerechtigkeit und allem Irrthum steht er doch in unüberwin-dlicher Gesundheit und Rüstigkeit da und erfreut jedes Auge; während dicht neben ihm der bei weiten Gerechtere und Belehrtere kränkelt und zusammenfällt, weil die Linien seines Horizontes immer von Neuem unruhig sich verschieben, weil er sich aus dem viel zarteren Netze seiner Gerechtigkeiten und Wahrheiten nicht wieder zum derben Wollen und Begehren herauswinden kann.*

...[T]here exists an intensity of sleeplessness, of rumination, of historical awareness, that actually damages the living organism and that can actually destroy it,
whether it is a person, a people or a culture. To determine this degree, and the
border at which the past must be forgotten before it becomes the gravedigger of
the present, it is necessary to have an exact measure of the plasticity of the life
force that inhabits a person, a people or a culture. Here I mean the force that
allows it to grow autonomously, to digest the past, to incorporate alien bodies,
to recover from wounds, to substitute losses and recreate broken forms. ... What
such a force cannot cope with, it is able to forget: it no longer exists, the horizon
is closed and whole — and nothing can bring it to believe that, across that horizon
exist other peoples, passions, teachings and purposes. ... [E]very living organism
can only be healthy, strong and fertile within such a horizon. If it is unable to
draw a horizon around itself ... then it will sooner or later suffer a premature
demise. Brightness, a good conscience, the happy deed and confidence in the future, whether in an individual or in a people, all depend on the maintenance of a
line that separates the calculable and the light from the incalculable and the dark:
... it depends on the instinctive ability to decide when it is necessary to think
historically and when it is necessary to act anti-historically. ... [T]he historical
and unhistorical are equally necessary for the health of a person, a people and a
culture. ... [T]he historical awareness and feeling of a people may be very limited,
his horizon may be as narrow as the horizon of an Alp-valley villager, in all of
his judgments he may be unjust and in all of his experiences he may be wrongly
convinced that he is the first — but despite [his] injustice and wrongheadedness
he still stands upright in unconquerable health and vigour. He is a joy to behold,
while next to him his much more just and wise neighbour falls ill and collapses,
because his neighbour has horizons that are unstable and shifting, because he can
no longer untangle the fine webs of his subtle judgments and truths and because
he can no longer attain blunt willpower and desire.

STUDY MATERIAL

Sources

Stat rosa pristina nomine, nomina nuda tenemus.

— BERNARD DE CLUNY

SAFE CONDUCT

The following list is primarily meant as a reference resource for young people in search of material for further research into the cultural-historical themes touched upon in *Alba Rosa*. It specifies all non-fiction books and movies referenced in *Alba Rosa*. The filmography has been added because young people rarely have time and patience for products from before 'their time'. To permit those interested to make a quick selection, indications of genre and relevance have been added.

It is important to also add some words of advice for young people who are attempting a study of materials relevant to Traditionalism without the benefit of a reliable teacher or guide. Under the aegis of contemporary Postmodern Cultural Nihilism, the young people of the West are facing an unenviable predicament: they are bereft of reliable academic leadership within the Humanities and Social Sciences. These disciplines have been destroyed by a fatal combination of 'valorization', 'internationalization', 'feminization' and 'xenification'. Without trustworthy professional guidance, it is not easy to acquire a solid foundation in philosophy, sociology and cultural history. Here only a few general pieces of advice and some rules of thumb can be given.

First: Be careful! There are many pseudo-Traditionalist traps and ambushes that can ensnare the unwary student. A significant — and increasing — proportion of both 'contemporary' and 'classic' Traditionalism-related literature now falls outside the public and academic consensus. Partially this is due to politically correct anathemas that have been pronounced over their contents, and partially this is due to the irregular — often downright 'fantastic' — approaches of their authors. It is important that a student of such materials develops an instinct for distinguishing between 'objective facts', '(meta)political theses' and 'genius inspirations': these three categories tend to fluidly overlap and for every serious thinker they necessarily complement each other. It is necessary to achieve a balance between hard-headed 'common sense' and legitimately inspired imagination.

Second: Investigate source material — and try to read it in the original language! Authentic research, — in cultural history as well as political philosophy, demands a skipping of 'summaries' and 'interpretations' and re-living the world in which source material was created. Even the most genius minds of human history had their *Sitz im Leben* — to grasp that basic reality is a prerequisite for understanding their creations.

Third, a rule of thumb for indecisive beginners: Read the 'classics', mostly written by authors born before the 'baby boom' (approximate cut-off date 1940)! There are only very few baby boomer and post-baby boomer authors who are saying something that is substantial as well as reliable — and, even then, mostly only concerning the *side-effects* of Cultural Nihilism, not about Cultural Nihilism *itself*. Following this rule of thumb, it is possible to spare oneself many wasted study-hours and much annoying confusion. But to help those students lacking the skill and time to concern themselves with 'classic' studies, the following bibliography starts with a short-list of interesting contemporary authors, headed 'contemporary themes'.

Bibliography: Contemporary Themes

Bellil, Samira, *Dans l'enfer des tournantes*. Paris: Denoël, 2002.

Benoist, Alain de, *L'éclipse du sacré: discours et réponses*. Paris : La Table Ronde, 1986.

Baudet, Thierry H.P., *Breek het partijkartel! De noodzaak van referenda*. Amsterdam: Prometheus, 2017.

Bernays, Edward L., *Public Relations*. Norman, OK: University of Oklahoma, 1952.

Bosma, Martin, *De schijn-élite van de valse munters: Drees, extreem rechts, de sixties, nuttige idioten, Groep Wilders en ik*. Amsterdam: Bakker, 2010.

Cliteur, Paul, Jesper Jansen and Perry Pierik (ed.), *Cultuur Marxisme. Er waakt een spook door Europa*. Soesterberg: Aspekt, 2018.

Dugin, Aleksandr, *Eurasian Mission: An Introduction to Neo-Eurasianism*. London: Arktos, 2014.

———*The Last War of the World-Island: The Geopolitics of Contemporary Russia*. London: Arktos (2015)

———*The Fourth Political Theory*. London: Arktos (2015)

Faye, Guillaume, *L'archéofuturisme*. Paris: L'Aencre, 1998.

———*La colonisation de l'Europe: discours vrai sur l'immigration et l'Islam*. Paris: L'Aencre, 2000.

———*Sexe et dévoiement*. La Fosse: Le Lore, 2007.

Fortuyn, Wilhelmus S.P., *Baby boomers: autobiografie van een generatie*. Utrecht: Bruna, 1998.

———*De verweesde samenleving: een religieus-sociologisch traktaat*. Uithoorn: Karakter, 2002.

———*De puinhopen van acht jaar Paars: de wachtlijsten in de gezondheidszorg: een genadeloze analyse van de collectieve sector en aanbevelingen voor een krachtig herstelprogramma*. Uithoorn: Karakter, 2002.

Fukuyama, Francis, *The End of History and the Last Man*. New York: Free Press, 1992.

Goodrich, Thomas, *Hellstorm. The Death of Nazi Germany 1944-1947*. Sheridan, Co: Aberdeen Books, 2010.

Herman, Edward S. and Avram N. Chomsky, *Manufacturing Consent: the Political Economy of the Mass Media*. New York: Pantheon, 1988.

Huntington, Samuel P., *The Clash of Civilizations and the Remaking of the World Order*. New York: Simon & Schuster, 1996.

Iserbyt, Charlotte T., *The Deliberate Dumbing Down of America: A Chronological Paper Trail*. 1999

Jorjani, Jason R., *Prometheus and Atlas*. London: Arktos, 2016.

———*World State of Emergency*. London: Arktos, 2017.

Klein, Naomi, *The Shock Doctrine: the Rise of Disaster Capitalism*. Toronto: Knopf, 2007.

Kevin B. MacDonald, *A People That Shall Dwell Alone. Judaism as a Group Evolutionary Strategy with Diaspora Peoples.* Lincoln: Writers Club, 2002.

————*The Culture of Critique. An Evolutionary Analysis of Jewish Involvement in Twentieth-Century Intellectual and Political Movements.* Long Beach, 2002.

MacDonogh, Giles, *After the Reich. The Brutal History of the Allied Occupation.* New York: Basic Books, 2007.

Moldbug, Mencius, *A Gentle Introduction to Unqualified Reservations.* Kindle ebook, 2009.

Molyneux, Stefan, *The Art of the Argument. Western Civilization's Last Stand.* Kindle ebook, 2017.

Murray, Douglas, *The Strange Death of Europe: Immigration, Identity, Islam.* London: Bloomsbury, 2017.

Peterson, Jordan B., *12 Rules for Life: An Antidote to Chaos.* London: Penguin Random House, 2018.

Raspail, Jean, *Le camp des saints: roman.* Paris: Laffont, 1973.

Scruton, Roger V., *An Intelligent Person's Guide to Modern Culture.* London: Duckworth, 1998.

Sieferle, Rolf-Peter, *Finis Germania.* Schnellroda: Antaios, 2017.

Sloterdijk, Peter, *Die schreckliche Kinder der Neuzeit: über das anti-genealogische Experiment der Moderne.* Berlin: Suhrkamp, 2014.

Steuckers, Robert, *EUROPA* I-III. Lille: BIOS, 2017.

Ulfkotte, Udo K., *Gekaufte Journalisten.* Rottenburg: Kopp, 2014.

Venner, Dominique, *Le choc de l'histoire: réligion, mémoire, identité.* Versailles: Via Romana, 2011.

————*Pourquoi je me suis tué. Avant-propos par un dernier verre.* La Chaire : Last Litany, 2013.

Vierling, Alfred, 'Nota Centrumdemocratisch beleid ter bescherming van het Nederlands staatsburgerschap'. Den Haag: SWOCI, 1985.

Zwitzer, Tom, *Permafrost: een filosofisch essay over de westerse geopolitiek van 1914 tot heden.* Groningen: De Blauwe Tijger, 2017.

BIBLIOGRAPHY: CLASSIC THEMES

Anquetil Duperron, Abraham-Hyacinthe, *Zend-Avesta, ouvrage de Zoroastre, contenant les idées théologiques, physiques & morales de ce législateur.* Parijs: Tilliard, 1771.

Altizer, Thomas J.J., *The Descent into Hell. A Study of the Radical Reversal of the Christian Consciousness.* Philadelphia: Lippincott, 1970.

————*History as Apocalypse.* Albany: State University of New York Press, 1985.

Coomaraswamy, Ananda, *The Dance of Siva. Fourteen Indian Essays.* New York: The Sunwise Turn, 1918.

Dumézil, Georges E.R., *Le festin d'immortalité : étude de mythologie comparée Indo-Européene*. Paris : Paul Geuthner, 1924.

———*L'idéologie tripartie des Indo-Européens*. Brussel : Latomus, 1958.

Dávila, Nicolás Gómez, *Einsamkeiten: Glossen und Text in Einem*; orig. *Escolios a un texto implícito*. Wenen: Karolinger, 1987.

Evola, Julius, *Men Among the Ruins. Post-war Reflections of a Radical Traditionalist*; orig. *Gli uomini e le rovine*. Rochester: Inner Traditions, 2002.

———*Revolt against the Modern World*; orig. *Rivolta contro il mondo moderno* Rochester: Inner Traditions, 1995.

———*Ride the Tiger*; orig. *Cavalcare la Tigre*. Rochester: Inner Traditions, 2003.

Fromm, Erich, *The Anatomy of Human Destructiveness*. New York: Holt, Rinehart & Winston, 1973.

Freud, Sigmund S., 'Zur Einführung des Narzissmus'. *Gesammelte Schriften* VI. Leipzig: Internationaler Psychoanalytischer Verlag, 1925.

Graves, Robert R., *The White Goddess: A Historical Grammar of Poetic Myth*. London: Faber & Faber, 1948.

Guénon, René, *La crise du monde moderne*. Paris: Gallimard, 1946.

Heidegger, Martin, *Sein und Zeit*. Tübingen: Neomarius, 1949.

Lasch, Christopher, *The Culture of Narcissism: American Life in an Age of Diminishing Expectations*. New York: Norton, 1979.

Lewis, Clive L., *The Discarded Image: an Introduction to Medieval and Renaissance Literature*. Cambridge: Cambridge University, 1964.

Merton, Thomas, *The Seven Storey Mountain*. New York: Harcourt, Brace & Company, 1948.

Müller, Max, *Anthropological Religion*. London: Longmans, 1892.

Nasr, Seyyed Hossein, *Islam and the Plight of Modern Man*. Londen and New York: Longman, 1975

———*Knowledge and the Sacred*. Edinburgh: Edinburgh University, 1981.

Needleman, Jacob (ed.), *The Sword of Gnosis. Metaphysics, Cosmology, Tradition, Symbolism*. London: Arkana, 1986.

Nietzsche, Friedrich W., *Unzeitgemässe Betrachtungen*. Nietzsches Werke II. Leipzig: Naumannm 1919.

Otto, Rudolf, *Das Heilige: über das Irrationale in der Idee des Göttlichen und sein Verhältnis zum Rationalen*. Breslau: Perthes, 1917.

Schmitt, Carl, *Politische Theologie*. München: Duncker & Humblot, 1922.

———*Der Nomos der Erde im Völkerrecht des Jus Publicum Europaeum*. Berlin: Dunker & Humblot, 1950.

———*Land und Meer*. Leipzig: Reclam, 1942.

Scholl, Inge, *Die weisse Rose*. Frankfurt-am-Main: Fischer, 1956.

Schuon, Frithjof, *De l'unité transcendante des religions*. Paris: Tradition, 1948.

Solzhenitsyn, Aleksandr I., *In the First Circle*; orig. *V kruge pervom*. New York: Harper Perennial, 1968.

Solzhenitsyn, Aleksandr I. (*cont.*), *Prussian Nights: A Narrative Poem*; orig. *Prusskye notsy*. London: Collins & Harvill, 1977.

Spengler, Oswald A.G., *Der Untergang des Abendlandes*.München: Beck, 1919.

Tilak, Bal Gangadhar, *The Arctic Home in the Vedas. Being also a New Key to the Interpretation of Many Vedic Texts and Legends*. Poona: Tilak Bros, 1903.

Weber, Max, *Die protestantische Ethik und der Geist des Kapitalismus*. Göttingen: Mohr, 1905.

Wolfe, Tom, 'The 'Me' Decade and the Third Great Awakening', *New York Magazine* 23 August 1976.

Wolfheze, Alexander, *The Sunset of Tradition and the Origin of the Great War*. Newcastle upon Tyne: Cambridge Scholars, 2018.

FILMOGRAPHY

Besson, Luc, *Lucy* (2014) genre: science fiction;
— relevance: trans-humanism, technological hubris;

Carpenter, John, *In the Mouth of Madness* (1994) genre: psychological horror;
— relevance: zombie apocalypse — occult arts, postmodern culture ;

Curtis, Tony, *The Century of the Self* (2002) genre: cultural-historical documentary;
— relevance: narcissism epidemy — psycho-analysis, marketing & consumerism;

Darabont, Frank, *The Walking Dead* (2010-) genre: post-apocalyptic horror;
— relevance: zombie apocalypse — social-psychological dynamics;

Devlin, Dean, *Geostorm* (2017) genre: science fiction disaster;
— relevance: climate catastrophe, technological hubris;

Emmerich, Roland, *The Day after Tomorrow* (2004) genre: science fiction disaster;
— relevance: climate catastrophe;

Fincher, David, *Se7en* (1995) genre: crime-thriller;
— relevance: hamartiology of Modernity;

Forster, Marc, *World War Z* (2013) genre: action-horror;
— relevance: zombie apocalypse, eschatological motives (Jerusalem);

Ivory, James, *The Remains of the Day* (1993) genre: historical drama;
— relevance: social implosion — Regression of the Castes;

Lee, Ang, *The Ice Storm* (1997) genre: drama;
— relevance: social implosion — urban-hedonist immorality;

Mendis, Sam, *American Beauty* (1995) genre: drama;
— relevance: social implosion — urban-hedonist immorality;

Mongillo, Michael, *The Wind* (2001) genre: psychological thriller;
— relevance: narcissism epidemy;

Nichols, Jeff, *Take Shelter* (2011) genre: psychological thriller;
— relevance: climate catastrophe — social-psychological dynamics;

Romero, George, *Dawn of the Dead* (1978) genre: horror;

— relevance: zombie apocalypse — socio-cultural dynamics;

Santoro, Matthew, *Higher Power* (2018) genre: science fiction;

— relevance: trans-humanism, technological hubris;

Scorsese, Martin, *The Wolf of Wallstreet* (2013) genre: black comedy;

— relevance: social implosion — hyper-capitalism & hyper-individualism;

Snyder, Zack, *Dawn of the Dead* (2004) genre: horror;

— relevance: zombie apocalypse — eschatological motives (Revelation).

EARLIER PUBLICATIONS OF 'ALBA ROSA' MATERIAL

Chapter 1 — 'The Harrowing of Hell' is a slightly expanded and adjusted version of the article 'Hellstorm: Ten Western Perspectives on the Eurasian Project' in the *Journal of Eurasian Studies*.

Chapter 2 — 'The Crisis of the Modern West' partially appeared earlier in the article 'The Dutch Ernstfall: A Traditionalist Diagnosis of Dutch Post-Modernity' on the website Geopolitica.ru — two introductory paragraphs and explanatory notes have been added to contextualize the present Dutch predicament and to clarify specifically Dutch themes.

Chapter 3 — 'The Dangers of Democracy' contains material from the author's article 'Dutch Democracy: A Warning from History' on the website Geopolitica.ru.

Chapter 4 — 'The Sword of Knowledge' contains material translated by the author from his own Dutch-language article '*Het Zwaard van Kennis*', originally written for the periodical *Zicht* of the Dutch Christian-Conservative study centre 'Guido de Brès'.

Chapter 6 — 'The Living Dead' appeared earlier as an article on the website Geopolitica.ru.

Chapter 8 — 'The Archaeo-Futurist Revolution' appeared earlier as a book review on the website Geopolitica.ru.

GLOSSARY

κατέχον, *katechon* — Greek: 'that which withholds', Biblical 'restrainer' of the Antichrist, Carl Schmitt's intellectualization of the *Christianum Imperium*

μολὼν λαβέ, *molōn labé* — Greek: 'come, take (them)', King Leonidas of Sparta's response to Persian Emperor Xerxes' demand that he lay down his weapons during the Battle of Thermopylae

φαρμακός, *pharmakós* — Greek: 'sacrificial victim', hence 'outcast'

Accipe quam primum; brevis est occasio lucri — Latin: 'take while you can; the moment of profit is brief' (Martial)

Acquirit qui tuetur — Latin: 'he that maintains, acquires'

'Aḏān — Arabic: 'Listening', Islamic call to prayer

Adhuc coelum volvitur — Latin: 'the heavens still turn' (Erasmus)

Agent provocateur — French: 'inciting agent'

Alba Rosa — Latin: 'White Rose'

Albus in albis — Latin: 'white among the white'

Albanizacija — Serbo-Croatian: 'Albanianisation'

Alieni juris — Latin: 'under the power of another'

Allochtoon — Dutch: 'alien born'

Alma mater — Latin: 'nourishing mother', a university that somebody attended

'Amīdah — Hebrew: 'The Standing', Jewish prayer

Anomie — French from Greek *anomia*, 'lawlessness': 'psycho-social void' (Durkheim)

Anti-genealogische Experiment der Moderne — German: 'Anti-genealogical Experiment of the Modern Age' (Peter Sloterdijk)

Après nous le déluge — French: 'after us the flood' (de Pompadour)

Archéofuturisme — French: 'Archaeo-Futurism' (Faye)

'Aṣḥāb al-Kahf — Arabic: 'People of the Cave' (Quran)

Auctoritas — Latin: 'authority', 'power of command'

Audax Iapeti genus — Latin: 'the audacious progeny of Iapetus' (i.e. Atlas and Prometheus)

Ausnahmezustand — German: 'state of exception' (Schmitt)

Aussteiger — German: 'drop-out', non-conformist

Aut viam inveniam aut faciam — Latin: 'either I find a way, or I make one' (Hannibal)

Avant garde — French: 'advance guard', 'artistic pioneer'

Ave, formosissima, gemma pretiosa, ave, decus virginum, virgo gloriosa, ave, mundi luminar, ave, mundi rosa! — Latin : 'Hail, fairest one, precious gem, Hail, brightness of maidens, glorious maiden, Hail, light of the world, Hail, rose of the world!' (Carmina Burana)

Ba'al teshuvah — Hebrew: 'master of repentance', penitent

Behouden Huys — Dutch: 'Preserved House' (location: Novaya Zemlya)

Bellum omnium contra omnes — Latin: 'war of all against all' (Hobbes)

Bewältigung — German: 'coping'

Blitzkrieg — German: 'lightning war', German WW2 strategy

Blut und Boden — German: 'blood and soil'

Canards, canaux et canailles — French: 'ducks, canals and riffraff' (Voltaire)

Ceci tuera cela — French: 'this will kill that' (Hugo)

Cet animal est très méchant ; quand on l'attaque il se défend ! — French: 'this animal is very mean; when it is attacked, it defends itself!'

Chambre introuvable — French: 'the chamber (of representatives) that cannot be found'

Chassez le naturel, il revient au galop — French: 'chase away nature (and) it returns at a gallop'

Chassidei 'umot ha-'õlam — Hebrew: 'the righteous peoples of the world'

Contradictio in terminis — Latin: 'contradiction in terms'

Créolisation — French: 'creolization', racial and cultural merger

Crise du monde moderne — French: 'Crisis of the Modern World' (Guénon)

Da'esh — Arabic acronym: 'Islamic State of Iraq and the Levant', islamicist terrorist organization

Damnés de la terre — French: 'The Wretched of the Earth' (Fanon)

De l'audace, encore de l'audace, toujours de l'audace et la Patrie sera sauvée! — French: 'Audacity, then again audacity, always audacity — and the fatherland will be saved! (Danton)

De verweesde samenleving — Dutch: 'The Orphaned Society' (Fortuyn)

De puinhopen van acht jaar paars — Dutch: 'The ruins of Eight Years Purple' (Fortuyn);

Début — French: 'beginning', 'formal introduction'

Der Untergang des Abendlandes — German: 'The Decline of the West' (Spengler)

Deutschland ad acta legen — German/Latin: 'to close the books on Germany' (Sieferle)

Devotio Moderna — Latin: 'modern devotion', late medieval religious reform movement in the Low Countries

Die fröhliche Wissenschaft — German: 'The Joyful Science' (Nietzsche)

Die protestantische Ethik und der Geist des Kapitalismus — German: 'The Protestant Ethic and the Spirit of Capitalism' (Weber)

Die Weisse Rose — German: 'The White Rose', anti-Nazi resistance movement;

Divide et impera — Latin: 'divide and rule'

Dolce far niente — Italian: 'sweet idleness'

Dura lex sed lex — Latin: 'the law is harsh, but it is the law'

Einführung des Narzissmus — German: 'An Introduction to Narcissism' (Freud)

Elan vital — French: 'vital impetus', spontaneous morphogenesis (Bergson)

Eminence grise — French: 'grey eminence', 'power behind the throne' (Tremblay)

Empyrean — from Greek *empyrus*, 'in the fire': 'highest heaven'

Endsieg — German: 'final victory' (Goebbels)

Entfremdung — German: 'alienation' (Marx)

Epistème — French from Greek *epistèmè*: 'knowledge system' (Foucault)

Ernstfall — German: 'case of seriousness' (Schmitt)

Ex factis ius oritur — Latin: 'the law arises from facts'

Evangelion — Greek: 'good news', 'gospel'

Ewige Wiederkunft — German: 'eternal return' (Nietzsche)

Excalibur — from Welsh *caled-bwlch* 'hard breach', magical sword of King Arthur

Faute de mieux — French: 'for lack of better'
Favela — Brazilian Portuguese: 'slum'
Finis Germania — Latin: 'Germany's End' (Sieferle)
Flucht nach vorne — German: 'flight forward'
Freiheitliche Partei Oesterreichs — German: 'Freedom Party of Austria'
Front National — French: 'National Front'
Führergeburtstag — German: 'Leader's Birthday' (Hitler's, 20 April 1889)
Führerprinzip — German: 'leader principle'

Gaia — Greek goddess of the Earth, deified personification of the Earth
Geest — Dutch: sandy, raised landform with poor soil, homophone with 'ghost'
Gekaufte Journalisten — German: 'Bought journalists' (Ulfkotte)
Ger Toshav — Hebrew: 'resident alien'
Ger Tsedek — Hebrew: 'righteous alien'
Génération identitaire — French: 'generation identity', the identitarian generation
Gesundes Geschichtsempfinden — German: 'healthy historical instinct'
Gidsland — Dutch: 'guiding nation'
Giyur — Hebrew: 'conversion (to Judaism)'
Gli uomini e le rovine — Italian: 'Men Among the Ruins' (Evola)
Gnade der späten Geburt — German: 'mercy of a late birth'
Götterdämmerung — German: 'Twilight of the Gods' (Wagner)
Gram — Old Norse: 'wrath', magical sword of mythical Norse hero Sigurd
Griff nach der Weltmacht — German: 'Grab for World Power' (Fischer)
Gutmensch — German: 'good human', politically correct hyper-altruistic 'nice guy'

Halacha — Hebrew: 'the way to walk', Rabbinic Law
Heimat — German: 'homeland'
Hitler Jugend — German: 'Hitler Youth'
HLM banlieue — French: 'rent-controlled public housing suburb'
Hohe Messe — German: 'High Mass'
Homo novus — Latin: 'new man', plebeian raised to higher rank
Hortus conclusus — Latin: 'enclosed garden', title of the Holy Virgin
Hudūd — Arabic: 'boundaries', extreme punishments under Islamic Law

Il nome della rosa — Italian: 'In the Name of the Rose' (Eco)
Imperium — Latin: 'highest command power', 'imperial remit'
Invidia — Latin: 'hostile look', 'envy'

Jabhat an-Nuṣrah — Arabic: 'Victory Front', islamicist terrorist organization
Jeunesse dorée — French: 'gilded youth', bullying affluent youth

Kali Yuga — Sanskrit: 'Age of Kali', cosmic 'Dark Age'

Katechon — cf. κατέχον above

Katharsis — Greek: 'purification'

Kohl's Mädchen — German: 'Kohl's girl', reference to former German Chancellor Helmuth Kohl's patronage of his present successor Angela Merkel

Kulturkreis — German: 'cultural circle', anthropological approach of separate culture complexes

La Gioconda — Italian: 'the Giocondo girl', a reference to Lisa del Giocondo and to da Vinci's painting, *Mona Lisa*

Laïcité — French: 'secularity', the secular 'state religion' of the French Republic

Landnám — Icelandic: 'land settlement', original act of taking possession

Landvoogd — Dutch: 'regional governor', associated with foreign administrators

Le Horla — French *hors là*, 'out there': 'The Outsider' (de Maupassant)

Liberté, égalité, fraternité — French: 'liberty, equality, fraternity', motto of the French Republic

Luctor et emergo — Latin: 'I struggle and emerge', motto of the Dutch province of Zeeland;

Luftwaffe — German: 'airforce'

Lügenpresse — German: 'lying press', politically correct system media

Machtergreifung — German: 'seizure of power', Nazi rise to power

Machtübernahme — German: 'take-over of power', Nazi rise to power

Manumissio — Latin: 'affranchisement', freeing of slaves

Métèque — French: 'metic', foreign resident without citizenship (Maurras)

Métissage — French: the creation of a population of mixed ethnicity

Moc bezmocných — Czech: 'The Power of the Powerless' (Havel)

Nomina nuda tenemus — Latin: 'we hold only naked names' (de Cluny, Eco)

Moment suprême — French: 'supreme moment'

Monachus- Latin: 'monk'

Mors triumphalis — Latin: 'triumphant death'

Narodnaya Volya — Russian: 'The People's Will', revolutionary terrorist organization

Negativ auserwähltes Volk — German: 'negatively chosen people' (Sieferle)

Nirvana — Sanskrit: 'extinction', Buddhist state of final redemption

Nomos — Latin: 'law', Carl Schmitt's intellectualization of Higher Order

Noodgeval — Dutch: 'emergency'

Nouveau riche — French: 'new rich', *parvenu* lacking a proper pedigree

Novus Ordo Seculorum — Latin: 'The New Order of the Ages' (Virgil), motto of the Great Seal of the United States

Odin den Ivana Denisowitsa — Russian: 'One Day in the Life of Ivan Denisovich' (Solzhenitsyn)

Oikophobia — from Greek: 'fear of home'

Ousia — Greek: 'being', 'essence', 'substance'
Oyfn Pripetshik — Yiddish: 'On the Hearth' (Warshawsky)

Par excellence — French: 'by excellence'
Partij voor de Vrijheid (PVV) — Dutch: 'Freedom Party'
Paschein — Greek: 'to suffer', philosophical category of affection by some other object (Aristotle)
Pax Eurasiatica — Latin: 'Eurasian Peace'
Penitentia — Latin: 'repentance', the good work of contrition and penance
Pensionado — Spanish: 'pensioner', wealthy retiree living the expat life-style
Perfectus — Latin: 'perfect human', Cathar *Bonhomme*
Plaasmoord — Afrikaans: 'farm killing', targeted killings as part of the ongoing genocide of White Afrikaners in South Africa
Plakkaat van Verlatinghe — Dutch: 'Placard of Abjuration', Dutch 'Declaration of Independence' (1581)
Pointe en relevé — French: 'rising up on the toes', ballet technique
Prinzipienreiterei — German: 'harping on about principles'
Proletariat — German from Latin *proletarius*, '(only) producing offspring': 'working class' (Marx)
Qalandar — Persian: 'defender (of the people)', wandering Dervish, Sufi saint
Quod licet Iovi non licet bovi — Latin: 'what is permissible to Jove, is not permissible for an oxen', 'what is permitted to one important person or group, is not permitted to everyone'
Quos Deus vult perdere prius dementat — Latin: 'those whom God wishes to destroy, he strikes with madness first'

Ragnarök — Old Norse: 'the doom of the gods' (*Edda*)
Raison d'être — French: 'reason for being'
Realmatriarchat — German: 'real-life matriarchy'
Realpolitik — German: 'real politics', pragmatic political realism
Regent — Dutch: 'patrician', non-noble semi-hereditary ruling class of the Dutch Republic
Regressione delle caste — Italian: 'Regression of the Castes' (Evola)
Rentier — French: 'someone living idly off investments', usurer
Res Publica Christiana — Latin: 'The Christian Commonwealth', Christendom
Restitutio in integrum — Latin: 'restoration to original condition', legal redress for damages incurred
Retraite — French: 'retirement', hence (temporary) spiritual (monastic) retreat
Revenant — French: 'returnee', ghost or animated corpse returning from death

Sacerdotus — Latin: 'priest'
Samizdat — Russian: 'self-published manuscript', dissident literature in Communist Eastern Europe

Samson Agonistes — Greek: 'Samson the Champion' (Milton)

Sara-la-Kali — French/Romani: 'Sara the Black', Saint Sarah

Schreckliche Ende/Schrecken ohne Ende — German: 'terrible end/terror without end'

Schrecklichen Kinder der Neuzeit — German: 'terrible children of the New Age' (Sloterdijk)

Sine qua non — Latin: 'without which nothing'

Singulärste Schuld auf Erden — German: 'the world's most unique debt' (Sieferle)

Sitz im Leben — German: 'setting in life', theological concept of context

Soixante-huitard — French: 'sixty-eight person', baby boom activist of '1968'

Soevereiniteit in eigen kring — Dutch: 'sphere sovereignty' (Kuyper)

Sonderkommando — German: 'special unit', work units of camp inmates involved in the operation of Nazi death camps

Sophia Perennis — Latin: 'Perennial Philosophy', epistemological basis of Traditionalism;

Sonderfall — German: 'special case', historical uniqueness

Sperrgebiet — German: 'prohibited area'

Spyashchaya krasavitsa — Russian: 'Sleeping Beauty' (Tchaikovsky)

Stat rosa pristina nomine, nomina nuda tenemus — Latin: 'the ancient rose remains [only] in name, naked names are all that we have' (de Cluny, Eco)

Stunde Null — German: 'Zero Hour', the caesura in German history, precisely marked by the midnight hour of 8 May 1945 (Unconditional Surrender of Germany)

Superbia — Latin: 'pride'

Tabula rasa — Latin: 'erased slate', blank wax tablet

Techne — Greek: 'craft', philosophical concept of use-conditioned reality

Temeraire — from French *téméraire*: 'rash', 'reckless'

Tesi samanunga was edele unde scona et omnium virtutum pleniter plena — 'Macaronic' Latin and Old Dutch: This community was noble and clean and filled with all virtues (Munsterbilzen Evangelarium)

Théâtre de l'absurde — French: 'Theatre of the Absurd', existentialist fiction

Theriomachy — Greek: 'animal struggle', archetypal human struggle with evil

Totaler Krieg — German: 'Total War' (Goebbels)

Tournante — French slang: 'turn over session', Maghreb-style gang rape

Tsadikim Nistarim — Hebrew: 'Hidden Righteous Ones'

Tutu — ballet costume

Tweede Kamer — Dutch: 'Second House', Dutch House of Representatives

Übermensch — German: 'superman' (Nietzsche)

Umvolkung — German: 'ethnic replacement'

Umwertung aller Werte — German: 'tranvaluation of all values' (Nietzsche)

Untermensch — German: 'subhuman', inferior people

Unus mundus — Latin: 'One World', philosophical concept of an underlying unified reality reflected in archetypes and synchronicities (Jung)

Unzeitgemässe Betrachtungen — German: 'Untimely Meditations' (Nietzsche)

Uradel — German: 'primordial nobility' (dating back to the 14th century or earlier), as opposed to *Briefadel* ('patent letter nobility') of later date

Urzeit — German: 'prehistoric time'

Uti possidetis — Latin: 'as you possess', legal possession resulting from the cessation of hostilities

Va banque — French: 'go bank', a gambler's all-in bet equal to all the money in the game's bet

Vae victis! — Latin: 'woe to the vanguished!' (Brennus)

Verelendung — German: 'immiseration', economic thesis of necessary relative wage reduction in capitalist development (Marx)

Vergangenheitsbewältigung — German: 'overcoming the past', post-war German preoccupation with national guilt complexes

Vindiciae contra tyrannos — Latin: 'Defences against Tyrants', Huguenot tract concerning peoples' right to resist unjust rulers

Völkerwanderung — German: 'migration of the peoples', era of Barbarian Invasions of Europe during the Migration Period (375–568 AD)

Volksgemeinschaft — German: 'people's community'

W Imię Boga: za naszą i waszą wolność — Polish: 'in the Name of God: for our and your freedom'

Wehr- und Waffen-Instinkt — German: 'defence and armament instinct' (Nietzsche alluding to Luther's hymn 'A mighty fortress is our God, a good defence and weapon)

Werdegang — German: 'developmental process'

Wiedergutmachung — German: 'restitution, compensation', reparation payments by post-war Germany to victims of the Nazi regime

Wilhelmus — Dutch national anthem, the oldest in the world and dedicated to Prince William of Orange, 'Father of the Nation'

Wir schaffen das — German: 'we can manage it', Angela Merkel's phrase defending her 'open borders' policy during the European Migrant Crisis of 2015

Wunderkammer — German: 'wonder-room', curiosity cabinet

Za vashu i nashu svobodu — Russian: 'for our and your freedom'

Zweiundzwanzig, Hoeringstrasse — German: 'Höringstrasse (number) 22' (Solzhenitsyn)

OTHER BOOKS PUBLISHED BY ARKTOS

	A Global Coup
	Sex and Deviance
	Understanding Islam
	Why We Fight
DANIEL S. FORREST	*Suprahumanism*
ANDREW FRASER	*Dissident Dispatches*
	The WASP Question
GÉNÉRATION IDENTITAIRE	*We are Generation Identity*
PAUL GOTTFRIED	*War and Democracy*
PORUS HOMI HAVEWALA	*The Saga of the Aryan Race*
LARS HOLGER HOLM	*Hiding in Broad Daylight*
	Homo Maximus
	Incidents of Travel in Latin America
	The Owls of Afrasiab
ALEXANDER JACOB	*De Naturae Natura*
JASON REZA JORJANI	*Prometheus and Atlas*
	World State of Emergency
RODERICK KAINE	*Smart and SeXy*
PETER KING	*Here and Now*
	Keeping Things Close
LUDWIG KLAGES	*The Biocentric Worldview*
	Cosmogonic Reflections
PIERRE KREBS	*Fighting for the Essence*
STEPHEN PAX LEONARD	*Travels in Cultural Nihilism*
PENTTI LINKOLA	*Can Life Prevail?*
H. P. LOVECRAFT	*The Conservative*
CHARLES MAURRAS	*The Future of the Intelligentsia*
	& For a French Awakening
MICHAEL O'MEARA	*Guillaume Faye and the Battle of Europe*
	New Culture, New Right
BRIAN ANSE PATRICK	*The NRA and the Media*
	Rise of the Anti-Media
	The Ten Commandments of Propaganda
	Zombology

OTHER BOOKS PUBLISHED BY ARKTOS

Made in the USA
Las Vegas, NV
23 January 2024

84691001R00187